European Public Spheres

The euro crisis has led to an unprecedented Europeanization and politicization of public spheres across the continent. In this volume, leading scholars make two claims. First, they suggest that transnational cross-border
communication in Europe has been encouraged through the gradual Europeanization of national as well as issue-specific public spheres. Second, the
politicization of European affairs – at the European Union (EU) level and
in the domestic politics of member states – is inevitable and here to stay.
Europeanized public spheres, whether elite media, mass media, or social
media such as the internet, provide the arenas in which the politicization
of European and EU issues takes place. *European Public Spheres* explores
the history of these developments, the nature of politicization in the public
spheres as well as its likely consequences, and the normative implications
for European public life.

THOMAS RISSE is Professor of International Politics at the Otto Suhr
Institute of Political Science at the Freie Universität Berlin, and he is
coordinator of the Research Center 700 "Governance of Areas of Lim-
ited Statehood" and co-director of the Research College "Transformative
Power of Europe," both funded by the German Research Foundation
(DFG). His publications include *A Community of Europeans? Transna-
tional Identities and Public Spheres* (Cornell University Press, 2010); *The
Persistent Power of Human Rights: From Commitment to Compliance*
(Cambridge University Press, 2013, co-edited with Stephen C. Ropp and
Kathryn Sikkink); and *External Actors, State-Building and Service Provi-
sion in Areas of Limited Statehood* (special issue of *Governance*, 2014,
with Stephen D. Krasner).

CONTEMPORARY EUROPEAN POLITICS

Consulting Editor:
Andreas Føllesdal, University of Oslo

Contemporary European Politics presents the latest scholarship on the most important subjects in European politics. The world's leading scholars provide accessible, state-of-the-art surveys of the major issues which face Europe now and in the future. Examining Europe as a whole and taking a broad view of its politics, these volumes will appeal to scholars and to undergraduate and graduate students of politics and European studies.

Other titles in this series:
Resilient Liberalism in Europe's Political Economy edited by Vivien A. Schmidt and Mark Thatcher
The Worlds of European Constitutionalism edited by Gráinne de Búrca and J. H. H. Weiler
European Identity edited by Jeffrey T. Checkel and Peter J. Katzenstein

European Public Spheres

Politics Is Back

Edited by
THOMAS RISSE

CAMBRIDGE
UNIVERSITY PRESS

University Printing House, Cambridge CB2 8BS, United Kingdom

Cambridge University Press is part of the University of Cambridge.

It furthers the University's mission by disseminating knowledge in the pursuit of education, learning and research at the highest international levels of excellence.

www.cambridge.org
Information on this title: www.cambridge.org/9781107441637

© Cambridge University Press 2015

First published 2015

Printed in the United Kingdom by Clays, St Ives plc

A catalogue record for this publication is available from the British Library

ISBN 978-1-107-08165-9 Hardback
ISBN 978-1-107-44163-7 Paperback

Contents

Figures

Tables

1 Introduction

THOMAS RISSE

The euro crisis has been arguably the most profound crisis in the history of European integration.[1] European Union (EU) and national policy makers have been regularly using references to war and peace, as well as the fate of the EU in general, to point to the severity of the crisis. As German Chancellor Angela Merkel stated: "The euro is our common fate, and Europe is our common future."[2] Or, to quote EU Commission President Josè Manuel Barroso: "We will defend the euro whatever the cost."[3] Core issues of European integration have assumed center stage in the domestic arenas of most member states:

- What should the future of the EU look like? Should the EU move toward a fiscal union that also includes joint economic policies and the transfer of financial support from the wealthier to the poorer member states? How should austerity policies be balanced with policies fostering economic growth in times of deep recession?
- How much "solidarity among strangers" (Habermas 2006a, 76) do Europe and the EU[4] need in times of crisis? Is the "community of Europeans" (Risse 2010) strong enough to sustain fiscal transfers

---

[1] I thank the participants of the two workshops in Berlin (April 29–30, 2011, and January 13–14, 2012) for their comments. This introduction owes much to Marianne Van de Steeg's input, which I gratefully acknowledge. I also thank Tanja Börzel and Vera van Hüllen for their critical comments. Support from the DFG-funded Research College "Transformative Power of Europe" is gratefully acknowledged.
[2] December 12, 2010. Available at www.nytimes.com/2010/12/16/business/global/16union.html?pagewanted=all (accessed March 10, 2012).
[3] May 8, 2010. Available at www.welt.de/politik/ausland/article7536673/Die-dramatische-Notoperation-am-Herzen-Europas.html (accessed March 10, 2012).
[4] Of course, Europe is more than the EU. Nevertheless, this book focuses on the EU as the relevant supranational polity in Europe. As a result, I use the terms "Europe" and "EU" interchangeably unless noted otherwise.

from Northern to Southern Europe to bail out countries facing the prospect of sovereign default?
- What about the future of European democracy at times when financial markets seem to determine the speed with which policy makers must make decisions involving billions of euros? What about the role of the European Parliament (EP) and of national parliaments in this?

The public salience of the euro crisis is unprecedented. A Google search for "euro crisis" results in 55.8 million hits, as compared to 8 million hits for "European constitutional treaty," and only 719,000 hits for "Maastricht Treaty" (as of June 27, 2014).[5]

Moreover, never have domestic and European politics been as intertwined as in the euro crisis. When the German Chancellor and the Greek Prime Minister speak to their domestic constituencies to assuage their fears and to win over majorities for bailouts or for stringent austerity policies, respectively, the rest of Europe (and the world) not only listens attentively but also feels obliged to comment and to participate in the debates. In short, this is transnational communication in action. The domestic has become European, and European politics has become an integral part of domestic politics. Three processes can be observed simultaneously: transnationalization, Europeanization, and politicization.

The euro crisis exemplifies the main premise of this book: namely, the Europeanization and increasing politicization of debates on EU-related issues in the various public spheres. Even in the days of permissive consensus, European-wide debates took place. "Brussels" and regular meetings of European and national policy makers created a common discourse and a political agenda. Yet, European decision making mostly remained insulated from the larger public. Behind closed doors, it was easier for the member states to find compromises and reach consensus. The larger public was informed after the fact and may have noticed the consequences of European decision making only years later, when the European decisions were implemented at the national level.

This era is over, as this book argues. The permissive consensus has given way to a "constraining dissensus" (Hooghe and Marks 2009).

---

[5] I owe this idea to compare Google hits to Stephanie Anderson.

During the past twenty years or so, since the Maastricht Treaty, the referenda in France and the Netherlands on the Treaty for a European Constitution, and now the euro crisis, the European polity has been transformed profoundly. EU politics is losing its technocratic and depoliticized nature and is becoming "normal" politics subject to similar debates and controversies, as in the case of domestic affairs. So far, political entrepreneurs – mostly on the far right – who disagree with moves toward more European integration have tried to seize the opportunity offered by the change in the political climate and to propagate Euroskepticism. European center-right and center-left politicians have been slow to react to increasing politicization of EU affairs and are realizing only gradually that they have to win the active support of their citizens; thin, top-down communication on deals struck at European summits will no longer suffice. Two-way communication on European politics between citizens and their elected representatives will be necessary (Schmidt and Radaelli 2004; Schmidt 2006).

Therefore, this book makes two claims. First, transnational cross-border communication in Europe – at the levels of both the elites and bottom-up social mobilization – is enabled through the gradual Europeanization of national- as well as issue-specific public spheres. We argue that European public spheres do not emerge above and beyond local-, national-, or issue-specific public spheres in some abstract supranational space but rather through the Europeanization of these various public spheres that then allows for cross-border communication in Europe (see Part I).

Second, the politicization of European affairs at both the EU level and in the domestic politics of member states is inevitable and here to stay, whether or not we like it (see Checkel and Katzenstein 2009a and Risse 2010 for similar assessments). This book explores the nature of politicization in the public spheres and its likely consequences (see Part II).

The book then asks three interrelated sets of questions. First, what do we know about the Europeanization of public spheres (see Part I)? To what extent do we observe the emergence of transnational communities of communication and on what levels? What are the major scholarly controversies with regard to theory-building, measurements, and empirical findings (see Chapter 2)? We argue that the main scholarly disagreements do not so much concern theories and concepts. Whether we approach public spheres from a Luhmannian perspective that focuses on mutual observation (Luhmann 1971) or a Habermasian concept that emphasizes communities of communication (Habermas 1980/1962) appears to be less relevant than methodological issues and how to interpret empirical results (e.g., what is the benchmark for establishing the Europeanization of public spheres? See Chapters 4 and 5 compared to Chapter 3.)

Second, how does the Europeanization of public spheres affect social and political affairs in Europe? Does it matter (see Part II)? We argue that Europeanized public spheres – whether elite media, mass media, or social media (e.g., the internet) – provide the arenas in which the politicization of European and EU issues takes place (see Chapter 6). The main controversy concerns the question of whether politicization and the increased salience of EU politics will contribute to the emergence of European identities and a European polity (see Chapters 6 and 7). In contrast, a more skeptical view holds that the politicization of European affairs does not affect identities and community-building directly but rather via party alignments and political cleavages. As a result, politicization might actually contribute further to the rise of Euroskepticism and to further alienation of voters in the EU (see Chapter 8).

Third, what are the implications of these findings for theory-building, on the one hand, and for normative questions related to European democracy and the so-called democratic deficit on the other (see Chapters 9 and 10)? In particular, Jeffrey Checkel (Chapter 9) asks critical questions about theoretical and methodological approaches. He also challenges assertions about the relationship of public spheres and collective identities as well as the generalizability of the book's findings with regard to wider Europe, particularly Eastern Europe. Andreas Follesdal (Chapter 10) takes a normative view and discusses the book's implications for deliberative as well as contestatory democracy in Europe.

The chapters in this book report empirical findings based on a variety of methods, including large-N statistical analyses (Chapter 8), claims analysis (Chapter 3), frame analysis and corpus-linguistics (Chapter 4), network analysis (Chapter 5), and experiments (Chapter 7). It is remarkable, therefore, that most of the contributors agree with the two core claims made previously: namely, that (1) we can observe the gradual Europeanization of various public spheres; and (2) the politicization of European affairs in these public spheres is here to stay.

This remainder of this introduction proceeds as follows. First, I define central concepts that are relevant for this book, such as public spheres, Europeanization, politicization, and Euroskepticism. Second, I introduce the book's central themes and controversies. Third, I conclude with remarks about the book's central findings and its contribution to the larger literature on European democracy.

European public spheres: concepts

Public spheres

There has been a long debate on what constitutes a public sphere, or *Öffentlichkeit*,[6] to use the German term. This discussion inevitably links normative and analytical perspectives (Trenz 2008). From a normative perspective of democratic theory, most observers deem crucial an open, pluralistic, and critical public discourse rooted in independent media for providing an interface between state and society in a democratic polity. Europe should not be an exception. As a result, the debate about a European public sphere is linked to the controversy about the democratic quality of the EU and its various problems (see Chapter 10).

The normative understanding of *Öffentlichkeit* as a necessary component of democracy has implications for the analytical conceptualization of a public sphere because it requires indicators with regard to its communicative quality. If public spheres as the "fourth estate" are supposed to inform citizens about the political process, monitor and critically evaluate governance, and enable a public discourse in a democracy (McNair 2000), then they must allow for meaningful communication and exchange, thereby satisfying certain normative criteria. This has implications for the development of indicators (see Chapter 2).

Depending on one's normative viewpoint about public spheres in a democratic polity, most conceptualizations of *Öffentlichkeit* are centered between a minimalist or Luhmannian understanding, on the one hand, and a more demanding or Habermasian concept, on

---

[6] The German term *Öffentlichkeit* usually is translated as "public sphere." Yet, this translation does not capture the normative connotations implied in the German term. See De Vreese 2007b, 4; Trenz 2008, 1–3.

the other. According to Niklas Luhmann's functional interpretation, public spheres constitute a societal subsystem devoted to the mutual observation of societal and political actors (Luhmann 1971). Accordingly, public opinion is the social subsystem through which a society observes and describes itself, thereby contributing to social integration (Luhmann 2000; Trenz 2005, 71–80). Communications through media then constitute second-order observations that not only enable participants and audiences to observe themselves and their contributions but also the observations of others and their construction of reality. By mirroring and communicating social conflicts, the media contribute to social order in a given society. In this understanding, communication through public media does not aim at mutual understanding and public discourse but rather at mutual observation.

Jürgen Habermas's understanding is normatively more demanding and linked to the challenging of public authority. He concentrated on the emergence of arenas of semi-public reasoning and deliberation among free citizens in the saloons, coffeehouses, and Masonic lodges of eighteenth- and nineteenth-century bourgeois society in Europe. These arenas constituted emerging public spheres in which private citizens challenged public authorities to legitimate themselves before the court of public opinion (Habermas 1980/1962, 25). Habermas's later work then systematically linked the concept of a public sphere to the institutionalized opinion-formation processes in a democratic political system that is governed by the rule of law (Habermas 1992; see also Kantner 2004). As a result, opinion formation in the public sphere no longer must single-handedly carry the burden of ensuring that deliberation occurs in a democratic polity. Rather, it is the legal and political institutional framework of a modern democracy that ensures its deliberative quality.

This book takes Habermas's conceptualization of public spheres as a forum for its starting point but uses a less demanding normative understanding. Following Friedhelm Neidhardt, we define a "public sphere" as "an open forum of communication for everybody who wants to say something or listen to what other speakers have to say" (Neidhardt 1994, 7; my translation; see Chapter 2). According to the forum model of public spheres, various actors engage in public speech acts within different public arenas addressing both their co-speakers and the audiences (i.e., in the gallery). As a result, each public sphere consists of

3. Common European themes and issues are addressed using similar frames of references (Eder and Kantner 2000, following Habermas 1996d, 306) or making claims across borders (Koopmans and Statham 2010a).

Thus, the Europeanization of public spheres includes issue salience, actors, and substantive content of communication. If Europe and the EU are not visible, then we do not need to be concerned about Europeanization. However, there is general agreement in the scholarly literature that coverage of EU issues in national media has increased substantially since at least the mid-1990s (e.g., Trenz 2005; Kantner, Kutter, and Renfordt 2008; Wessler et al. 2008; Koopmans and Statham 2010a; see also Chapter 4 in this volume).

Regarding the actor dimension, Koopmans distinguishes between *vertical* and *horizontal* Europeanization. The former refers to the degree to which EU actors are present in the various public spheres, whereas the latter concerns the presence of actors from other EU member states (Koopmans, Erbe, and Meyer 2010; see also Chapter 3 in this volume). Political demands or claims are Europeanized when they are directed across borders (e.g., the Greek trade unions protesting Chancellor Merkel's austerity policies) or when they involve EU-related issues (e.g., Greek trade unions protesting against Greek austerity legislation to qualify for a bailout at the European Financial Stability Facility [EFSF]).

Regarding the substantive content, the "Eder–Kantner criteria" involve similar framing across transnational space (see the previous discussion and Chapter 4). Frame analysis has become a common tool to measure the Europeanization of public spheres that center on specific debates and controversies across borders (see Chapter 2 for a more detailed discussion; see also Risse 2010, ch. 6). The idea behind this conceptualization is that public spheres are considered Europeanized if and when similar frames are used in the various public arenas so as to allow cross-border understanding and communication. Of course, this includes cross-border contestation and controversies about which frame is the most appropriate to tackle a particular policy issue. As mentioned previously, whether budgetary discipline and/or economic growth are the most important cures to save the euro is being hotly debated across the EU, and there is no end in sight for the controversy. However, this discussion is only possible if speakers across various public spheres agree – at least implicitly – that, indeed, these are the major choices and if they understand the implications.

We submit that all three indicators – salience, actors, and content – are necessary to speak of the Europeanization of public spheres in a meaningful sense. If Europe and the EU are not visible in the public spheres, it does not matter if the actor and content dimensions are Europeanized because hardly anyone notices. Similar frames of reference might be used purely coincidentally in various public spheres without the respective speakers and their audiences knowing about one another. An earthquake in Japan might spark similar media reactions in France and, for example, China, including similar frames of references, but we would not call this a common public sphere. At the same time, it is not enough that speakers from various European countries or from EU institutions are present and being quoted in several public spheres if there is no common frame of reference. As an extreme example from the euro crisis: When the Greek newspaper *Dimokratia* depicted German Chancellor Merkel as a Nazi on its cover together with the headlines "Dachau" and (in German) "Memorandum Macht Frei,"[8] such a frame was set explicitly against any form of cross-border communication because it dehumanizes the other (see Chapter 6).

Politicization and Europeanization

The third concept in need of clarification for this book is politicization (see Chapter 6). Whereas Europeanization entails that Europe "hits home" in terms of both the presence of other European speakers (and audiences) and the cross-border use of frames or claims (see previous discussion), it does not necessarily imply politicization. We could envisage, for example, highly visible media reporting on a European Council and Heads of State meeting without any mention of the controversies at the summit. This news reporting then might be Europeanized without being politicized at all. The same holds true for the presence of other European actors in the various public spheres, as well as

[8] Available at www.washingtonpost.com/blogs/blogpost/post/angela-merkel-depicted-as-nazi-in-greece-as-anti-german-sentiment-grows/2012/02/10/gIQASbZP4Q_blog.html (accessed March 12, 2012). "Memorandum Macht Frei" ridicules the "Arbeit macht frei" slogan at the entrance of the Auschwitz concentration camp.

the similarity of frames of reference. In other words, Europeanization does not equal politicization. At the same time, politicization may or may not be Europeanized with regard to actors or frames of reference. For example, Europe and the EU are heavily politicized in the British public spheres, but they are not very Europeanized with regard to the presence of other European speakers or relative to meaning structures (Koopmans, Erbe, and Meyer 2010).

Following De Wilde (2011, 566–7), we define "politicization" as "an increase in polarization of opinions, interests, or values and the extent to which they are publicly advanced towards the process of policy formulation within the EU." In other words, European issues are politicized if and when the following statements are true:

- There is an increase in issue salience of EU-related questions in various public spheres.
- There also is growing controversy and polarization with regard to EU issues (for further discussion, see Chapter 6 in this volume).

Inevitably, politicization is about political conflict and the intensification of political debates in the public spheres (see Schattschneider 1960, 16). EU policies are politicized when they become an integral part of "normal politics." Politicization of EU affairs can occur with regard to different thematic dimensions and at different levels (Kriesi et al. 2008; De Wilde 2011; Statham and Trenz 2013b; Zürn and Ecker-Ehrhardt 2013). The literature on the politicization of European public spheres appears to agree that the "sleeping giant" – that is, the mass mobilization of public sentiment in response to EU policies (Franklin and Van der Eijk 2006) – is gradually awakening and that EU issues are becoming increasingly politicized in the various public spheres (see also Chapter 8 in this volume). Political elites across the EU are slowly realizing that silencing of necessary debates is no longer acceptable.

With regard to themes, politicization may involve the institutional level, including constitutional issues such as the balance of power among the European Commission, the EP, and the Council of Ministers. Some of the debates about a European constitution – particularly the national referenda debates in various countries – involved the institutional level (Oberhuber et al. 2005; Jentges, Trenz, and Vetters 2007; Trenz 2007; Pfetsch, Adam, and Eschner 2008; Statham and Trenz 2013b). Moreover, decision-making processes in the EU become politicized through greater involvement of politicians rather than bureaucrats or expert groups. Finally, politicization involves policy issues on the EU agenda itself. We could even argue that the EU has become a "normal polity" as the more specific EU policies, rules, and decisions are scrutinized and debated controversially in the various and interlinked public spheres. The controversy about the Bolkestein directive concerning freedom of services connotes an early example of a politicized EU issue across borders (Laffan and O'Mahony 2004; Grossman and Woll 2011). The current euro crisis also serves as a prominent example for such a politicization of EU affairs in transnational public spheres (see Chapter 6).

Politicization of EU affairs usually does not take place above and beyond the domestic politics of the member states. As with the Europeanization of public spheres in general, politicization of EU issues occurs in and through the various national-, local-, and issue-specific public spheres. In addition, politicization can manifest in the various interconnected transnational public arenas. What is less clear, however, is how politicization of European themes and the Europeanization of public spheres relate to one another. Among the various dimensions of Europeanization, only the first – issue salience and visibility of European issues – seems to be necessary for politicization. Even here, however, cause and effect are not clear-cut. News-value theory (discussed previously) argues, for example, that increased political conflict – that is, politicization – should lead to growing issue visibility in the media. The other two dimensions of Europeanization – actors and content – are orthogonal to politicization (see Chapter 6). It could be possible, for example, that EU questions are thoroughly politicized in national public spheres even though other European actors – from the EU and from member states – do not have a voice at all. Regarding the substantive content and various interpretative frames, it is not clear whether politicization per se leads to greater Europeanization of public spheres in terms of emerging transnational communities of communication. Whether or not issues are framed as questions of common European concern that require European answers is orthogonal to politicization. Some would argue, for example, that the increasing politicization of EU policies leads to greater renationalization rather than Europeanization of public spheres – in conjunction with the rise of Euroskepticism (see Chapters 8 and 9).

PART I

How to grasp the Europeanization of public spheres: theory, methods, empirics

2 | Theorizing communication flows within a European public sphere

BARBARA PFETSCH AND ANNETT HEFT

The values and ideas of European integration often have been threatened in previous and current political and economic crises. The ongoing financial crisis, however, has made acute the discussion about transnational spaces for political debate because it has brought about an unprecedented level and intensity of communication and provoked a pressing public debate about the future of the market, the common currency, and the individual and collective costs of European solidarity for both countries and citizens. For scholars and public intellectuals, the political situation seems to offer a vivid example to observe in real time that European integration proceeds together with profound disagreement about its fundamental meaning. This communication also can be seen as a core constituent of a European public sphere. The question remains, however, about whether the public debate in the given circumstances is sufficient to meet the requirements of a true European community of communication that will eventually enhance a common identity.

Against this background, this chapter aims to understand the concepts and meanings of a European public sphere and the factors that are linked with various degrees and levels of transnational communication within and across Europe. We discuss the research on theories and measures of a European public sphere, thereby focusing on the communication flows, their interdiscursivity, and their convergence. Whether the actual communication is sufficient to qualify with respect to the normative requirements of true European democracy is still a contested theme. Since the early studies in the 1990s, scholars have debated how inclusive and convergent European communication within national public spheres must be to constitute a democratic European public sphere (Gerhards 1993, 2002; Wessler et al. 2008). Some researchers concentrate on the Europeanization of communicative flows as instances of transnational communicative interaction (Koopmans and Statham 2010b). Other scholars question

whether and under what conditions transnational communication provides a space for an emerging European community of communication and the construction of a European identity (see, e.g., Wessler
et al. 2008; Tobler 2010; and, in particular, Risse 2010; Van de Steeg
2010).

In this chapter, we pursue the discussion in three steps. First, we
discuss theories about the basic question of what exactly constitutes a
European public sphere. We show that the chosen theoretical models
involve different normative requirements and, consequently, demands
and expectations on the functions of a public sphere. We also discuss
empirical measures and approaches that are used in studies on the
unresolved research questions.

Second, we argue that public communication is strongly connected
with the emergence of European identity and that we must understand
exactly the empirical patterns of horizontal and vertical transnational
communication before we can assess the state and the future of the
European public sphere. We highlight that the nature and the degree of
Europeanization rest on a multitude of contingent conditions, such as
the interests and constellations of actors that have a stake in European
communication. We also discuss their communication patterns and the
role of the media.

Bringing together the actors' objectives of public communication
and theoretical claims about the functionality of Europeanized public
spheres is a necessary but insufficient condition to explain transnational communication across Europe. In fact, research points out that
Europeanization also depends on contexts and opportunity structures
in the political realm. European Union (EU) governance, public opinion, and conflict over EU issues have been shown to influence the
emergence of Europeanized public spheres. Thus, in the third section,
we discuss these issues with respect to the interrelationships among
issue characteristics, communication strategies, and media effects.

It is in public debate that collective identities are constructed and
reconstructed and publicly displayed, thereby creating political communities. Risse (2010) stresses that the processes of arguing and debating issues of common concern lead to collective identification and create a community of communication as Europeans (see also Chapters 6
and 7 in this volume). These debates automatically raise questions of
self-definition, European values, and the common political future of
Europe (Risse 2010, 125–6). In this line of thought, communication

national and the European levels. Here, national actors may address European actors or make claims on European issues (i.e., "bottom up"). Conversely, European actors (e.g., the European Commission) may address national governments and thus intervene in national policies and debates (i.e., "top down") (see Koopmans and Erbe 2004, 101; Koopmans and Statham 2010b, 38). Such communicative linkages make European institutions and their representatives, as well as European policies, visible within national public spheres.[3] "Horizontal Europeanization," conversely, consists of communicative linkages between different member states. The authors distinguish between a weak and a strong variant. The weak form means that the media in one country cover debates and political developments in another member state without direct linkages between the countries. Communicative linkages of actors from one country that explicitly refer to actors or policies in another country build the strong variant of horizontal Europeanization (Koopmans and Erbe 2004, 101; Koopmans and Statham 2010b, 38; see also the dimension of "discursive integration" in Wessler et al. 2008, 11f.). Hence, horizontal Europeanization serves as a sign of the interconnectedness of national publics in different member states and of real exchange between discourse arenas (see also the indicator of "discursive interaction" in Van de Steeg 2003, 181).

The main advantage of the approach of conditional Europeanization is that it stresses the dynamic and relational character of public communication that allows measurement of how public debate develops over time and across national spaces. By assessing communication flows, it is possible to capture public spheres of various types without a priori determining their extension. In this framework of analysis, it is an empirical question whether and to what degree the discussion of issues remains within a nationally bound communication space or whether it transcends it and becomes Europeanized. Thus, we can compare degrees of Europeanization over time or across policy areas and in relation to the extent of non-Europeanized communication. The process of Europeanization is assessed by "the extent that a substantial – and, over time, increasing – part of public contestation goes beyond a particular national political space ... and does not bypass Europe

---

[3] For a similar approach, see the dimension of "monitoring governance" in Wessler et al. (2008, 10–11). The attention to European issues, of course, also is captured by the model of concurrent issue publics.

by referring only to non-European supranational and transnational spaces..." (Koopmans and Statham 2010b, 43). By contrast, a completely closed national public sphere according to this theory is characterized by communication flows that remain confined to national actors discussing national issues within this scope.

If debates are studied over time, the concept of conditional Europeanization also allows for assessing whether national debates converge over time. This convergence may occur in relation to speakers, discourse coalitions, cleavage structures, or frames and patterns of justification (Wessler et al. 2008; Tobler 2010).[4] Moreover, we also can study whether and how a European "community of communication" (Wessler et al. 2008; Risse 2010; Van de Steeg and Risse 2010) emerges through public communication over time and eventually generates symbols of collective identity. Thus, an increasing degree in the use of expressions of belonging to the same European community is understood as a sign that a collective identity of Europe is acknowledged (Wessler et al. 2008, 32).

How can we identify and measure Europeanization?

Theories of European public sphere not only present concepts of how to define and determine communication flows within and across Europe. These concepts also are consequential for the empirical study of how far the transnationalization of communication has come to date. The study designs and methods applied to measure Europeanization all have strengths and weaknesses, so there is no superior solution or better methodological approach. Nevertheless, the designs developed and the methods applied are a consequence of the chosen theory and its particular analytical angle.

Measuring communication flows across Europe

Analyzing the Europeanization of national debates requires study designs that capture the degree to which European issues and actors have become visible in media coverage as compared to non-European

---

[4] With regard to this dimension, the difference between the model described here and the model of concurrent issue publics is that the latter is in its original conceptualization a static model, whereas the concept of Europeanization presupposes a relational and dynamic approach.

items. Furthermore, to cope with the dynamic character of Euro-peanization, longitudinal research designs are needed. Cross-sectional data collected at one point in time provide only a snapshot of "Euro-peanness" (i.e., whether European issues or actors have surfaced at the moment). Such a study design falls short of documenting the process of Europeanization.

Empirical studies that relate to the theory of conditional Euro-peanization use the method of claims analysis to assess the density of communicative linkages between actor types and issues within and between national and transnational spaces. The method attempts to reconstruct public contestation by examining how actors establish arguments in public by addressing other actors and making claims on them (Koopmans and Statham 2010b, 53–7). Claims analysis is an elaborate approach to investigate the spatial reach, interconnected-ness, and relative density of public communication within and between different political spaces (Koopmans and Erbe 2004; Koopmans and Statham 2010b; see also Chapter 3 in this volume).[5]

In the analysis of a European public sphere, claims analysis serves as a tool to measure the density, the direction, and the scope, as well as the content of communication, and to determine the degree to which these elements of communication remain national or become European. The source material for claims analysis is national media coverage.

Erbe developed a further approach in this tradition (Erbe 2005, 2006, 2012). She captures horizontal Europeanization in press reviews of national media by recording the mutual quotation and referencing. Press reviews are indicators of mutual observation of media outlets across Europe; by pointing out the structure of their opinion geograph-ically, she is able to reconstruct transnational flows of communication.

Analyzing the synchronization of frames and discourse coalitions

Studies that adhere to the theory of concurrent issue publics work with designs that focus on single issues of European concern. They measure and compare the attention given to an issue in various countries at one point in time. The comparative approach allows for assessing the

---

[5] However, claims analysis also comprises the substantive issue of a claim and the justification given for the claim, thereby capturing parts of the framing of an issue.

similarity or difference arising from the conflict lines under which these issues are discussed. This design accounts for evaluations of the Europeanness of issues of public communication, but it is unable to measure the dynamic development of public sphere. Capturing the synchronization and possible convergence of meaning structures on European matters across Europe over time requires longitudinal and cross-country comparative study designs.

Another method applied in the investigation of concurrent issue publics is frame analysis, which tries to capture " . . . interpretive packages that give meaning to an issue" (Gamson and Modigliani 1989, 3). Framing involves the selection and accentuation of arguments with regard to problem definition, causal interpretation, moral evaluation, and/or treatment recommendation (Entman 1993, 52). The analysis of frames allows for measuring the similarity of discourses at a given point in time (i.e., cross-sectional and cross-country design) or the gradual convergence and divergence of public debates on European affairs (i.e., longitudinal and cross-country design). However, with the analysis of framing over time alone, we are unable to determine the actual interconnectedness. The similarity of communication in different arenas, for example, could be a simple result of similar news values leading journalistic selection processes. As Trenz points out, " . . . the simultaneity of communication about the same issues does not by itself define the criteria of a European public sphere (it is still possible that communication takes place in different arenas which ignore each other)" (Trenz 2004, 308). Thus, we cannot be certain that the simple coincidence of issue agendas or frames among national media at a given point in time actually indicates Europeanness. Another problem is that the analysis of single-issue careers does not allow for a relational perspective on the overall Europeanization of public spheres. Therefore, although we obtain a spotlight on the issue analyzed, we cannot assess whether European issues gain increasing relevance and attention over time and, more important, in relation to other national and international issues discussed in mass media or other arenas.

Network analysis

The study of the European public sphere has greatly profited from network analysis, which is both a statistical method for analyzing the connections between different agents (Scott 1991, 3) and a theoretical perspective that underlines the relevance of actors' embeddedness in network structures (Jansen 2002, 11). Network analysis was used in studies on Europeanization as an approach to map actor relationships constituted by communication flows within and across Europe. Also, the data of claims analysis can be used because they contain basically subject–action–object relationships (Adam 2008b). Claims data allow the reconstruction of discourse networks and actor coalitions relating to either issues or geographical scope (Koopmans and Statham 2010b, 57). When used within a cross-country and longitudinal design, network analysis can provide answers to the questions of whether transnational discourse coalitions in Europe build up around issues or countries and whether they are similar and converge or diverge over time (Adam 2008b, 192–5).

Another approach to measure communication and interconnectedness in networks within and across Europe takes advantage of digital communication technologies as a data source. For instance, Bennett, Lang, and Segerberg (see Chapter 5 in this volume) conducted hyperlinked web analyses, thereby revealing the relationships among actors and organizations that gather around an issue. These networks evolve on the basis of internet communication, which supplements traditional mass-mediated communication. Mapping digital communication and interaction networks is a further approach to grasping the inclusiveness and scope of European public communication.

The juxtaposition of research designs and methods demonstrates well that the empirical study of European public communication has advanced and reached a high level of methodological rigor and sophistication. Also, depending on the theories about a European public sphere, the empirical study takes different angles and approaches. Yet, most scholars agree that the limitation of one single method can be overcome by combining the strategies of analysis. For instance, Trenz proposes when studying the mechanisms of Europeanization of public sphere, "the interdiscursive and the resonance mechanisms should be considered as complementary" (Trenz 2010, 25). This claim is reflected in recent studies that combine the measurement of communication flows and interdiscursivity within actor constellations, on the one hand, and the analysis of convergent argument structures and frames, on the other.

Who has a stake in transnational European communication and the emergence of Europeanized public spheres?

The nature of Europeanized public spheres as a dynamic interaction of segmented or transnational publics implies that Europeanization must not be seen as a unilinear or continuously growing flow of communication. Instead, it is a process that is highly dependent on various conditions that promote or restrain the development. We address these constraints in two steps. First, with regard to actors and their communicative needs and strategies, we ask: Who has a stake in Europeanization? What are the motives, functions, and possible outcomes of communication of political actors in the centers of national and European policy making, as well as their challengers from civil society? What intentions do political actors pursue, and what consequences follow from their strategic choices for the emergence of Europeanized public spheres?

Second, actors engaging in speech about other European actors or topics have different access to resources and political power. They use a wide range of communication strategies and have different incentives to target the national or supranational level of publics and policy making. In our assessment, we first distinguish between actors at the center of the political system and actors on the inner and outer periphery (Peters 1993; Habermas 2006b). We then discuss the media in their role as political actors and potential motors of or obstacles to Europeanization.

Supranational EU actors, domestic-state actors, and parties

According to their institutional background, actors at the supranational level of EU decision making and domestic state actors face different needs for communication. In the 1990s, it was argued that institutions, including the European Commission, the European Parliament (EP), and the European Council, neglect professional communication functions and therefore lack media visibility (Gerhards 1993). Since then, we have witnessed a change from "politics behind closed doors" to more transparency (Brüggemann 2008, 2009). The "Plan D for Democracy, Dialogue and Debate" declared by the European Commission in 2005,[6] the activities around the "Europe

---

[6] Commission of the European Communities 2005, COM (2005) 494 final.

Direct" program,[7] and the web television channel "europarltv" established by the EP[8] are examples of increasing communication activities
and their professionalization by EU institutions.

The proliferation of EU communication efforts also must be interpreted in light of the increasing politicization of European affairs.
Although the institutions in Brussels are prepared and eager to invest in
their own communication capacity, they are in strong competition with
national governments that are not willing to relinquish their predominant role in EU communication (Meyer 1999). Studies of information
policies toward the media demonstrate this competition. National governments are the only actors that target journalists regularly and most
frequently, followed by national-interest groups and national parties.
EU institutions rank only fourth in their attempt to supply information
to the press (Statham 2010b, 132–5).[9] However, within the EU opportunity structure, supranational actors are more active in addressing the
EU level than the domestic level. In the perception of journalists, European institutions target EU correspondents considerably more often
than other journalists (Statham 2010b, 135).[10] Thus, in stimulating
European public debate, EU correspondents clearly acquire a special
transmitter role for European institutions.

The communication of national politicians in Brussels faces a
twofold challenge: they are responsible for EU policy making at the
European level and they also remain primarily national actors accountable to national governments, parliaments, and their national electorate (Kriesi et al. 2010, 225). Their interest is to activate accep-
tance and generate legitimacy at home for political decisions reached
in EU functions. Thus, with national elections and contention in mind,
these actors may avoid excessive internal discussion on unpopular EU
decisions. According to a recent analysis by Gerhards et al. (2009),
national actors employ a twofold framing strategy: they attribute

---

[7] Available at http://europa.eu/europedirect/index_en.htm (accessed March 15, 2013).
[8] Available at www.europarltv.europa.eu/en/home.aspx (accessed March 15, 2013).
[9] To assess who makes the most effort to supply information, journalists were asked to describe the frequency with which they were contacted by a list of political actors, by actor type and political level (Statham 2010b, 133).
[10] On a scale ranging from 0 to 1, European institutions target EU correspondents with a mean score of 0.76 and other journalists with a mean score of 0.28 (Statham 2010b, 135).

positive outcomes of EU politics to their own record whereas they blame others, especially the European Commission, for negative outcomes. This is important because we know that within Europeanized national public spheres, domestic state actors generally gain considerably more visibility than their counterparts at the supranational level (Koopmans et al. 2010, 65). Thus, national politicians have a better chance of promoting their views and of shaping public opinion and the perception of EU politics through national media. Moreover, the national actors that play a role in European claims making primarily represent the governments and their administrations (Wessels et al. 2003, xvf.). Parliamentary arenas and national-party organizations are less well represented (Koopmans 2010, 108).

Interest groups and social-movement organizations

Examining the importance that interest groups and social-movement organizations (SMOs) attribute to communication on the European level, we find that these actors prefer traditional lobbying activities to public-media strategies in Brussels (Kriesi et al. 2010, 238f.). This especially applies to groups with the easiest access to policy makers, such as business-interest associations. They value inside activities more than unions, farmers' associations, and other groups do (Kriesi et al. 2010, 240). Therefore, interest groups are not agents that we should expect to regularly trigger European public communication.

However, SMOs turned out to have a stronger preference for public strategies. Looking at the standing of interest groups and other civil-society groups in Europeanized public debates, it is especially the civil-society actors such as nongovernmental organizations (NGOs) that are rather weakly represented in Europeanized claims making (Koopmans 2007). Although peripheral actors gain a certain amount of public visibility in specific issue fields (e.g., agriculture and monetary politics), a closer review reveals that these are primarily actor groups with strong institutional or organizational power and resources (e.g., farmers, employers, and businesses or economists and financial experts) (Koopmans 2007, 198–9).

The mass media as infrastructure and political actors of Europeanization

European communication must be seen as a process that takes various forms and dynamics. Public assemblies, demonstrations, online

Although Europeanization features certain peculiarities in the new Eastern European countries, the overall pattern appears to be similar to developments in the Western European member states. Scholars term this a "pattern of a catch-up Europeanization" (Kleinen-von Königslöw and Möller 2009, 101) with increasing reporting on EU matters and issues of other European countries but at a later date than in the old member states. In the course of time, differences in the Europeanization of old and new member states seem to vanish. In a review of the news addressing the 2004 and 2009 EP elections, Schuck et al. (2011) show that the higher visibility of election news in the new EU member states detected in 2004 did not recur in 2009 (see also De Vreese and Boomgaarden 2009). The authors conclude that differences in Europeanization " . . . appear to be more country-specific than indicative of any East-West or North-South divide" (Schuck et al. 2011, 47).

Within national publics, the amount and the level of Europeanization differ among media types and formats. Regarding the print media, we witness differences in the level of Europeanization and the positioning on European policies among quality newspapers, on the one hand, and tabloid and regional papers, on the other. Research reports a significantly lower level of vertical forms of Europeanization (i.e., attention to European institutional actors and European issues) in tabloid newspapers and also slightly lower levels of horizontal references (Kleinen-von Königslöw 2010b). Also, there is evidence that regional newspapers report on European issues in a more parochial and less Europeanized manner (Vetters 2007). Koopmans (2010, 120) maintains, however, that the newspaper type is of minor importance for *explaining* the overall patterns of Europeanization, except for the greater probability of expressing critical views on Europe. Euroskepticism and negative judgments on Europe are significantly higher in the tabloid press than in broadsheets.

Differences in Europeanization levels also are found in audiovisual media (Lauf and Peter 2004; Peter and de Vreese 2004). For example, public-service broadcasters in Germany and Austria feature considerably more references to Europe, European institutions, and European countries in their nonfictional news, magazines, documentaries, and talk-show formats than commercial television channels in those countries (Woelke et al. 2010). This pattern is explained by the fact that public-service broadcasters are required to devote a greater share of their programming to information formats. The pattern, how-ever, also persists in a relative sense considering the overall broadcast-ing time of these formats (Woelke et al. 2010, 57). The mission and self-commitment of public-service broadcasting (e.g., in Germany and Spain) favor European integration and understanding among nations (Holznagel 1999), and the objective is to foster the exchange of infor-mation among citizens of the EU (Harrison 2010).

National media as political actors

The proactive role of the national media in Europeanization relates to their editorials and commentaries and the question of whether they actively promote or restrict European scopes and angles (Pfetsch 2008; Pfetsch and Adam 2008). The assumption is that the national media may open up the discursive space for European angles, even though other political actors insist on national scopes or downplay the Euro-pean positions (Koopmans and Pfetsch 2006, 118f.).

Comparative research on newspaper editorials in seven countries in the early 2000s revealed that three factors influence the level of Euro-peanization of the press, as measured by the openness to European actors, the framing of European issues, and the support for the EU (Pfetsch 2008; Pfetsch et al. 2008, 2010). First, Europeanization was higher in the outlets of Continental European countries that are fully involved in the European integration process than in the press of coun-tries with a lesser depth of integration. For example, in Spain, Italy, France, and Germany, the press showed more European views com-pared to the media in the United Kingdom and Switzerland (Pfetsch 2008, 28f.). An exception was the Netherlands, where the level of Europeanization was low in the media despite the country's political involvement in the EU (Pfetsch et al. 2008, 473). Moreover, the press portrayed Europeanization mainly with respect to two transnational frames: (1) the relationship between the member states and the EU, and (2) the alternative between widening or deepening EU integration (Pfetsch et al. 2008, 2010). It is interesting that the media advocated a supranational model of deepened integration before EU enlargement (Pfetsch et al. 2008, 481). The only exception was the UK press, which stressed the distance between the country and the EU and showed an overall negative attitude toward Brussels.

Second, the openness to European scopes in the press varies signif-icantly across policy fields. Issue fields with deeper integration where the political decision-making power has shifted from the national to the supranational level of policy making feature better conditions for Europeanization. Monetary policy and European integration issues are debated within an overall European frame of reference, whereas education and pension issues are discussed only from the national perspective. This finding is consequential because it confirms that the media engage in the transnational public debate if the issues at stake are linked to the political power structure in Brussels (Pfetsch 2008, 30–3).

Third, newspaper types feature variation in the Europeanization of media commentary. As in the news coverage, the tabloid and regional press turned out to advocate national views to a higher degree than the quality press, and journalists of the tabloid press expressed more negative opinions on average than commentators in the quality press (Pfetsch 2008, 31–3). In countries where the depth of integration is a contentious issue, the tabloid press seems to be a frontrunner in presenting this polarization (Pfetsch et al. 2008, 473).

Opportunity structures of Europeanization

Active claims making and communication infrastructures are necessary but not sufficient conditions to explain the level and dynamics of European public debate. Both political elites and challengers position themselves using their framing strategies within a given political space established by, for example, the setting of multilevel EU governance, public opinion, cleavages, and actor networks, as well as general attitudes about European integration. These factors create important political-opportunity structures of communication that impose on the degree and level of Europeanization.

EU multilevel governance

First, the chance of Europeanization depends on the way in which decision-making power in specific issue fields is structured. The distribution of power between the national and the EU levels varies among issue fields, as does the extent of Europeanization. Where the EU has gained strong supranational competencies – such as in monetary politics and European integration – European actors and policy contexts are highly visible (Koopmans et al. 2010). Conversely, this beneficial condition does not exclude other issues to become strongly Euro-peanized if other context factors, such as politicization (see the following discussion), stimulate this development.

A second set of structural factors comprises a country's involvement in the European integration process. Cross-national variations in types of Europeanization depend on EU membership and how deeply a country is involved in the different steps of European integration, such as the euro and the Schengen Agreement (Wessler et al. 2008; Koopmans et al. 2010; see also Chapter 3 in this volume).

Furthermore, communication patterns within Europe depend on the size and power of a country, thereby determining the transnational hierarchy of influence on news geography and flows of opinion. There is evidence that the media in smaller and less powerful countries more often discuss the affairs of neighboring European countries. They also tend to include more actors from other European countries in their national debates (Wessler et al. 2008, 73f.).

Public opinion

Public opinion about European politics is an essential condition of the emergence of the European public sphere that plays out in two ways. First, public opinion constitutes an important parameter of the political opportunity structure and thus an important precondition of debate on European issues. The results of continuous surveys and the debates about the variation in people's opinions about Europe and the EU affect the agenda-setting and framing strategies of political actors (discussed previously). Political debate within nation-states and positioning on EU issues certainly are constrained if Euro-barometer data indicate an opinion climate of decreasing trust in the EU.

Second, and at the same time, public opinion is also an "output" of communication and therefore a consequence of a (more or less) Europeanized public debate (Gerhards and Neidhardt 1991). In this respect, public opinion plays out as media effects. There is empirical evidence that the framing of EU politics within mass media has an impact on media users' attitudes and their perceptions of EU integration. Heavy media users accessing several media sources for EU-related information have been shown to adopt more positive attitudes toward the EU and Europe as a community (Scharkow and Vogelgesang 2009).

However, media effects are not independent of the tone and framing of EU coverage. Several studies show that the more often EU news mentions that one's own country has benefited from the EU or frames EU policy in terms of opportunity, the higher is the share of people who support European integration. Conflict or risk framing as well as news about European politics framed in terms of strategy, by contrast, can lead to a decrease in EU support and greater Euroskepticism (Schuck and De Vreese 2006; De Vreese 2007a; Vliegenthart et al. 2008; De Vreese et al. 2011).

Media effects seem to have important consequences for European identity building. Bruter's work shows that not only the attitude toward the integration process but also the identification with Europe are influenced by media messages and the use of EU symbols. He points out that " . . . the mass media, by disseminating good or bad news on Europe and European integration, has a strong identity-building power over the citizens of the European Union" (Bruter 2005, 124). The study provides evidence that the exposure to "good news" influences citizens' likelihood of identifying with Europe, whereas "bad news" makes them less likely to feel like Europeans (Bruter 2005, 126f.). This research also confirms that different levels of European identity must be considered (see Chapter 7 in this volume).

Conflict and politicization

The ongoing financial crisis in Europe has provided ample proof that issue-specific conflict constellations among political elites, the public, and intermediary actors are mobilizing attention to European issues. Cleavages and conflict constellations are crucial to understanding variations in the amount and quality of Europeanization in national arenas. This applies to (1) the degree of conflict within a country's political elite differentiating between polarized and consensual issues, (2) the presence or absence of actors from the political periphery mobilizing public attention, and (3) the relationship between national elites' attitudes and public opinion (Adam 2007a, 413). Research has shown repeatedly that the common input from the EU is filtered at the national level (Risse et al. 2001; Adam 2007b, 2008a). Thus, national political actors are important to the chances of Europeanization. National political elites strategically decide whether to actively put a European issue on the agenda or to avoid broader public discussion. Adam argues that if national political actors cannot profit from the domestication of an issue, the topic likely will become a low-salience issue (Adam 2007a). In France, where a clear majority of citizens rejected EU enlargement, whereas the French political elite supported it, the media tended to play down the issue (Adam 2008a).

Politicization of EU issues is another condition that fosters the salience of European issues on the public agenda. Following De Wilde, we understand politicization as "an increase in polarization of opinions, interests, or values and the extent to which they are publicly advanced towards the process of policy formulation within the EU" (De Wilde 2011, 566–7; see also Chapter 1 in this volume). Conflicts and political events such as the European Council summits, EP elections, changeovers of the European Commission, and changes in the presidency have been shown to open opportunity windows for media attention and politicization (Eder 2000; Peter and de Vreese 2004; Boomgaarden et al. 2010; Tobler 2010). Next to these special times, the integration process is considered to modify the context of political communication. As Neidhardt et al. (2000, 289) point out, we can expect that stronger integration will lead to increasing demands for public communication, to increasing news values, and to more conflicts initiating European debates.

In addition, scholars suggest that the potential for such public contestation might be higher in countries where strong Euroskeptic voices exist. Adam and Maier (2011), for example, argue that parties at the fringes of the left–right spectrum could turn out to be driving forces for the public articulation of Europskeptic positions, thereby acting as politicizers of Europe. Their analyses of parties' televised advertising slots during the 2009 EP election campaign in six countries show that EU issues and actors are more prominent on the campaign agenda in countries with several Euroskeptic parties. This means that the more Euroskeptic voices existing within a country, the more likely is EU articulation (Adam and Maier, 442). This relationship has been shown not only in the context of advertising slots but also with respect to broader media coverage of European integration in different European countries (Adam and Pfetsch 2009). Except for the United Kingdom, the question of deepening European integration versus national demarcation is more strongly addressed in countries with Euroskeptical parties and more critical stances within the national public (Adam and Pfetsch 2009).

Conclusions

Our discussion began with the premise that far-reaching inclusive communication across national public spaces stands for a European public sphere, which is a first and necessary condition for the development of a political community and European identity. Against this background, we present theories and empirical studies on the European public sphere that basically highlighted the manifold conditions that enhance and restrain the development of transnational European communication. Eventually, research points to the fact that the requirements of communication make the European public sphere a rather fragile and fluid phenomenon, for various reasons. First, our discussion shows that – notwithstanding the theory of a European public sphere – political constraints and media attention to horizontal and vertical communication linkages are subject to change over time. Thus, we need studies of transnational communication in longitudinal cross-national study designs.

Second, the many actors in various national arenas have different and often controversial stakes in the EU. Therefore, they apply various and, in many cases, competing communication strategies that are not always conducive to a common European discourse. We also see from our discussion of communication goals and solutions of different actors that Europeanization might not necessarily increase but instead stagnate or decrease when political conflict constellations, governance in EU institutions, or public opinion changes. As a result, we should observe debates through framing or claims analysis and also continuously study the actor constellations.

Third, we emphasize the role of the media as infrastructures and active voices in transnational European communication. For the most part, the quality broadsheets and public broadcasters seem to open up spaces for transnational debate and also argue in favor of European transnational communication. However, regional media and the tabloids, which are quite widespread in many European countries, may easily counteract this tendency and provoke rather parochial tones, a national closure of public debate, and even Euroskeptic opinions. Finally, we suggest that political constellations, public opinion, and national and social cleavages can provoke situations of communication that are rather dysfunctional for a European public sphere.

We began this chapter with a reference to the ongoing financial crisis in Europe that has intensified communication and contention to an unprecedented level and nevertheless reveals the core of a European public sphere. However, because so many conditions and constraints of transnational communication enter the picture, we cannot assume that media attention, coverage of European issues, and support for European integration are growing permanently. Even if we were to observe a continuing level of contention, we cannot be certain that a high level of attention leads to a stable community of communication, a sense of togetherness, and eventually European identity. We argue that a political community of Europeans requires communication; however, from the discussion of constraints, we may doubt whether communication inevitably leads to a stronger political community of citizens. Although we have evidence that good news about Europe enhances the sense of identity among European people, we can only speculate about the effects of bad news about Europe. In the end, the dynamic of intense contention – even if conducive to a European public sphere – may provoke more national partitions and exclusion of countries and social groups from communication. Avoiding the consequences of bad news about Europe, however, is a political task. This is when politics must be brought back in.

3 How advanced is the Europeanization of public spheres? Comparing German and European structures of political communication

RUUD KOOPMANS

If anyone still had any doubt, the euro crisis put the increasing politicization of the European Union (EU) and its policies in plain sight. Research on the Europeanization of public spheres had previously pointed out that if there is a European public sphere deficit, it certainly does not consist of a lack of media attention for European affairs (e.g., Koopmans and Statham 2010a). However, high degrees of visibility and politicization alone are not sufficient to provide the communicative underpinnings for a viable European polity. If politicians and institutions in the EU or other member states appear only as targets of claims by domestic actors and never as speakers in their own right, then media consumers will never have a firsthand view of the opinions and arguments of actors beyond their own national boundaries; they will learn only how domestic actors view the outside world. Similarly, if domestic actors never appear as the targets of claims by actors from the European level or other member states, ordinary citizens will never hear the opinions and arguments that prevail among domestic actors in the critical light of opinions from beyond their own national boundaries. If this were the predominant shape that the politicization and increased visibility of European affairs takes, transnational public-opinion formation could not occur, a genuine understanding of the motivations and interests of nondomestic actors could not arise, and – consequently – there would be no basis for transnational consensus formation or solidarity. Politicization of Europe that takes such a nationally centered shape would not advance beyond the preceding era of depoliticized European politics behind closed doors, and it would have destructive rather than constructive impacts on the European project.

Despite the numerous studies about the Europeanization of public spheres that have appeared in recent years, we still lack a reliable answer to the question of the shape that the politicization of European affairs is taking. Is this politicization of the type that is an integral part of domestic politics and, therefore, a healthy sign of a normalization of European public debates? Or does politicization take the parochial shapes previously described and does it threaten rather than support further progress in European integration?

An important reason why our answers to these questions are tentative and inconclusive is that a standard of comparison is lacking in studies of the Europeanization of public spheres. As a result, the same data on flows of Europeanized communication can be interpreted positively by some and negatively by others. How much Europeanized public debate and how much exchange of information and viewpoints across national boundaries and between supranational and national levels are necessary to provide the communicative basis for a European polity? These questions can be answered only by comparing Europeanized public debates to something that we know fulfills these functions: that is, public debates within the confines of nation-states. As self-evident as this may seem, such an empirical comparison has not yet been undertaken. Many of the earlier studies of the Europeanization of public communication sampled on the dependent variable by investigating cases preselected for their European-wide scope and relevance, such as the Haider debate (Van de Steeg 2005), European election campaigns (De Vreese et al. 2006), the introduction of the euro (De Vreese et al. 2001), and political scandals involving EU institutions (Meyer 2002; see also Chapter 2 in this volume). Other studies focused on a wide range of issues but selected for analysis only those media articles that contained keywords such as "Europe" or "EU" (Kantner 2004; Trenz 2005), thereby excluding those claims that make no reference to European actors or policies. A smaller number of studies, including the "Europub" project (Koopmans 2007; Koopmans and Statham 2010a), included acts of political communication regardless of whether they referred to European dimensions. Such studies have the advantage that they allow comparisons of degrees of Europeanization across countries, issues, and time and, moreover, they allow us to compare the relative importance of national and Europeanized communication. Even these studies, however, based conclusions regarding degrees and forms of Europeanized communication on rather intuitive assessments of the sufficiency or insufficiency of such communication for undergirding a viable European polity.

In this chapter, I go beyond such intuitive assessments by comparing the structure of political communication within two polity types and their constituent components. In the literature on Europeanization in general and on Europeanization of political communication in particular (see Koopmans and Erbe 2004), a distinction between vertical and horizontal forms of Europeanization is made: the former refers to relationships between the European and national levels, and the latter pertains to relationships among national polities within Europe. A similar distinction can be applied to communicative relationships within national polities. The vertical dimension then refers to relationships between the national level, on the one hand, and regional and local polity levels, on the other. Within national polities, the horizontal dimension refers to relationships among different regional and local polities. As the Europeanization of political communication can be described by the shares of vertical references to the European polity level and horizontal references to other European countries, so can the nationalization of political communication be described by the degrees to which attention is vertically focused on the national center and horizontally on actors, events, and policies in other regions and localities. Conceptualizing communicative relationships in the national and European arenas along similar conceptual lines allows a direct comparison of the structure of communication within national and European arenas, thereby putting our assessments of the (in)sufficiency of current degrees and forms of Europeanization on a more solid footing.

National polities, of course, come in different shapes, and one of the most crucial dimensions of variation concerns the degrees of institutional centralization and regional and local autonomy. It is important to consider this in a comparative assessment of Europeanized and national public debates because, from the point of view of functional communicative integration, there is no need for European public debates to resemble highly centralized policy debates in strongly centralized countries. National polities with a federal institutional structure, such as Germany, are therefore of particular interest because they indicate minimally required degrees of vertical and horizontal integration. As such, they offer a fairer standard of comparison for Europeanized communication than the more centralized communicative structures of polities such as France and the Netherlands.

The data used for my analysis are drawn from the Europub project, which covers claim making in print media in seven European countries – Germany, France, the United Kingdom, Italy, Spain, the Netherlands, and Switzerland – in seven issue fields during the period 1990–2002. Switzerland was excluded from the analyses in this chapter because it is not an EU member. Because it is the most decentralized country within my sample and therefore the most realistic benchmark for an assessment of Europeanized public debates, I give special attention to the structure of political communication in Germany. To investigate to what extent the patterns found for the period 1990–2002 have changed in the most recent period of European politicization concerning the financial crisis, I also draw on a content analysis of the coverage in German media of the crisis in the period 2010–12.

Claim makers in national and European communicative arenas

Koopmans and Statham (2010a, 55) define "claim making" as purposeful communicative action in the public sphere consisting of a public-speech act that articulates political demands, calls to action, proposals, or criticisms, which – actually or potentially – affect the interests or integrity of the claim makers and/or other collective actors. For the Europub project, claims were coded on the basis of a random-sampling frame of newspaper issues irrespective of the actors involved or whether they had a European dimension. A full account of the sampling frame and coding rules is included in Koopmans and Statham (2010a, 53–8). Of the seven issue fields included in the Europub study, two – European integration and military troop deployment – were omitted from this analysis. By definition, they have an issue scope that extends beyond the level of national polities and therefore do not allow an analysis of the structure of purely domestic public debates. The remaining five issue fields for which the structures of public debates in domestic and European arenas can be compared are monetary politics, agriculture, immigration, pensions and retirement, and education (see Koopmans and Statham 2010a for a more precise topical delineation of these issue fields). For my purposes, it is important that this encompasses fields of strong (i.e., the first-pillar fields of monetary politics and agriculture) and weak (i.e., pensions and education) institutional Europeanization, as well as an intermediary case (i.e., immigration). The appendix at the end of this chapter lists the twenty-nine newspapers included in this study and their respective national and regional bases.[1]

Claim data offer the possibility to analyze the structure of political communication from two different perspectives: (1) the actors who make claims (i.e., claim makers or speakers); and (2) those who are addressed, held accountable, criticized, or supported (i.e., the targets of claims). In the first step of the analysis, I focus on the most basic aspect of the structure of political communication – namely, the actors who appear in the media debate as claim makers. For the European communicative arena, this implies that I examine the degree to which print media present the opinions of actors from the European level or from other European countries compared to the share of domestic claim makers from the newspapers' own countries. In a similar manner, I investigate within the national arena to what extent actors from the national polity level and from other regions are cited compared to claim makers from the domestic regional base of the newspaper in question.

National communicative arenas

To delimit the national communicative arena, I selected all claims included in newspapers from a particular country that were physically made within that country; that had a national, regional, or local issue scope (i.e., the geopolitical context in which the issue was framed by the claim-making actor; see Koopmans 2007); and that were made by an actor from that particular country. Within that arena, I investigate whether the actors whose claims are cited are from the national center (e.g., national government, courts, political parties, labor unions, and

---

[1] I do not analyze differences across newspaper types in this chapter. The sample includes quality newspapers of left and right political leaning, as well as tabloids and regional newspapers. Results for right- and left-leaning newspapers are virtually identical. Regional newspapers and tabloids display both a stronger focus on their own region in the domestic arena and a stronger focus on their own country in the European arena. In other words, regional and tabloid newspapers generally have a more parochial focus. However, because this parochial bias affects the domestic and European arenas in the same direction and to a similar degree, the findings on differences of structures of communication across domestic and European arenas also hold for these newspaper types. Results of analyses by newspaper type are available from the author on request.

Table 3.1. *Vertical and horizontal dimensions of claim makers in national communicative arenas, by country*

	D	NL	E	UK	F	I	All
National	70.1	88.0	81.6	85.6	82.7	82.8	81.2
Own region	7.2	4.6	4.9	4.9	6.2	5.1	5.6
Other region	22.7	7.5	13.5	9.4	11.1	12.1	13.2
Total	100%	100%	100%	100%	100%	100%	100%
N =	766	415	266	849	369	859	3,524

Table 3.2. *Vertical and horizontal dimensions of claim makers in national communicative arenas, by issue field*

	Monetary politics	Agriculture	Immigration	Pensions and retirement	Education	All
National	96.7	78.3	79.5	92.5	75.2	81.2
Own region	1.5	6.3	4.1	1.8	8.3	5.6
Other region	1.8	15.4	16.4	5.7	16.5	13.2
Total	100%	100%	100%	100%	100%	100%
N =	275	318	659	663	1,609	3,524

NGOs); from the region (or localities within that region) in which the newspaper is based; or from another region within the same country. Regions were generally defined along administrative–political lines (i.e., Bundesländer, cantons, provinces, and autonomous regions) except in France, where I chose larger regions rather than *départements* because of the latter's small size and limited political clout.[2] Tables 3.1 and 3.2 present the results of this analysis of national communicative arenas across countries and issue fields, respectively.

Regarding country differences, Table 3.1 shows that national-level actors dominate the public debate very strongly in all countries,

---

[2] This decision for France affects the results only to the extent that a choice for *départements* as the regional unit would have resulted in much lower shares of actors from the same region, and higher shares for actors from other regions, without affecting the overall balance between national and regional actors.

varying between 88 percent in the Netherlands and 70 percent in Germany. Germany's domestic public sphere is significantly less centralized, which reflects the fact that Germany has a strongly federalized institutional structure. This suggests that if we want a national public sphere that can best serve as a standard of comparison for a European public sphere, Germany is the country. The table also shows that in all countries, coverage of actors from other regions is greater than that of actors from the newspapers' own regional base. Regarding differences across issue fields, Table 3.2 shows that national actors dominate strongly in all issue fields but clearly more so in monetary politics (97 percent) and pensions and retirement (93 percent) than in education (75 percent), with agriculture (78 percent) and immigration (80 percent) in intermediary positions. Coverage of actors from other regions clearly outweighs that of own regional actors in all issue fields.

The European communicative arena

I now apply the same procedure to communication structures within the European arena. As in the national arena, I vertically distinguish two polity levels in this case, the European and the national. Claims with a regional or local issue scope, as well as those with a supranational or international issue scope beyond Europe, were deleted from the current analysis. The European communicative arena, therefore, is defined by all claims that had a national or European issue scope and were made by an actor from a European country. Within that arena, I investigate whether the actors whose claims are cited are from the European center (e.g., the European Commission, European-level courts, or European-level NGOs), from the country in which the newspaper is based, or from another country within Europe. Analogous to the analysis of the relationships across levels within national arenas, Tables 3.3 and 3.4 show the structure of the European communicative arena across countries and issue fields.

In sharp contrast to the communication structures in the national arena, in which the central national level is strongly dominant (compare to Table 3.1), Table 3.3 shows that actors from the European center command considerably more modest levels of attention, ranging from 10 percent of all claims in UK newspapers to 30 percent in the Spanish press. Instead, the majority of claims are made by actors from a newspaper's own country, with percentages ranging from

Table 3.3. *Vertical and horizontal dimensions of claim makers in the European communicative arena, by country*

	D	NL	E	UK	F	I	All
European	21.4	17.8	29.5	9.8	24.3	24.2	20.6
Own country	57.9	62.7	51.6	77.9	53.3	61.0	61.8
Other country	20.7	19.5	18.9	12.3	22.4	14.8	17.6
Total	100%	100%	100%	100%	100%	100%	100%
N =	1,869	1,038	956	1,647	1,053	1,795	8,358

Table 3.4. *Vertical and horizontal dimensions of claim makers in the European communicative arena, by issue field*

	Monetary politics	Agriculture	Immigration	Pensions and retirement	Education	All
European	29.8	29.8	10.6	6.1	1.3	20.6
Own country	47.2	52.8	67.5	86.9	94.2	61.8
Other country	23.0	17.4	22.0	7.0	4.6	17.6
Total	100%	100%	100%	100%	100%	100%
N =	3,690	1,435	1,211	753	1,269	8,358

52 percent in Spain to 78 percent in the United Kingdom. Not only the vertical focus on the center but also the horizontal focus on other polities on the same level is more weakly developed than in the national arena. Whereas in the national arena coverage of actors from other regions clearly outweighed that of actors from the newspaper's own region, within the European arena it is the exact reverse. The UK press is the most outspoken in this regard, with more than six times as many claims by UK actors as by all actors from other European countries combined. However, if the number of horizontally Europeanized claims is evaluated not in relation to the number of claims by own national actors but rather in relation to the importance of the horizontal dimension of communication in the domestic arena, the picture looks different. Within the European communicative arena, 18 percent of all claims are made by actors from other European countries, compared to 13 percent of claims by actors from other regions within the

national arena. Again, the exception to this pattern is the only federal country in our sample – Germany – where the horizontal dimension is somewhat more strongly developed within the national arena (23 percent of claims by actors from other regions) than in the European arena as covered in German newspapers (21 percent of claims by actors from other European countries). Thus, on the actor level, the structure of political communication in the European arena is characterized by a weak center but also by moderately strong horizontal communicative exchanges that are almost on a par with those in the national arena of a federal state such as Germany.

Of course, the relatively weak position of the European center may be due to the fact that in some of the issue fields selected, European institutions have only limited influence. Indeed, Table 3.4 shows that there are strong differences across issue fields. Education along with pensions and retirement are issue fields in which attention is almost exclusively given to domestic actors and European-level actors; actors from other European countries are virtually absent. In the field of immigration, the role of European-level actors also is limited (11 percent). The common-market issues of monetary politics and agriculture clearly show the highest levels of Europeanization in both the vertical and horizontal variants. However, even in these fields with strong supranational European competencies, domestic actors continue to dominate European-level actors (i.e., 47 versus 30 percent in monetary politics; 53 versus 30 percent in agriculture). Regarding the horizontal dimension, it is again a matter of the standard of comparison. Compared to the share of domestic actors, the level of attention for foreign-national actors is modest. Relatively speaking, foreign-national actors carry the most weight in monetary politics (23 percent), but even that is only half the share commanded by domestic actors (47 percent). Conversely, levels of horizontally Europeanized communication can easily stand comparison with horizontal communication structures in national arenas, especially in European debates on monetary politics, agriculture, and immigration, all of which have shares of horizontal communication (between 17 and 23 percent) that exceed the percentages in the issue fields with the strongest horizontal communication flows within the domestic arena: immigration and education (compare to Table 3.2). In summary, I conclude that controlling for the level of competencies of European institutions somewhat diminishes, but certainly does not eliminate the sharp contrast between the national and European communicative arenas where the relevance of actors from the center is concerned. Horizontal structures of communication, however – at least in those fields in which European competencies are substantial – are even somewhat more strongly developed than on the national level.

Claim makers in a decentralized national polity: the case of Germany

In the comparisons between national and European structures of political communication presented so far, I either aggregated over issues – including issues with strong and weak European competencies – or over countries – including both highly centralized and strongly decentralized countries. To provide a more realistic standard of comparison for judging sufficiencies and deficiencies of Europeanized political communication, I now compare the nature of claim makers in European political communication as previously defined to the country that the analyses have shown to have the least centralized communication structure: Germany. As in all federal polities, the degree of institutional decentralization in Germany varies strongly across policy areas. The *Länder* have little input regarding monetary politics and pensions and retirement, but they have substantial competencies on immigration (e.g., naturalization and expulsion) and agricultural policies. They have clearly the most power in the area of education. Educational systems vary strongly across *Länder*, including crucial issues such as the age at which children are selected for different strands of secondary education; the structure of the system of secondary education; the availability of religious education in state schools; and how schools deal with crucifixes, headscarves, and other religious symbols. The *Länder* control the majority of expenditures in the educational domain, and the role of the federal ministry of education is limited. Most decisions in the educational realm that are of more than regional relevance are taken in the so-called *Kultusministerkonferenz*, where education ministers of the *Länder* regularly meet. The decision-making system in German education politics, therefore, is reminiscent of the way in which decisions are taken in the EU, where the central bureaucracy is relatively weak, control over expenditures resides almost exclusively with the member states, and most of the important common decisions are taken in the Councils of Ministers. For these reasons, Germany – and the field of

in the United Kingdom (18 percent). Across issues (the results are not displayed in the table), European targets are negligible in the field of education (1 percent) but they account for almost half (48 percent) of all targets in monetary politics and agriculture. In sharp contrast to national arenas, however, the majority of targets are domestic actors (52 percent in the European arena versus only 5 percent in national arenas), and almost half (47 percent) of claims are fully domestic in the sense that both speakers and targets are from the country in which the newspaper is based. Fully Europeanized claims (i.e., speakers as well as targets are situated on the European level) comprise only 12 percent of claims in the European arena, compared to 75 percent of fully nationalized claims in national arenas.

In line with the structure of EU decision making, multilevel types of claim making, however, are more widespread in the European arena. All forms of multilevel claim making together comprise 41 percent of claims in the European arena, compared to 22 percent in national arenas. Additionally, 20 percent of claims are bottom-up vertically Europeanized, with national actors targeting European-level actors. Another 6 percent are of the top-down vertical variant, in which European-level actors address claims at national targets. Horizontal forms of multilevel claim making also are more developed in the European than the national arenas. Most of these are of the weak variant, in which newspapers report domestic claims from other countries (10 percent). However, in contrast to national arenas, there also are claims of the strong horizontal variant in which domestic actors make claims on targets in another country, or vice versa (together, 4.5 percent). Although these are small percentages, they show that in the European arena, direct communicative interaction occurs between actors from different countries, whereas in the national arena, virtually all communicative interaction between regional actors passes indirectly through the national center – even in decentralized countries such as Germany.

Figure 3.1 graphically summarizes the results from across all countries and issue fields. The size of ellipses indicates the share of the respective actor category among claim makers; the arrows indicate the direction of claims, from claim maker to target; and the thickness of the arrows represents the relative importance of a specific communicative link.[3] The figure illustrates the stark contrast between

[3] I thank Jutta Höhne for producing Figures 3.1 and 3.2.

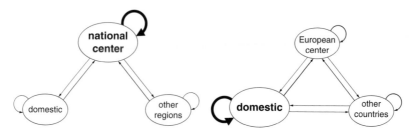

Figure 3.1. Graphical representation of the structure of political communication in national (left) and European (right) arenas across five issue fields and six countries.

the degree of vertical centralization of debates in national and European arenas. National debates are heavily dominated by actors from the national center, as both claim makers and targets of claims. Actors from the European center, by contrast, are relatively marginal in debates in the European arena and – to the extent that they are present – it is more often as targets of claims by others than as claim makers in their own right. Horizontal communicative linkages, however, are somewhat more strongly developed in the European than in the national arenas. Perhaps more important than this modest quantitative difference, debates in the European arena are also more strongly horizontally linked in a qualitative sense. This is because a small but non-negligible share of communication is encountered in which actors from the newspaper's own country directly address actors in other countries and, even more important, where domestic actors are targeted by actors from other member states. Still, these signs of horizontal communicative integration cannot undo the fact that debates in the European arena have a strong parochial focus on actors from the newspaper's own country (i.e., 63 percent of claim makers; 52 percent of targets). Taking a broad view on public debates across all issues and countries arrives at a rather sobering conclusion regarding the degree of integration of the European communicative arena, which remains heavily dominated by domestic national actors and their opinions and arguments.

This comparison across all issue fields, however, can provide only a first rough idea of the differences between the communicative structures of national and European arenas. As emphasized previously, we would not empirically expect or normatively require that communication patterns in the European arena are similar to those found in

Table 3.8. *Claim makers and targets in the European communicative arena in the field of agriculture*

CLAIM MAKERS	TARGETS			
	European center	Own country	Other countries	All
European center	18.5	6.2	3.2	27.9%
Own country	21.3	28.8	2.9	53.0%
Other countries	8.5	2.2	8.4	19.1%
All	48.3%	37.2%	14.5%	100%
N = 485				

national communication on highly nationalized issues such as pensions and retirement. It would be similarly misconceived to judge the sufficiency of levels of Europeanization of communication by measuring them against the yardstick of the degree of nationalization of public spheres in highly centralized countries such as France. Finally, we would not expect or require communication in the European arena to be strongly Europeanized in issue fields where the EU has few competencies, such as education policies.

Therefore, I focus on two issue fields – agriculture and monetary politics – in which the EU and its institutions have gained important competencies that can be meaningfully compared to the competencies of national governments in national policy fields. Moreover, regarding monetary politics, I exclude claims made before the introduction of the euro; for the same reason, I entirely exclude the United Kingdom, which has retained its own currency. As the national comparison, I focus again on the most federalized country in the sample, Germany, and on the issue field in that country in which the competencies of the federal states are strongest: education.[4]

Table 3.8 demonstrates the agriculture issue in the European arena. Compared to Table 3.7, in which all issue fields were considered together, the most important change is that in the field of agriculture, European-level actors become the most important targets of claims,

---

[4] An analysis of the agriculture issue in Germany is not possible because the number of cases for which targets are known is too small to allow a meaningful quantitative analysis.

Table 3.9. *Claim makers and targets in the European communicative arena in the field of monetary politics (since 2000 and excluding the United Kingdom)*

| | TARGETS | | | |
CLAIM MAKERS	European center	Own country	Other countries	All
European center	22.3	4.6	6.6	33.5%
Own country	23.8	14.4	2.1	40.3%
Other countries	14.6	1.6	10.0	26.2%
All	60.7%	20.6%	18.7%	100%
N = 1,214				

with 48 percent (compared to 32 percent in Table 3.7), whereas the share of claims with domestic targets strongly decreases (37 percent compared to 52 percent in Table 3.7). This also results in a strong reduction of the share of claims that are purely domestic to 29 percent (compared to 47 percent in Table 3.7). Against this massive shift in the targets of claims stand significantly more modest changes regarding the actors that make claims. Here, too, the share of European-level actors increases (28 percent compared to 18 percent in Table 3.7) and that of domestic actors decreases (53 percent compared to 63 percent in Table 3.7). Domestic actors remain, however, by far the most important category of claim makers on agricultural issues.

Table 3.9 shows that the Europeanization of structures of communication has progressed even further in the field of monetary politics than in the field of agriculture. No less than 61 percent of claims on monetary politics are aimed at European-level actors, putting domestic targets (21 percent) far behind. However, although less outspoken than in the agriculture field, domestic actors remain the dominant category of claim makers (40 percent), and there is a significant gap between the importance of European-level actors as targets and their more modest role as claim makers in their own right (34 percent). In contrast to the agricultural field, a modest strengthening of horizontal communication structures also can be discerned in debates on monetary politics. Actors from other countries are responsible for 26 percent of monetary-politics claims (compared to 20 percent in Table 3.7) and

Table 3.10. *Claim makers and targets in the German national communicative arena in the field of education*

CLAIM MAKERS	TARGETS			
	National center	Own region	Other regions	All
National center	33.7	2.4	12.4	48.5%
Own region	2.4	8.9	0.0	11.3%
Other regions	10.6	0.0	29.6	40.2%
All	46.7%	11.3%	42.0%	100%
N = 169				

appear in 19 percent of claims as targets (compared to 16 percent in Table 3.7). The reason for this increased presence of foreign countries in debates on monetary politics is mainly that they appear more often as sources of claims targeted at the European center (15 percent) or as targets of claims made by the European center (7 percent).

How do these patterns of Europeanized communication about agricultural and monetary politics compare to those in a decentralized political issue in a federal national polity? Table 3.10 provides an answer for education politics in Germany. Regarding the actors that are addressed, there is a fair amount of similarity to debates on monetary politics in the European arena, with actors from the national-polity center as the most important targets (47 percent compared to 61 percent in Table 3.9) and a modest role for domestic targets (11 percent compared to 21 percent in Table 3.9). Unlike European monetary politics, however, domestic (i.e., own-regional) actors also are quite marginal in German education politics concerning their role as speakers of claims (11 percent compared to 40 percent in European monetary politics in Table 3.9), and actors from the national center (49 percent) appear as the most important category of claim makers. The reasons for these differences lie mainly in the differential importance of two types of claim making. German education debates include a stronger centralized component with a high share of claims by national actors directed at other national targets (34 percent). European monetary debates, by contrast, stand out by their comparatively high share of vertical bottom-up claims by domestic actors targeted at the European

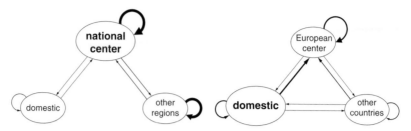

Figure 3.2. Graphical representation of the structure of political communication in German education politics (left) and European monetary politics (right) (since 2000 and excluding the United Kingdom).

center (24 percent). Another crucial difference is that the horizontal dimension of communicative interaction is generally more developed in German education politics, with actors from other regions responsible for 40 percent of claims (compared to 26 percent of claims by actors from other countries in European monetary politics in Table 3.9) and appearing as targets in 42 percent of claims (compared to 19 percent of foreign-national targets in European monetary politics in Table 3.9). However, as these percentages indicate, the horizontal dimension is by no means absent in European debates on monetary politics. In one key respect, moreover, the horizontal dimension is even more developed in the European than in the German domestic arena. There are at least some direct communicative linkages between actors in different countries, whereas when publicly visible communication is concerned, German regional actors never directly address one another.

   Figure 3.2 summarizes the results of this comparison for the two best comparable cases of German education politics and European monetary politics. Contrasting this figure to Figure 3.1, it is immediately clear that a comparison that takes into account differences across issue fields and national polities reveals a much stronger resemblance between the communicative structures within national and European arenas. German education debates and European debates on monetary politics both appear as strongly vertically and horizontally integrated. In monetary politics, however, the European center is more important as a target of claims than as a speaker, which is related to a high share of bottom-up vertical claims in which national actors address European actors and institutions. However, although domestic actors comprise the largest category of claim makers on monetary politics, this hardly makes debates on European monetary politics parochial because the majority of opinions and arguments that reach citizens through the press are from European-level actors and those from other member states. Altogether, these results reveal a rather well-balanced structure of communication within the field of European monetary politics that gives roughly equal voice to domestic, foreign-national, and European-level actors. Also revealed is a pattern of communicative linkages among these actor types that includes the entire gamut of multilevel relationships between speakers and targets. The only imbalance identified is that the European level is significantly more present as a target than as a speaker of claims.

Recent developments: public debates on the European financial crisis, 2010–12

Of course, the fact that the data used so far refer to the period up to 2002 raises the question of to what extent the findings can be extrapolated to more recent years – in particular, the period of intense European-wide public debates and politicization around the financial crisis in the Eurozone from the end of 2009 onward. Unfortunately, there currently are no data available that allow the same kind of detailed analysis of multilevel communicative linkages among claim makers and targets across several issue fields and countries that the Europub data allow. Nevertheless, we can grasp the most recent developments by a simpler and much less labor-intensive approach that focuses on the extent to which various types of actors are mentioned in newspaper coverage – without distinguishing whether they appear as claim makers or targets.

For this analysis, I used the LexisNexis database of German newspapers, focusing on the coverage of the European financial crisis using the following keyword search string: "financial crisis AND Euro AND (currency OR interest rate OR debts)."[5] The string was checked for consistency and returned very few articles that were not related to the financial crisis in the Eurozone; most articles that did refer to the crisis were picked up. The search was conducted for a total of twelve months throughout the years 2010–12 (i.e., January–March 2010, April–September 2011, and October–December 2012). The searches

---

[5] Finanzkrise UND Euro UND (Währung! ODER Zins! ODER Schulden!).

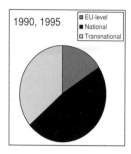
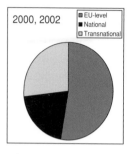
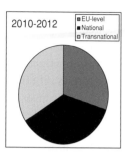

Figure 3.3. Relative shares of national, European, and transnational actors in media coverage of monetary politics and the European financial crisis, 1990–2012.

N (actor mentions) = 156 (1990, 1995); 348 (2000, 2002); 42,445 (2010–20). Note that because of different sample densities, N cannot be compared across time periods.

combined the topical keyword string with a range of actor search strings. For instance, the search string "financial crisis AND Euro AND (currency OR interest rates OR debts) AND (EU-Commission OR European Commission)" returned articles mentioning the European Commission relative to the financial crisis.[6] I compared the obtained results for 2010–12 to the Europub results for the field of monetary politics in the German press for the two periods of 1990–95 (before the introduction of the euro) and 2000–2002 (around and immediately after the introduction of the euro). To make the Europub results congruent with the data for 2010–12, I combined the number of claims in which specific actors were mentioned as claim makers or as targets; this was done because returns from the LexisNexis searches are the combined result of these two types of actor mentions.

Figure 3.3 illustrates the relative frequency with which these three types of actor were mentioned in media coverage of monetary politics and the financial crisis. European-level actors included the European Commission, European Council, European Central Bank (ECB), and European Parliament (EP), as well as the two major European-level political parties and parliamentary fractions: the conservative European People's Party (EPP) and the Party of European Socialists

[6] Finanzkrise UND Euro UND (Währung! ODER Zins! ODER Schulden!) UND (Europäische! Kommission ODER EU-Kommission). The other actor-specific search strings are available from the author on request.

(PES). German national actors included the federal government (Bundesregierung), the federal bank (Bundesbank), and the federal parliament (Bundestag), as well as the two most important parties and parliamentary fractions: the Christian Democrats (CDU/CSU) and Social Democrats (SPD). Finally, transnational coverage of foreign European actors was measured by references to the four most important countries in the Eurozone other than Germany – France, Italy, Spain, and the Netherlands – as well as the most important EU member state outside of the Eurozone: the United Kingdom.

The first panel in Figure 3.3 shows the relative shares of these actors in the pre-euro era. Almost half (48 percent) of the actors mentioned in German media relative to monetary issues in 1990 and 1995 were national political actors. Another 36 percent were from the five other member states, whereas only 16 percent were from the European polity level. The second panel in the figure shows how this balance of discursive forces shifted dramatically from domestic actors toward European-level actors in the period around and immediately after the introduction of the euro. In 2000 and 2002, more than half (53 percent) of all actors mentioned were from the European polity level, another 26 percent were from the five other member states, and German national actors comprised only 21 percent of all mentions. By 2010–12 (the results for the three separate years are not displayed because they are virtually identical), the picture again had changed significantly, with European-level actors declining in relative importance (30 percent), national actors making a comeback (36 percent), and the share of transnational actors remaining fairly stable (34 percent). Overall, Figure 3.3 suggests that the introduction of the euro initially resulted in a strong loss of influence of domestic actors but more recently produced an almost equal balance among domestic, transnational, and European-level actors.

What about the democratic deficit?

So far, these conclusions about the structure of Europeanized political communication are mostly positive. When a comparison with national communicative structures can be made most meaningfully (i.e., between strongly Europeanized policy fields and decentralized national polities and policy fields), the multilevel structure of European public debates is generally not less balanced and multidirectional than communication within national public spheres. The single exception is that European-level actors are not nearly as strongly present as speakers as they are as targets of claims. The recent politicization of European affairs in the context of the financial crisis seems to have added to this balanced communicative structure.

However, there is one important caveat that I highlighted in earlier work (Koopmans 2007): the evidence for the period 1990–2002 shows that the shift in discursive influence away from the national level toward the European and transnational levels also implied a major increase in the discursive weight of executive political actors (i.e., European Commission, European Council, ECB, and domestic and foreign-national governments) to the detriment of civil-society actors as well as parliamentary and political-party representatives. Has this changed during the recent period of increased polarization in the context of the financial crisis? Precisely answering this question again would require the kind of detailed analysis that the Europub data allow. However, an answer using results of the LexisNexis searches can again be reached. I disregard transnational actors because this would require numerous complicated search strings to differentiate foreign-national actors by type. However, from earlier research, we know that the overwhelming majority of transnational actors mentioned in domestic newspapers tend to be foreign-executive actors, such as heads of state and ministers (Koopmans 2007). Within the categories of national- and European-level actors, moreover, I cannot analyze the role of civil-society actors because of the multitude of different civil-society actors. However, the field of monetary politics is one in which the discursive influence of civil society is limited, even in fully nationalized public debates (Koopmans 2007). Therefore, the most important question regarding the field of monetary politics is how the changes from the pre-euro phase to the largely consensual early euro phase and, subsequently, the politicized phase of the financial crisis affected the balance of discursive power between executive actors, on the one hand, and parliamentary and party actors on the other.

Figure 3.4 shows the shares of different actors as a percentage of all mentions of German or European-level actors relative to monetary politics and the financial crisis. European-level (i.e., European Commission, European Council, and ECB) and German (i.e., federal government and federal bank) executive actors are shown on the left

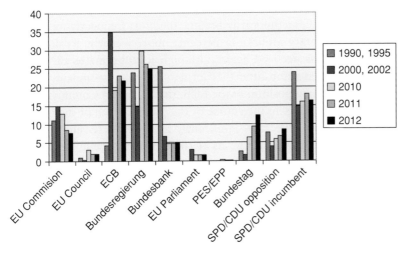

Figure 3.4. Shares (in percentages) of executive and parliamentary/political party actors from the European and national polity levels in media coverage of monetary politics and the European financial crisis, 1990–2012.
N (actor mentions) = 117 (1990, 1995); 256 (2000, 2002); 3,435 (2010); 16,884 (2011); 7,066 (2012). Note that because of different sample densities, N cannot be compared across time periods.

side of Figure 3.4. European-level (i.e., EP and European Socialist and Conservative parties) and German (i.e., federal parliament and SPD and CDU/CSU parties) legislative and party actors are shown on the right side of the figure. For the German parties, incumbent parties are distinguished from opposition parties. In judging the relative weight of executive as well as legislative and party actors, incumbent parties are ambiguous because an important segment of their spokespersons are also members of government – even when they are not, they often support the government's point of view. Therefore, the share of opposition-party voices provides a better indicator of the weight that nonexecutive voices carry in the public debate.

The most significant but also the least surprising change that occurred in the period 1990–2012 is the rise of the ECB as a central player and the concomitant reduced discursive influence of the German federal bank. In 1990–95, it was still the most frequently mentioned actor (25 percent) but, by 2010–12, it was responsible for only 5 percent of mentions. In the period around the introduction of the euro, the ECB temporarily became the most frequently mentioned actor on monetary affairs (35 percent); more recently, its discursive prominence has declined again, although it still remains the second most-mentioned actor, after the German federal government. In contrast to the strong position of the ECB, the European Commission has a more modest role. In the course of the politicization of the financial crisis, its influence became significantly reduced, decreasing to a level of only 8 percent of all mentions in 2012. The European Council and its chairman, Herman van Rompuy, are even less prominent, never rising above 3 percent of mentions. The role of the European executive in monetary and financial affairs, therefore, is largely limited to the ECB, whereas the European Commission has lost important influence in this field and the European Council and its president have not been able to gain any influence. This does not mean that the meetings of heads of state during European Council and other summit meetings are not important. However, their impact on public debates takes the form of statements by representatives of various national governments, and it does not generate much discursive prominence for the Council as an institution or for van Rompuy as its president. In that sense, European summits are reflected in public debates as intergovernmental exchanges between nation-states – especially between a few key players among them – and not as a coherent supranational body with independent authority. This is likely a fairly accurate representation of how the power politics within these summits actually operates.

From the point of view of the democratic deficit, the question is to what extent legislatives and political parties can exert influence in public debates to counterbalance the strong position of the ECB and the German national government. The results show that such a role is certainly not played by the EP or by the European-level political parties. The EP has never had any significant role in debates on monetary and financial affairs, and this situation has not improved during the period of politicization in the context of the financial crisis: in the period 2010–12, the EP accounted for a meager 1.6 percent of actor mentions. European political parties and parliamentary fractions are even more marginal; their presence in public debates on monetary and financial matters can be detected only at the microscopic level.

Politicization has had an effect, however, on the prominence of national legislatives and parties. Initially, the introduction of the euro went along with reduced prominence of the German federal parliament and of the main opposition party (at the time, it was the CDU/CSU). However, in the period of the financial crisis, the share of articles mentioning the Bundestag rose steadily to 12 percent in 2012; a similar trend is observed for the main opposition party in this period: the SPD. Taken together, these results indicate that the politicization of European monetary politics during the financial crisis has strengthened the discursive influence of legislatives and political parties. Their role at first declined as a result of the Europeanization of monetary politics, from 35 percent of all mentions in 1990–95 to 23 percent in 2000–2002. However, during the financial crisis, their share bounced back to 30 percent in 2000 and 36 percent in 2011 and 2012. This was due entirely to the waning and waxing of the influence of national parliaments and parties. If anything, the EP and European-level parties declined in relevance over time, from an already marginal level. Thus, the politicization of monetary politics during the financial crisis reduced the democratic deficit of European monetary politics, but it has done so entirely by a domestication of controversies and an enhanced role for national parties and parliaments.

Discussion and conclusions

The key point of departure for this chapter is that if we want to judge how far the Europeanization of public debates has proceeded, which shapes it has taken, and whether these shapes are of a type that is functional or dysfunctional for further European integration, then we must establish a standard of comparison. In the absence of reliable and comparable historical data on the emergence (and occasional breakdown) of national public spheres, the most suitable standard for such a comparison consists of the communicative structures found in contemporary national public spheres in stable democracies. If politicized public debates in the European arena increasingly resemble the structures of communication in national political debates, which are certainly not lacking in conflict and controversy, then we may welcome politicization as a sign of the normalization and growing maturity of European public spheres. However, European public debates might be decidedly different from those in national arenas, and this difference might take the form of a parochial perspective strongly dominated by the opinions and arguments of domestic actors, with European-level institutions and actors from other member states only appearing as the passive targets of claims by domestic actors. In this case, there is reason to believe that politicization will have destructive rather than constructive consequences for the prospects of further European integration – or even the maintenance of what has been achieved so far.

In addition, there is the important issue of which actors have a voice in Europeanized public debates. Earlier research revealed that Europeanization in the past has occurred together with a concentration of discursive power in the hands of European and national executive actors. Whether this erosion of the influence of legislative, political party, and civil-society actors – that is, a deepening of the famous "democratic deficit" – has intensified or abated in the recent period of politicization during the financial crisis has important repercussions for the legitimacy and future course of the European integration project.

I addressed these questions empirically by comparing the claim makers and targets of claims that appear in public debates in twenty-nine European newspapers in six EU member states across five issue fields during the period 1990–2002, supplemented by an analysis of public debates on the financial crisis during the period 2010–12 in the German press. Within both the national and European arenas, I distinguished between domestic references to actors from their own region or country, horizontal linkages to actors in other regions or countries, and vertical linkages to the national respectively the European center.

In a first step, I examined public debates across all issues and countries. This perspective suggests a rather sobering conclusion regarding the degree of integration of the European communicative arena, which remains heavily dominated by domestic-national actors and their opinions and arguments. However, as I argued, such a conclusion would be doubly premature. First, national polities are not uniform in their degrees of centralization, and neither are all national issue fields within the same polity equally centralized. European public debates need not resemble highly centralized policy debates in strongly centralized countries. It is sufficient for them to reveal patterns of communicative interaction similar to those found in relatively decentralized policy fields in federal polities. Second, there is an important variation to consider across issues within the European arena: in some, European institutions and regulatory frameworks play a key role, in others they are marginal. Only in those issue fields in which European integration has advanced is there a need for strong horizontal and vertical communicative integration.

Therefore, I complemented the analyses of overall structures of communication in national and European arenas with a more focused comparison of two European issue fields with strongly developed European-level competencies – monetary politics and agriculture – to a relatively decentralized issue field in a federal polity: education politics in Germany. This perspective leads to a more positive assessment of the structure of Europeanized political communication. Especially in monetary politics, there is a rather well-balanced pattern that gives roughly equal voice to domestic, foreign-national, and European-level actors, which refer to one another as targets in ways that reflect the multilevel structure of the European polity. The European level, however, is more present as a target than as a speaker of claims. This could undermine the legitimacy of European-level monetary policies and institutions, which quite often appear as objects of criticism and responsibility but are less often present with their own opinions and arguments. Still, with one third of claims coming from these European-level actors (mainly the ECB), they make a substantial contribution to opinion formation.

Extending the perspective to debates on monetary and financial politics in Germany in the most recent period of 2010–12, I investigated to what extent increased politicization altered the discursive balance of forces. This longitudinal perspective shows that, initially, in the period 2000–2002, the introduction of the euro led to a strong rise in the prominence of European-level actors, mainly at the expense of domestic German actors who, during the 1990s, were still the dominant actors in monetary politics. However, politicization during the financial crisis redressed this imbalance. During the period 2010–12, discursive influence was almost equally balanced among domestic, transnational, and European-level actors. This is important evidence of the maturity of Europeanized political communication, at least for the German case.

Politicization also contributed to reducing the democratic deficit of Europeanized political communication – at least, that is what the evidence for Germany and for the field of monetary and financial politics suggests. Initially, the introduction of the euro led to a (further) marginalization of legislative and party actors in public debates, but politicization during the financial crisis helped them to regain or even exceed the level of discursive influence that they had on monetary politics in the pre-euro era. This can be attributed entirely to the rising voices of national parliaments and parties, however. The EP and European-level political parties are marginal voices, whose discursive influence declined further during the financial crisis. Were the EP abolished tomorrow and European-level parties dissolved, as far as debates on monetary and financial politics are concerned, no one would notice.

Altogether, these results show that Europeanized political communication by now can easily stand the comparison to the yardstick of national public debates – at least if we realistically and fairly compare strongly Europeanized issue fields (e.g., agriculture and monetary politics) to multilevel issues in federalized polities (e.g., Germany). However, evidence from debates on the financial crisis in Germany suggests that the changes wrought by politicization have not only meant more but also a different type of Europeanization. From the perspective of the democratic deficit, this is good news because after a period of eroding influence, national parliaments and parties are regaining influence in debates over monetary and financial affairs – especially, of course, because the enormous financial-aid packages and budget cuts cannot be passed without their consent and without concern for potential electoral fallout. For adherents of a vision of a supranational, federal Europe, the news is not as good. With the exception of the ECB, all other European-level key institutions have experienced significant losses in discursive influence during the financial crisis, whether the European Commission, which at least retains a modest voice, or the EP and European-level political parties, whose influence was already marginal. The contours of a supranational European polity therefore seem more distant than ever, whereas a new, more intergovernmental and more domesticated Europe seems to emerge from the crucible of the financial crisis. Needless to say, further research is necessary to ascertain to what extent these conclusions hold beyond the German case and beyond monetary and financial politics.

Appendix: List of newspapers included in the study

	Country	Regional base
Frankfurter Allgemeine Zeitung	Germany	Hesse
Süddeutsche Zeitung	Germany	Bavaria
Bild	Germany	Hamburg
Leipziger Volkszeitung	Germany	Saxony
Le Monde	France	Île de France
Figaro	France	Île de France
L'Humanité	France	Île de France
Ouest France	France	Lower Brittany Normandy, Pays de la Loire
Guardian	United Kingdom	Greater London
The Times	United Kingdom	Greater London
Sun	United Kingdom	Greater London
Scotsman	United Kingdom	Scotland
Repubblica	Italy	Lazio
Corriere della Sera	Italy	Lombardy
Il Mattino	Italy	Tuscany, Umbria
La Nazione	Italy	Campania
El País	Spain	Community of Madrid
Abc	Spain	Community of Madrid
El Mundo	Spain	Community of Madrid
La Vanguardia	Spain	Catalonia
Volkskrant	Netherlands	North-Holland
Algemeen Dagblad	Netherlands	South-Holland
Telegraaf	Netherlands	North-Holland
Leeuwarder Courant	Netherlands	Friesland
Neue Zürcher Zeitung	Switzerland	Zürich
Le Temps	Switzerland	Geneva
Journal de Genève	Switzerland	Geneva
Le Matin	Switzerland	Vaud
Blick	Switzerland	Zürich

4 National media as transnational discourse arenas: the case of humanitarian military interventions

CATHLEEN KANTNER

The often aggressive tone prevalent in public debates on the current European sovereign-debt crisis is seen by many observers as evidence of the long predicted impossibility of democratic governance beyond the nation-state, the lack of a European *demos*, and the lack of a resilient European identity. In this chapter, I argue that transnational political communication in the European Union (EU) is well developed and that we can clearly observe a gradient in comparison to non-EU countries such as the United States.[1] In the national media, people find information and competing interpretations that enable them to form their opinions on the important issues concerning the shared economic, legal, and political space of the EU. Moreover, the various publics are not simply speaking past one another, in that they do share common themes, but they occasionally have conflicting opinions rooted in different interests and sometimes different values. Although in cases such as the European sovereign-debt crisis, the opposing camps seem to coincide with countries or groups of countries, the picture is more complicated because also within countries, the important issues are highly controversial. The European sovereign-debt crisis is an excellent example of an intense and highly politicized transnational debate.

This chapter proceeds as follows. The second section briefly introduces my conception of transnational political communication to prepare the background for the empirical analysis in the third section. There, data from two research projects are presented, both of which content-analyze newspaper articles published in the leading conservative and liberal newspapers of several EU member states, with the

[1] I thank the authors of this volume and Eric Sangar for their helpful comments on earlier drafts, as well as Joshua Rogers and Barty Begley for the language editing.

United States as a comparative case. I argue that we can clearly observe transnational debates about many important European issues. A *common agenda* of European issues already exists. Taking a closer look at one particular issue of high importance in the years after the end of the Cold War – namely, the issue of humanitarian military interventions – I describe the sequence charts of sixteen years of media coverage on this issue and compare the "national" *issue cycles*. I demonstrate that even for this "hard case," the issue cycles in the various national media arenas were highly intercorrelated and reacted to the same trigger events. With respect to the *framing* of these debates, competing master frames and ideological cleavages are compared cross-nationally – contributing to a mosaic of commonalities as well as of more or less pronounced differences between the EU member states and the United States. The fourth section summarizes the results of my empirical investigations and counterclaims regarding the lack of visibility of Europe within national media or the widely suspected mutual closure of national public spheres. Ordinary citizens who use the national media to be informed about politics are informed about European issues. However, transnational political communication is currently not satisfactorily fed into representative democratic institutions at the EU level. It is therefore premature to speak of the existence of a full-fledged European public sphere. Presumed "hermetic communicative borders" between national publics and the often-lamented "public-sphere deficit," however, are a poor excuse for a lack of political will to democratize the EU.

Transnational political communication: background and conceptualization

An informed public is a precondition for democratic politics (Grimm 1995; Habermas 1998a). We can conceptualize transnational political communication as the possibility for ordinary citizens to have access on an everyday basis to news and commentary on the complex, conflict-ridden, and often also ethically highly controversial issues that emerge in our interdependent globalized and Europeanized societies. In other words, transnational political communication can be seen as the process that enables ordinary citizens who are part of different national media arenas to discuss issues the relevance of which is not confined to national borders.

Is transnational political communication actually taking place? The results of my empirical analysis show that, indeed, we can observe the emergence of transnational political communication. First, however, I briefly describe theoretical arguments that help to understand the operationalization used in the empirical part of this chapter.

The established theoretical conceptualizations of political communication start with the nation-state. In the democratic nation-state, various speakers in different arenas of the "public sphere" compete for the attention of the audience and try to convince it of their interpretations of events and issues, as well as of their solutions to problems. The result of this is a "national debate" that emerges through the thematic intertwinement of these contributions and discourses that take place in a plurality of individual arenas.

On a theoretical level, there is no intrinsic argument that would exclude the possibility of similar communication processes beyond the nation-state (Eder and Kantner 2000, 2002; Kantner 2004). Certainly, beyond the nation-state the audience often is composed of members that do not share a common language, common values, and common political preferences. However, the same applies to national audiences: indeed, many countries – such as Canada, Spain, Switzerland, and the United Kingdom – have been able to construct well-functioning democracies despite the fact that their populations speak different languages. Migration further adds to linguistic and cultural heterogeneity in many countries.

I explain elsewhere (see Kantner 2003) that an essential precondition for the emergence of communication in any given social context is the perception of common problems: people start talking once they perceive that they are "in the same boat." I argue that this insight also applies to contexts beyond the nation-state. Globalization, but Europeanization even more so, has pushed the transnationalization of economic, legal, and political interactions among nation-states toward degrees of intensity, density, and interdependence formerly unknown. Especially in the European context, societies have become so interlocked that many problems and conflicts require common reactions and solutions.

In such a context, it becomes likely that common problems would be publicly articulated by concerned speakers. The occasions and motives for actors and speakers to publicly address the same transnational issues therefore multiply with the increase of common experiences and problems. This might lead to politicized debates and mobilize the attention of international press agencies and journalistic, policy and civil-society networks. Once discourse actors start to turn latent problems into political issues and to draw others into exchanging arguments, bilateral, transnational, and international institutions and decision makers are more likely to become frequent objects of public debate: their visibility in the media is likely to correspond to the degree of supranationalization (Koopmans and Erbe 2004; Della Porta and Caiani 2006; Neidhardt 2006; Koopmans, Erbe, and Meyer 2010, 64f.). Building on these arguments, we are observing *transnational political communication* to the degree that in different countries:

- the *same transnational issues* are discussed
- at the *same time* and
- under similar *aspects of relevance* (Habermas 1998b, 160; Eder and Kantner 2000, 81; Kantner 2004); that is, with similar frames of interpretation but not necessarily with the same opinions

The primary channels of transnational political communication are national mass media because ordinary people turn to whatever media they use to be informed about all of the different issues they consider important –whether local, national, European, or global. Therefore, the empirical analysis of transnational political communication becomes, in practice, a search for transnational interlinkages among national media arenas (Eder and Kantner 2000, 2002; Van de Steeg 2006; Risse 2010). The next section describes the three dimensions through which this search for transnational interlinkages can be conducted. My aim is to empirically detect the occurrence of debates across different national arenas of political communication and to measure:

- to what degrees the same transnational/European issues and agendas (same issues)
- have been discussed with similar issue cycles (same time)
- and similar "frames" of interpretation (similar aspects of relevance)

Agendas, issue-cycles, and frames: measuring transnational political communication

Can ordinary citizens inform themselves in the national media about common transnational issues and the complex processes of multilevel politics? Are the debates in different national arenas interconnected? Recent comparative media-content analyses on EU-related political communication in general and European policy issues in particular came to the empirical result that many issues are debated cross-nationally. The media cover EU issues on a regular basis and their share of coverage compared to national issues is larger than initially thought (Habermas 1996b; Peter and de Vreese 2003; Trenz 2004, 2005; Kantner 2006; Wessler et al. 2008; Koopmans and Statham 2010a). European integration is not only covered in relation to distinct EU issues but also has become an integral part of national political and economic coverage (Semetko, De Vreese, and Peter 2000, 129).

The following section describes the empirical analysis of the first dimension discussed previously: To what extent can we speak of transnational political communication in terms of issues and agendas that are debated across national boundaries? This analysis focuses on European issues because the EU is commonly seen as the most prominent and densest form of transnational political cooperation.

Same transnational issues and agendas?

There are still almost no comparative media-content analyses that would cover a broad range of transnational and European policy issues and events. Among the few exceptions are Kevin (2003) and Koopmans and Statham (2010a), who covered several selected political issues. Only Trenz (2004, 2005) and Kantner (2006) reconstructed the complete European agenda in the media of different countries for a period of one year (January to December 2000).[2] The study

[2] The data presented in this section derive from an empirical research project, "*Transnationale Öffentlichkeit und die Strukturierung politischer Kommunikation in Europa*," funded by the German Research Foundation (DFG, ED 25/13–1) and conducted by Klaus Eder, Cathleen Kantner, Hans-Jörg Trenz, and Cornelia F. Dereje at Humboldt–University Berlin from 2000 to 2003. This comparative media-content analysis used a representative random sample of newspaper reporting and commentary on Europe from January to December 2000. The study included the following broadsheets: *Frankfurter Allgemeine Zeitung (FAZ)* and *Süddeutsche Zeitung (SZ)* (Germany); *Le Monde* and *Libération* (France); *Guardian* and *The Times* (United Kingdom); *La Repubblica* and *La Stampa* (Italy); *El País* (Spain); *Standard* and *Die Presse* (Austria); and as the non-European comparative case, the *New York Times (NY Times)* (United States). The articles were drawn from the full-content CD-ROM of the newspapers. The sampling procedure used EU-related keywords. Political news and commentary

revealed an unexpectedly high amount of newspaper reporting and commentary referring to a broad spectrum of European issues, a few of which became European top issues. In the context of the Nice Summit, a short but intensive discussion about the institutional reform arose. The participation of Jörg Haider's radical right-wing Freedom Party of Austria (*Freiheitliche Partei Österreichs* [FPÖ]) in the Austrian government coalition and the following "sanctions" by the EU were broadly discussed. Also, the euro was a top issue in all countries investigated. Finally, the Eastern Enlargement of the EU, a possible European constitution, and the developing common European foreign and security policy were important top issues on a common European media agenda in 2000. However, in some countries, additional topics with high practical relevance to the country concerned occurred on the top list. *El País*, for example, argued in 2000 that Basque Homeland and Liberty (*Euskadi Ta Askatasuna* [ETA]) terrorism was a European issue. The French *Libération* discussed economic issues (i.e., company mergers and mad cow disease) more intensely than other papers. *FAZ* and *La Stampa* ranked EU monetary politics among the top issues (for more details, see Trenz 2004, 2005; Kantner 2006).

In comparison to the overall amount of political reporting and commentary, the share of articles that addressed problems and issues located in the context of common European political decision making was very high for all European newspapers examined. The Austrian *Standard* and the German *FAZ* scored even higher than 50 percent, whereas the Italian *La Repubblica* and the British *The Times* scored only 28 and 31 percent, respectively, of all political newspaper articles that had a European dimension. For the other European papers, the value was at least one third (Kantner 2006).

The widespread claim that there is a dramatic deficit in European political communication cannot be confirmed. The national press gives considerable attention to Europe. Moreover, volume and density of political communication with a European dimension were much higher

without explicit relation to the EU (including reporting about other member states, bilateral relations, and EU issues that were addressed without explicitly mentioning the EU) were excluded from the analysis. Media debate concerning the Council of Europe or the Organisation for Economic Co-operation and Development without explicit involvement of the EU was classified as "international politics." The huge raw sample was reduced by random selection and then cleaned. The coded dataset encompassed 4,225 newspaper articles.

than in the US control sample. In the *New York Times,* only 8 percent of all political articles had a European dimension. Therefore, the EU countries proved to be indeed a "compacted" space of transnational communication.

These findings can be further specified. The depth of the European dimension varied between the analyzed articles (Trenz 2004, 2005; Kantner 2006). European issues often stood at the center of the article; I called those articles "European articles." At 44 percent, this was the biggest group among the EU-related articles. However, in articles with a subnational, national, or international main issue, one or more European issues often were raised as side issues; I called these articles "Europeanized articles." Those articles comprised 21 percent of the EU-related debate. The explorative sampling strategy that did not focus on selected issues resulted in the discovery of a third type of article: articles with a subnational, national, or international main issue mentioned the EU only rhetorically, without a distinct argument about European policies; I called these articles "European rhetoric." Rhetorical references to Europe included, for example, the "European welfare state model," a "European identity," EU events, and EU actors. Of the EU-related discussion, 35 percent was rhetorical. This last category can be seen as an indicator of shared implicit background knowledge about the EU.

Although there also are differences among the EU countries, Table 4.1 shows that the most important difference in scope was between the EU press and the *New York Times.* I observed that in the latter, whereas articles focusing mainly on EU issues are rare, "Europeanized reporting" that acknowledges the role of the EU in a multilevel political system as well as articles that contain "European rhetoric" are almost absent in the US newspaper.

Are EU-related media reporting and commentary indeed too weak to allow us to speak of the existence of transnational European political communication? Authors including Koopmans (see Chapter 3 in this volume) argue that in comparison to national political communication, the EU-related debate is still very deficient. Is an EU debate still very much playing second fiddle?

First, no one has claimed that national, EU-related, or other "multilevel"-related political communication has exactly the same volume. Moreover, EU politics involves national representatives on the EU-level and national institutions. Given that the Council of the

Table 4.1. *Share of EU-related articles among the overall political newspaper reporting and commentary, September–December 2000 (in percentages)*

	FAZ	SZ	Guardian	The Times	Standard	Presse	El País	Le Monde	Libération	La Stampa	Repubblica	New York Times	Average EU
European articles	24.1	17.6	11.9	13.4	28.0	19.9	16.1	18.1	10.7	12.9	8.1	4.2	16.4
Europeanized articles	9.6	6.5	14.9	4.1	10.0	11.1	6.9	6.2	6.7	9.2	6.1	1.2	8.3
European rhetoric	17.9	16.5	9.0	13.2	17.7	8.7	10.3	17.8	8.8	10.6	13.5	2.7	13.1
Sum	51.6	40.6	35.8	30.7	55.7	39.7	33.3	42.1	26.2	32.7	27.7	8.1	37.8

European Union, which consists of the *national* ministers, and the European Parliament (EP) must co-agree on any legislative proposal; that the most complex acts of European law, the directives, must be transposed into *national* law to become effective; and that the implementation of EU law is a task conducted by the *national* states, we can reasonably assume that national politics dominates in the media.

Second, contrary to this widely held expectation, the presented findings – even if more long-term-oriented investigations might complete the picture – are surprising. The broad agenda and the high share of EU-related reporting and commentary in the EU countries are astonishing. The clear difference in volume and density of EU-related political communication between the EU and the US papers lends strong support to my theoretical claim that political interdependence in a common economic, legal, and political space can motivate speakers in the public and the media to address common problems, conflicts, and issues.

Third, the significant amount of Europeanized articles in the EU countries (as well as the impressive lack thereof in the United States) supports the empirical claim that in the EU countries, ordinary citizens have access to debates involving the intertwined national, European, and other levels of political decision making. Furthermore, many problems are debated in neither an exclusively national nor an exclusively European context. This empirically confirmed overlap of transnational and national political communication disconfirms assumptions about a clear distinction among levels of political communication separated along the levels of the EU multilevel system. In other words, the influence of transnational communication can be felt even in articles that, at first glance, discuss issues belonging to the national sphere.

The next section assesses to what extent there is emerging transnational political communication in terms of similar issue cycles.

Same issue cycles? The case of humanitarian military interventions

If people in Finland debate an issue today and people in Greece discussed it four months ago and people in Romania discuss it in two years' time, we can hardly understand this as a common debate. Common issues should be characterized by common-issue cycles. Whereas agendas of publicly discussed issues and the ranking of top issues in different countries can be studied with a synchronic approach, the cross-country comparison of issue cycles demands diachronic methods. Only if we choose as long a period of investigation as possible can we see the development of the topic.[3] Whereas most existing media-content analyses cover only snapshots of a few weeks before and after particular events, my empirical investigation comprises a *continuous* period of sixteen years (i.e., from January 1990 to March 2006) of

[3] The data presented in this section derive from an extensive quantitative-qualitative content analysis conducted at Freie Universität Berlin. The project "In Search of a New Role in World Politics: The Common European Foreign, Security, and Defence Policies (CFSP/ESDP) in the Light of Identity Debates in the Member States' Mass Media" was directed by Thomas Risse and Cathleen Kantner. For the generous funding of this project, we are grateful to the German Research Foundation (DFG, RI 798/8–1, -2) and the European Commission's Sixth Framework Programme, within which this study was supported as part of the integrated FP6-Project RECON (FP6–028698). My special thanks go to our colleagues Amelie Kutter and Andreas Hildebrandt, who with astonishing creativity developed and refined the corpus-linguistic methods that generated the data analyzed in this section. I also thank Jana Katharina Grabowsky for providing the Dutch data and Swantje Renfordt for supervising the qualitative part of the content analysis.

news coverage and commentary on humanitarian military interventions in seven European countries and the United States.[4]

For the systematic comparison of the issue-attention cycles, I chose the issue of humanitarian military interventions. The debate on this topic is a "hard case" for the study of European transnational communication because diplomacy and the use of force in international conflicts are perceived to be the exclusive domain of nation-states. Moreover, the transatlantic alliance (i.e., North Atlantic Treaty Organization [NATO]) and the United Nations (UN) are far more important international actors than the EU. The EU's Common Foreign and Security Policy (CFSP) was introduced only in 1993 and continues to be a field of intergovernmental decision making. The Common Security and Defence Policy (CSDP) was developed even later and it has been able to conduct independent military operations only since 2003. If the visibility of transnational issues and actors in the media corresponds to the degree of supranationalization, transnational European public communication is least likely to be observed in this case.

Figure 4.1 lists the issue cycles of newspaper articles covering humanitarian interventions. Those using the specific wording for humanitarian military interventions comprise approximately 20 percent of all articles on wars and interventions in France, Poland, the United Kingdom, and the United States; 25 percent in Germany; and almost 30 percent in the Netherlands, Ireland, and Austria. It is interesting that there is no evidence for across-the-board claims about a long-term upward trend in the debate since the early 1990s.[5] The curves follow the exogenous impulses given by important crisis events that result in the random appearance of the issue cycles.

---

[4] The European countries were chosen to cover the range of diverse positions in foreign, security, and defense policy preferences prevalent in the EU. Small and large countries, with both post-neutral and Atlanticist foreign-policy traditions, were included. The choice fell on Austria (AU), France (FR), Germany (GER), Ireland (IR), the Netherlands (NL), Poland (PL), and the United Kingdom (UK). The United States (US) was included as a comparative case.

The selected broadsheets are *Der Standard* and *Die Presse* (AU); *Le Monde* and *Le Figaro (1997–2006)/Les Echos (1993–1996)* (F); *Süddeutsche Zeitung* and *Frankfurter Allgemeine Zeitung* (GER); *The Irish Times* (IR); *NRC Handelsblad* and *De Volkskrant* (NL); *Gazeta Wyborcza* (PL); *Guardian* and *The Times* (UK); and the *New York Times* and *Washington Post* (US).

[5] A straightforward upward trend in the amount of European political communication over time was suggested by Wessler et al. 2008.

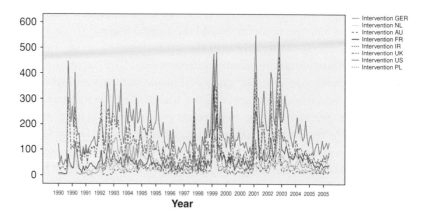

Figure 4.1. Issue cycle "humanitarian military interventions" (absolute numbers).

Notes: N = 112,729, intervention subsample; method used: corpus-linguistic frequency analysis, data aggregated on a monthly basis. Period of investigation: January 1990–March 2006 (195 months).[6]

At first sight, these highly volatile curves of the intervention issue cycles are difficult to interpret. There are no clear-cut long-term trends or seasonal patterns visible. Rather, four waves of higher quantitative levels and several peaks can be identified: 1990–91 (Iraq/Kuwait), autumn 1992 to autumn 1996 (Balkan crises and African conflicts), 1999–2000 (Kosovo), and 2001–2003 (9/11, Afghanistan, and Iraq War). Because the Iraq War was debated in many countries in terms of an "ordinary war" and not military intervention for humanitarian reasons, March 2003 is not the month with the maximum coverage, except for Ireland and the United Kingdom. Instead, the instances of maximum coverage are April 1999, the month in which the Kosovo conflict escalated and UN diplomacy failed, and March 1999, when the NATO Operation Allied Force started bombing Yugoslavia.

Thus, simultaneous peaks in several countries were triggered by the same international conflict events. In addition to crisis events such as the Kosovo crisis in April 1999 and Afghanistan in October 2001,

---

[6] Our sampling strategy focused on the issue itself, regardless of which policy level was active, and it did not include any EU-related keywords. For the description of the sampling strategy, the methods developed for cleaning the text corpus, and the corpus-linguistic methods, see Kantner et al. 2011; Renfordt 2011; and Kutter and Kantner 2012.

another group of conflicts – mainly in Africa – lead to simultaneous peaks: Somalia 1992–93 and 1995, the genocide in Rwanda in 1994, and the civil war in Sierra Leone in the late 1990s.

Even if at first sight the curves do not seem "harmonious," all curves correlate extremely strongly and significantly with one another, ranging from slightly more than 0.70 (AU/US, AU/UK, NL/UK, NL/US) to values around 0.80 among the Continental European countries and 0.90 between the Irish and the British papers, as well as between the United States and the United Kingdom (see Kantner 2011, 10). This is a strong indicator for synchronous, thematically intertwined debates about the normative justification (or lack thereof) of the use of military force for humanitarian purposes. The Polish issue cycle correlates the strongest with the German and the French cases and the least with the American case. Therefore, it seems that the debate in the new member state under study also was impressively on a European rhythm.

Not only the visible common peaks of the issue cycles but also the extremely correlated intensity of the discussion about humanitarian military interventions in the different countries indicate that, from the end of the Cold War, there was a broad international debate on violent crisis events in the European *and* American newspapers. Comparing the average correlations between different groups of countries, the issue cycles of all countries under study (0.80) clearly correlate less among each other than among only EU member states (0.84). Even if all issue cycles reacted to the same trigger events, there seems to be more exchange and mutual observation between the EU countries.[7] Very high correlations between countries with the same language may be caused by direct exchange, direct media competition, and stronger-than-average media cooperation. The findings also indicate no stronger or even separate transatlantic Western discourse because the European media are more thematically intertwined than either the NATO members or the neutral countries under study (i.e., both were 0.78).

Another indicator for the surprisingly pronounced difference between the American and the EU media arenas (with the United Kingdom and Ireland as a type of bridge) is the share of articles in which explicit references to Europe in a broad sense (including simple

---

[7] In a different analysis, I tested whether those issue cycles converge over time (Kantner 2011).

Table 4.2. *Share of "Europe" and "EU and its institutions" in articles on humanitarian military interventions (in percentages)*

Country	N intervention	% Europe	% EU
Austria	3,695	41.0	30.8
France	12,097	43.6	32.4
Germany	15,946	38.6	26.6
Ireland	8,018	38.1	28.2
Netherlands	9,871	38.8	25.7
United Kingdom	22,899	35.1	21.3
United States	36,151	33.7	16.4
All	108,677	38.4	25.9

Notes: N = 108,677, intervention subsample; method used: corpus-linguistic analysis. Period of investigation: January 1990–March 2006 (195 months). Because of missing months, three countries include fewer months: AU 163, IR 166, and GER 182.

geographical notions) as compared to the EU and its political institutions occurred (Table 4.2).

Using elaborated corpus-linguistic methods (Kutter and Kantner 2012), I discovered that as far as Europe in general is concerned, the differences between the countries were still quite moderate. The Continental European countries and Ireland mentioned "Europe" in about 40 percent of all articles on humanitarian military interventions, whereas in the UK and the US papers, "Europe" mattered 5 percentage points less. The generally high proportion of "Europe" mentions certainly is related to the fact that important crisis events and later humanitarian military interventions took place on the European Continent (as in Bosnia and Kosovo).

However, when searching for specific references to "political Europe," the differences increase dramatically: in the media arenas of Continental EU member states France and Austria, as well as in Ireland, about a third of all articles on humanitarian military interventions explicitly refer to the EU or even the emerging EU institutions of the CFSP/CSDP. In Germany and the Netherlands, it is every fourth article on the issue, whereas in the United Kingdom (20 percent) and the United States (16 percent), references to the EU are significantly lower.

In summary, citizens in different countries who use the national media can build informed opinions about the same international issues at the same time. Debates on humanitarian military interventions certainly were not restricted to a European community of communication; they were part of broader Western if not global news coverage. However, as in the previous analysis regarding the agenda of European issues, there is a marked difference between communication among EU member states and the non-EU control case (i.e., the United States). The issue cycles for debates on humanitarian military interventions show that although the debates are transnationally interconnected, this interconnectedness is decidedly more pronounced among EU countries. Moreover, the national media arenas of EU countries – with the exception of the United Kingdom – are marked by unexpectedly high levels of references to the EU and its institutions within the context of these debates. This finding is even more surprising because the actual competencies, diplomatic resources, and military power of the EU institutions were created only slowly during the period of investigation and are commonly perceived to still be limited today.

In the final section of my empirical argumentation, I focus on the detection of the use of similar frames as an indicator of transnational political communication.

Similar frames? Analyzing sets of competing interpretations

Most studies on transnational political communication in the EU come to the conclusion that – despite important differences – similar interpretations and structures of meaning, or "frames," prevail across the national media arenas when EU-related subjects are debated. The framing (although not the majority opinion) of European and Europeanized issues is astonishingly similar across national borders. Empirical studies demonstrate that transnational debates are not limited to the government positions on the international political level. Rather, in each country under study, there are many competing frames, yet the same set of important frames and arguments structures the discourse in different countries (see, e.g., Eder and Kantner 2000; Van de Steeg 2000; Kantner 2004, 2006; Trenz 2004, 2005).

Surprisingly, this also holds true with regard to ethical issues: instead of twenty-seven different national frames of meaning on each topic, there are only two normative positions that are critically debated in all countries. This can be shown in a cross-national frame analysis of the Haider debate.[8] With regard to this issue, we would expect opposing interpretative frames and opinions across Europe. Instead, the same four frames dominated the debate in all countries studied by the authors (Risse 2002, 15, 2010; Van de Steeg et al. 2003; Van de Steeg 2006). Discussion largely remained within this set of important competing views on the topic; the many other frames "on the market" did not find followers.

Is the issue of humanitarian military interventions also discussed under the same "aspects of relevance" across the countries? Is it similarly "framed"? In attempting to answer these questions, I investigated several dimensions of the interpretative framing of the debate. First, I distinguished among three master frames as an answer to the question of what is at stake: interests, identities, or universal principles? Second, I measured contestation along different ideological cleavages to capture opinions on competing principles for action.

The first step of this analysis was the identification of master frames. Was the topic discussed as a matter of particularist interests (e.g., power, money, or geostrategic interests)? Was it treated as a matter of collective identities (e.g., national, European, or Western identities)? Or was the issue framed in terms of universal human rights (in the sense of either abstract philosophical principles or their institutionalization in international law)?

As Figure 4.2 illustrates, interest frames dominated only in the Dutch and the French papers (21.32 and 16.70 of 100 articles, respectively). They were least prominent in the Irish and the Austrian papers (9.87 of 100). Except for Germany, the issue was strongly framed in terms of collective identities. Identity aspects were especially frequent in the English-speaking media arenas and in the Netherlands. In the Irish, the American, and the British press, identity frames prevailed over the other two master frames (20.93, 19.14, and 19.21 of 100, respectively). This also holds true for Austria (14.61), although not by a significant margin. Universalist frames occurred less often than the two particularist master frames in the English-speaking countries and the Netherlands. They ranged from 12.47 (Germany) to 15.87 (the

---

[8] In 2000, the right-wing populist Freedom Party (FPÖ), led by Jörg Haider, and the conservative People's Party (ÖVP), led by Wolfgang Schüssel, formed a new Austrian coalition government. The EU reacted with diplomatic sanctions to demonstrate that an extreme right-wing party in government was at odds with a European identity.

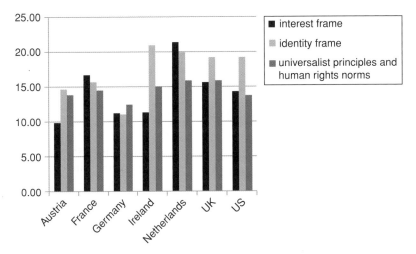

Figure 4.2. Master frames in the debate on "humanitarian military interventions" (weighted absolute numbers).
Notes: N = 5,850 articles (weighted: 100 articles per country); method used: human coding.[9]

Netherlands and the United Kingdom). Overall, the debate was somewhat "cooler" in Germany, France, and Austria, where a smaller share of articles used master frames and where the identity dimension did not exceed 18 percent of the articles in which humanitarian military intervention was the central issue.

Another way in which I operationalized the framing of humanitarian military interventions was to search for the use of ideological cleavages along which the politicization of the debate was structured. The following figures show only the weighted numbers for the activation of these cleavages when a clear ideological position could be identified in articles in which humanitarian military interventions were the main issue. Neutral stands or the gradualist discussion of the pros and cons are not presented in the figures in order to trace more clearly the way the issue was contested.

---

[9] A master frame could not be identified in all articles. Many articles, however, discussed combinations of two or even all three master frames. Polish data were not available in time for the qualitative content analysis. Therefore, they are missing in the following analysis.

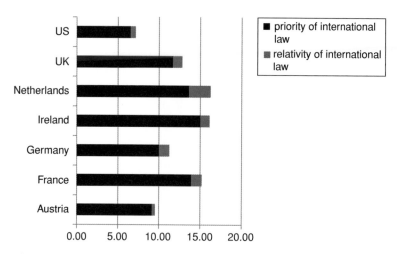

Figure 4.3. Cleavage "legality of humanitarian military intervention" in the debate on "humanitarian military interventions" (weighted absolute numbers).

Notes: N = 5,850 articles (weighted: 100 articles per country); method used: human coding.

One of the major ideological cleavages was the question of the importance of international law for the legitimacy of humanitarian military interventions. Does international law assume priority over other considerations – even pressing ethical dilemmas connected to the need to protect the victims of massive human-rights abuses in crisis countries in Africa or the Balkans? Or can international law – given its poor state of development, given its sometimes tendentious interpretation by the Great Powers in the UN Security Council which often did not reach agreement over UN mandates for interventions, or given national interests (e.g., upcoming elections and available military budgets) – be used *à la carte,* relative to other considerations? Especially in the context of the Iraq War in 2003, a severe split between the administration of US President George W. Bush and many European governments actually was framed along this cleavage.

Figure 4.3 illustrates that the controversy about priority or relativity of international law assumed different degrees of intensity. In Ireland, for instance, for every 100 articles, only 16.09 addressed this cleavage. Fifteen of those articles took the position that international law has priority in determining the legality of humanitarian military interventions, whereas only 1.09 articles argued that depending on the circumstances and other considerations, international law was not always the ultimate source of legal legitimacy of interventions. The position that international law was of relative importance compared to other considerations only rarely was approved in all countries. Comparatively, the highest approval of the relativist position was observed, surprisingly, in the Netherlands (2.64 per 100 articles), which may be due to the country's traumatic experience in Srebrenica.[10] Overall, the international media were obviously much less split on this cleavage than some governments. With regard to this aspect, Habermas and Derrida's (2003) impression that the European peoples had fewer differences than their governments with regard to the Iraq War can be confirmed. It is intrerresting that in the US media arena, this cleavage was politicized much less frequently.

Another important cleavage is closely connected to the question regarding the legality of humanitarian military interventions in terms of international law. How intensely was the debate polarized in terms of multilateral decision taking (e.g., in the framework of the UN, international organizations, or the EU) versus unilateral decisions by individual states or ad hoc "coalitions of the willing"?

With regard to this ideological cleavage, cross-country differences are not at all strong (Figure 4.4). Multilateralism is the preferred approach in the media of all countries. A plea for unilateralism is everywhere the exception rather than the rule. However, this aspect was debated least intensely in the American papers (14.73 in 100), followed by Germany and Austria. In all three countries, this cleavage was not as contested as in the United Kingdom and France (i.e., the EU military powers); the Netherlands, shocked by the tragedy of Srebrenica; or Ireland, one of the post-neutral countries under study. Unilateral decision taking in matters of war and peace received low approval in all countries. In Austria, it received none; it received the highest value in the Dutch press (2.45 in 100) – which also is probably a Srebrenica effect.

These findings confirm other researchers' findings. In her recent qualitative study, Swantje Renfordt (2011) used the same subsample of the

---

[10] In 1995, Dutch UN troops failed to protect Bosnian civilians from Serbian militias' atrocities in the "safe haven" of the city of Srebrenica.

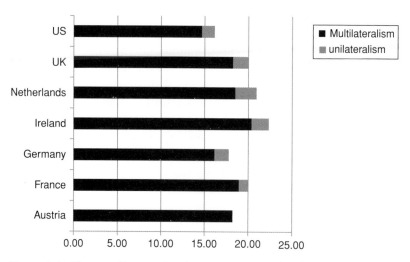

Figure 4.4. Cleavage "international cooperation" in the debate on "humanitarian military interventions" (weighted absolute numbers).
Notes: N = 5,850 articles (weighted: 100 articles per country); method used: human coding.

articles on humanitarian military interventions (n = 5,850) and an additional, even more specific set of variables on how the norms of international law were addressed in the press. She investigated the discussion of the "social validity" of the norms of international law on the use of force in the debates on humanitarian military interventions, providing more qualitative analysis of the debates. Renfordt found that legal framing is the most frequent frame in the debate – on both sides of the Atlantic. Of all crisis episodes between January 1990 and December 2005, the Iraq Wars (with peaks in 1998 and 2002–2003) and the Yugoslav Wars (1992–93, 1995, and 1998–99), which proved crucial for the debate in general, also were discussed most intensively under legal frames. They differ, however, in the fact that they are marked by two variations: human-rights aspects dominated during the 1990s, whereas procedural aspects focusing on multilateral decision making within the UN have been dominant since 2000, especially with regard to the Iraq War in 2003. The US media focus more on the human-rights motives, whereas the European media put the procedural aspect of multilateral legitimation center stage (Renfordt 2011, 205).

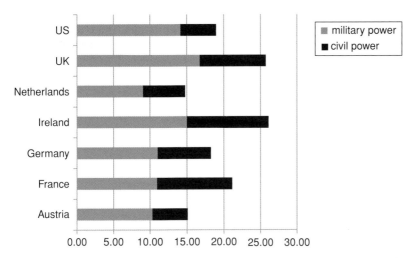

Figure 4.5. Cleavage "rule enforcement" in the debate on "humanitarian military interventions" (weighted absolute numbers).
Notes: N = 5,850 articles (weighted: 100 articles per country); method used: human coding.

Because public as well as scholary discourse assumes a strong cultural cleavage between Europe and the United States with regard to the preferred method of rule enforcement at the international level, I also coded this framing dimension. Europeans often become associated with a preference for "civilian power" that focuses on diplomatic means and economic cooperation. The dominant attitude toward the use of force is seen as rather "dovish." The United States, in contrast, is seen as more prone to military power and marked by a rather "hawkish" attitude toward the use of force in international conflict. How should international rules be enforced: by means of military or by means of civilian power? The results of this study (see Figure 4.5), however, do not confirm the expectations.

The cleavage concerning the means of rule enforcement was activated with different degrees of intensity in the different countries. It was most prominent in Ireland, a post-neutral EU member state, and the United Kingdom, the member state with the strongest and most modern military capabilities. It is surprising that in all countries except France, expressions of approval for military power rate higher than approval for civilian power. This certainly is due to the specific historical and political context of the issue under investigation. In the face of systematic, large-scale human-rights violations in the "new wars" after the end of the Cold War, military force was considered a necessary means – and one underdeveloped in the EU and its member states. Many speakers in the public arenas wanted to generate support for military reforms, participation in missions, and development of the CFSP/CSDP as well as related military capacities that they considered urgently necessary. Nation-building in Iraq and Afghanistan had not yet failed. Therefore, optimism was widespread that foreign interventions could not only stop the violence but also help to establish the rule of law and even democracy in the crisis countries.

Yet, the figures already indicate much more contestation, polarization, and politicization of the debate than could be observed with regard to the cleavages of "legality of humanitarian military intervention" and "international cooperation," in which the overtone in the media was quite cosmopolitan. Currently, in all countries both positions receive noteworthy approval. In France, both positions are almost evenly present, whereas the difference in favor of military power is highest in the American and the British papers.

To summarize, is the issue of humanitarian military interventions also discussed under the same "aspects of relevance" across the countries? Is the issue similarly "framed"? First, we can observe that all three master frames resonated in all countries. In the English-speaking countries and the Netherlands, the debate was "hotter"; master frames were activated more often and especially identity aspects mattered more. Country-specific experiences with the issue at stake (e.g., the Srebrenica trauma for the Netherlands) can give credibility to these findings. The interest master frame (i.e., encompassing economic as well as geostrategic interests) was the most prevalent only in the Netherlands and France.

Second, some ideological cleavages did not lead to much transnational difference. However, with regard to the choice between military and civilian power, intense politicization can be observed within as well as between countries. With respect to the cleavage of "legality of humanitarian military intervention," the international media were much less divided than national governments. Similarly, with regard to the cleavage of "international cooperation," a plea for unilateralism was always the exception. Again, at least at the level of public discourse, Europeans seem to have more in common than their national governments. This also applies to US citizens (although in the American debate, this cleavage did not matter as much as in Europe). This is an important finding: in scholary literature as well as in public discourse, the assumption that public opinion, media discourse, and governmental positions are identical seems to persist despite all evidence to the contrary. However, within democratic countries, there is a pluralistic discourse. Furthermore, this pluralistic discourse is not confined within national borders.

The cleavage that had significant potential for contestation concerned the means for "rule enforcement" on the international level. Due to the specific historical and political context of the debate on humanitarian and military interventions, in most countries, approval for military power rated somewhat higher than approval for civilian power. This cleavage obviously went to the heart of the debate: Who do we want to be and what role do we want to play in international conflicts and the newly emerging multipolar world order that is beginning to take shape in our lifetime?

To conclude, with regard to the analytic dimension of similar frames, national differences proved to be more insignificant than presumed by much of the scholarly debate that laments the lack of a European public sphere. An issue of global scope can very well provoke transnationally intertwined debates – both within the EU and beyond.

Conclusions

The findings of the research presented in this chapter support the claim that the same transnational issues (i.e., the similar agendas of common issues) are being debated at the same time (i.e., with similar issue cycles) under similar aspects of relevance (i.e., with a similar set of competing interpretative frames) across national borders. In many aspects, a strong difference between the EU member states and the United States could be observed. This was the case regarding the agenda of European issues, in which the United States only participated to a very low degree when its economic or foreign policy interests were concerned. Among the EU countries, the issue cycles of humanitarian military intervention correlated more strongly. The share of articles on humanitarian military interventions that explicitly referred to the EU and its political institutions also was marked by a US EU difference: The US (and, to a lesser degree, also the British) media lagged far behind most EU countries in the intensity of discussion of the EU as a political force.

In other aspects, the difference between the EU and the United States was rather moderate. This was the case for the correlations of the issue cycles on humanitarian military interventions and for the framing of the intervention debate. The US American media did not resonate much with the cleavages of "legality of humanitarian military intervention" and "international cooperation." However, to the extent that they did address the respective ideological choices, they shared a common theme with the EU countries. The moderate results regarding the in-depth content analysis of the debate on humanitarian military interventions do not change the general argument of this chapter because the chosen issue is a "tough case" within European political communication. It is rather surprising that with regard to an issue in which the EU initially had no role and only became a relevant foreign policy and military actor at the end of the period of investigation, we could observe a transnational European debate in which the Europeans are trying to come to terms with new international challenges.

The results of this analysis show that if citizens want to be informed about transnational political issues, they can do so in their mother tongue through the national mass media. The resulting debates do not emerge as a result of central coordination or identity politics. Speakers in the public realm, editorial staff, and journalists from various national contexts seem to perceive some issues as common transnational problems of public interest. Today, many important issues are intensively discussed transnationally via the national media – and among these issues, some raise fundamental questions such as "How do we, as EU citizens, want to live together?" and "What is good or better for us to do as Europeans?"

The findings presented in this chapter have important implications for the prospects of democracy beyond the nation-state. Currently, the quality newspapers fulfill their function in civil society. They report on important common issues and give ordinary citizens the opportunity to build informed opinions about them. The communicative infrastructure for democratic-opinion formation – whether national, European, or even global – can be considered to exist, as long as the national media report freely on the common issues at stake, according to sufficient journalistic standards (which include the presentation of various perspectives and views on the issue), and as long as a critical

Civil society issue publics and European public spheres

Networks of civil society advocacy actors have emerged in many policy areas with transnational implications (e.g., environmental protection, economic and trade justice, food safety, and gender) at both the national and supranational levels in the EU. Civil society in such areas is "Europeanizing" in how organizations frame causes, in the institutions they target, and in efforts to network transnationally around action and events (Balme and Chabanet 2008; Della Porta and Caiani 2009). At the same time, studies repeatedly find that the civil society voice is weak in mass-mediated public spheres (e.g., Koopmans 2007, 2010; Della Porta and Caiani 2009). We propose that to evaluate the civil society dimensions of European public spheres, it is crucial to look beyond mass media (online and offline) to analyze the forms in which civil society's own "public sphere-ing" is done (see also Haug 2010). In particular, the public digital communication that these actors use to inform and organize action is increasingly relevant now that digital media forms (e.g., websites and Facebook pages) become the primary public face of many advocacy organizations (Bennett 2003; Della Porta and Mosca 2007). In addition, we propose that from a public sphere perspective, it is important to consider specifically the openness to public engagement displayed in such communication: that is, the extent to which individuals are enabled and encouraged to attend and contribute to information, discussion, and action around issues. Our measures of public engagement can be taken in two ways: (1) as direct indicators of how publics encounter these issue networks online, and (2) as indirect indicators of how networks of similarly focused organizations operating in different political contexts value the importance of spending scarce resources on public engagement.

Because our approach departs from more familiar studies of mass-mediated public spheres, it is important to understand what bringing in these civil society communication and engagement measures adds to the existing picture of the European public sphere. The core ideas running through the study of mass-mediated public spheres are that the national press reaches large audiences, and that mass-media arenas thereby may carry political claims made by actors in other nations or in Brussels to national publics. "Gallery publics" then attend to the selected transnational issues that seem likely to affect them, resulting in opinion formation and the development of European identities (see Chapters 1 and 4). The criteria adopted by most scholars who embrace the national media perspective on European public spheres include looking for issues that: (1) involve some transnational impact (i.e., Is the issue European in the sense of being commonly framed?); (2) reach large mediated publics (i.e., Is the media reach inclusive?); and (3) involve a political conflict (i.e., Is it contested?). These largely intuitive standards are based loosely on Habermas (2006c) and have been used by researchers to study the development of a European public sphere over time (e.g., Koopmans and Statham 2010a) as well as to assess the emergence of a European political identity on the part of national publics (e.g., Risse 2010).

By contrast, our approach to analyzing civil society networks from a public sphere perspective focuses on "issue publics" and their effect on generating sustainable citizenship practices. We conceive of an "issue public" as constituted by a communication and networking process in which various actors come together to define an issue and establish a configuration of actors connected to that issue. The core of the potential issue public is the "issue network": that is, a set of actors connected primarily in a hyperlink network around an issue (Marres and Rogers 2005). There are often different types of actors involved but, in our cases, the most prominent actors are NGOs and SMOs. Issue networks develop into full-fledged issue publics to the extent that they are open to connection and contestation among organizations but also with citizens (Marres 2006; Lang 2012). Engagement in issue publics, in turn, exposes citizens to public advocacy practices that transcend a single issue focus (in part because networks centered on different issues tend to overlap), which means that issue publics may feature significantly in broader public spheres.[2]

As with all approaches to public spheres, this one centers on communication processes; however, issue publics entail communication of a different type than conventionally assumed in mass-media studies. Digital media in the present case are defining modes of network interaction. Various social technologies can be used to carry information and coordinate action across networks and to enable interaction with and

---

[2] This approach reflects the assumption that public life harbors "multiple but unequal publics" (Fraser 1992, 128) such that there is no single public sphere but rather a multiplicity of communication channels and locations of contestation resulting in the "contestatory interaction of different publics."

among citizens. Hyperlinked relationships among those organizations also are forms of communication that signal levels and directionalities of mutual recognition. These linkages provide channels across which campaigns, protests, and other common activities may flow, contributing to the strength of ties among the networked organizations. Beyond this, the opportunities for public engagement communicated by organizations across networks may offer pathways to individuals to navigate in seeking outlets for their political concerns. Communication is in this way is also a structuring agent in issue publics, not only a means of exchanging information: digital communication mechanisms such as servers, social networking platforms, and hyperlinks are active agents that are directly implicated in structuring networks (Bennett and Segerberg 2013; cf. Latour 2005).

Conceived in this way, issue publics may display the core defining properties of public spheres as outlined here but often with different engagement patterns than found in mass media publics. Although the networks are public, it is difficult to ascertain how many people actually witness or act in an issue public "arena." Although mass media audiences can be estimated through market metrics (i.e., viewers or subscribers), the sum of organizational memberships is not the best indicator of the reach of issue networks. Advocacy organizations increasingly use social media to reach potential supporters who may never become members or make donations (Karpf 2012), and people may encounter organizations in the networks in deliberate and less deliberate ways. Indirect measures can be devised to estimate levels of network engagement such as size of turnout at protest events, posts on sites, and visits to websites in the network. An indication of the broad reach of some of the issue networks considered here is their ability to mobilize hundreds of thousands of demonstrators in street protests (Bennett and Segerberg 2011). However, estimates are complicated by the considerable overlap between issue networks, as well as between them and the mass media.

For these reasons, it is difficult to assess the reach of networked issue publics and to compare their number with the audiences that the mass media claim. That said, the impact of particular news stories on gallery publics is also difficult to assess. Indeed, mass media studies indicate that substantial segments of potential audiences (particularly younger demographics) are not meaningfully engaged in elite-dominated issue discourses most of the time (Bennett 2012). Meanwhile, citizens have greater potential to use the media that constitute an issue public to interact with one another and to contest and/or to co-produce issue claims than mass media audiences. A large NGO site such as Oxfam may have several hundred thousand unique visitors per month, but only a small fraction may be interested in learning what they can do about a specific issue (e.g., promoting fair-trade consumerism in their workplace, church, or community). At the same time, those who actually take action may affect hundreds or even thousands more citizens offline with their projects and initiatives. Thus, the dynamics of online and offline participation is an important area of future research to complement the empirical indicators we offer here.

A tradeoff in thinking about mass-mediated versus civic issue publics in public sphere terms may be one of balancing the potential audience reach against the depth of potential engagement. In examining these networks, we therefore modify the mass media public sphere criterion of inclusiveness (i.e., absolute reach) for measurable levels of openness to public involvement. In particular, we conduct inventories of various interactive media features or affordances to determine how interested organizations across a network seem to be in engaging publics.

Regarding contestation, in which mass media gallery publics are most often exposed vicariously to contestation among elites, networked issue publics are more likely to be directly involved in producing contention. Many organizations in issue networks relate critically to political authority but also use communication technologies to invite differences of opinion within the network. Research by Bennett and Segerberg (2011) suggests that far from imposing a common line on citizens, issue networks may enable personalized expression of views and direct contestation between individuals and decision makers. In these ways, there may be interaction among people who do not agree about an issue and its framing. Indeed, the defining quality of an issue public is not its ability to spread information or to represent a given stakeholder. Rather, it is the continuous work involved in "formatting" an issue and communicating how different actors come into it: it is precisely through such connection and contestation that an issue public emerges (Marres 2006). In this sense, the issue public constitutes something similar to Calhoun's description of a public sphere as "a setting for communication and participation in collective action that can shape identities and interests, not only reflect them" (Calhoun 2003, 4).

For the purpose of analyzing European public spheres, this means that methodologies similar to those applied to mass media spheres in the preceding two chapters could also be applied to civil society issue publics. It is clearly possible to treat the issue public as an arena, analyzing the extent to which fellow European actors voice claims within it, and the extent to which common European themes develop in the use of similar frames and references. It is interesting, for example, to trace how common frames and action plans travel transnationally across issue networks, both horizontally across borders (e.g., when NGOs with multiple national branches share campaigns) and vertically to transnational hubs (e.g., the EU civil society platforms) and back down to national-level networks (see, e.g., Zippel 2006). Thus, future research on civil society issue publics from the perspective of Europeanization would do well to explore the extent to which the issue spheres include fellow European claim makers and audiences as well as common European themes occurring across national borders.

In contrast to the traditional study of mass media public spheres, however, networked issue publics also entail a different type of analysis. As already indicated, the possibility for active citizen engagement is a defining quality of issue publics and constitutes a primary point of analysis in the assessment of the quality of issue publics from a public sphere perspective. This means that in this chapter, the primary marker of civil society issue publics being "Europeanized" is the extent to which they have the capacity to directly engage numerous citizens in various causes at the same time that they have the capacity to bring them into contact with EU institutions and decision makers, on the one hand, and fellow Europeans (organizational or individual), on the other. The analysis of public communication spheres that the organized civil society actors produce grants an important perspective on the state of civil society dimensions in the European public sphere.

The remainder of this chapter explores the conditions under which NGO-centered issue networks engage citizens in contesting matters of common interest, both within issue networks at the national and EU levels and between these networks and various decision-making institutions. In a move similar to that pursued by Koopmans (see Chapter 3), we propose to treat national issue networks as baselines of public engagement quality against which we may evaluate the quality of the networks that emanate from the EU "Civil Society Contact

Group" (i.e., the so-called EU civil society issue platforms) in the same policy area.

Mapping issue networks and measuring public engagement capacity

The study analyzes issue networks in two issue areas (i.e., environment/climate change and economic development/fair trade) in two countries (i.e., the United Kingdom and Germany) to assess the public engagement quality of the issue publics at the national and EU levels. These two cases introduce interesting variations in terms of levels of public commitment to the EU project and different national political systems (although we were able to collect our data during a time in which the respective governments were roughly comparable in terms of political leanings). We selected issue clusters with transnational implications in which the EU has civil-society platforms: the platforms on the environment (i.e., The Green Ten) and trade and development (i.e., Concord) coordinate contact between organized civil society from different EU countries and EU institutions and decision makers.

The two selected issue areas are interesting for our purposes for two reasons beyond their representation at the EU platform level. First, they can be expected to generate different types of issue networks. Fair trade organizations are loosely organized around a federation of fair trade labeling and certification organizations in twenty-four nations. These gatekeepers provide structure for the terms of engagement with fair trade (i.e., by subscribing to common definitions of the issue and promoting similar norms for production and consumption) and also introduce variation in national networks as conflicts between business partners and economic-justice activists arise and become resolved (Bennett, Foot, and Xenos 2011). By contrast, environmental networks and climate change advocacy lack such central organization. Therefore, we anticipate that these networks may be even more variable, creating the potential for greater differences in the modes of engaging publics across networks.

The second reason for selecting these issues is that there may be interesting national-level differences in public engagement due to the political-institutional contexts in which these issue networks operate. We chose the United Kingdom and Germany as comparison cases in part because the Green Party was in government for several years in Germany, raising the potential to directly incorporate a degree of public engagement on the environment and climate change into governing institutions through elections. This participation in government by the Green Party might have diminished levels of direct public engagement in the German national environmental issue network. By contrast, the economic justice networks in both the United Kingdom and Germany operated at the time of our study within the contexts of Labor and Centrist governments that – although relatively sympathetic to some of the aims of fair-trade advocates – also bargained with business and world free-trade regimes. Thus, we might expect more direct public engagement focus in fair trade networks than across environmental networks in Germany.

Public engagement quality is at the heart of the comparison between the issue networks, and we propose that the arc of citizen engagement resulting in the constitution of an issue public may be assessed at two levels. At the most general level of network structure, it involves the capacity of organizations to link strategically among themselves to form common networks for communicating about issues and taking various types of orchestrated action. Therefore, the first step in analyzing public engagement quality requires attention to the networking profile of an issue network. At the next level, we analyze the public interaction profile of the network by inventorying the information and action engagement mechanisms that organizations use to inform and mobilize publics. The variety of indicators outlined herein enables us to build systematic profiles of the public engagement capacities of individual organizations. By summing the profiles of individual organizations, we can characterize the public engagement orientations and capacities of entire issue networks.

Throughout the analysis, these measures can be perceived in two mutually compatible ways: (1) as abstract indicators of the public-regarding or public-disregarding tendencies of organizations and their networks, and (2) as mechanisms that engage citizens and structure action. At the organization level, patterns of interlinking trace organizational relationships across networks but also create pathways for visitors to find information. Similarly, the presence or absence of public interaction mechanisms can be taken as evidence of interest in sharing policy initiatives and engaging citizens, as well as providing actual ways for individuals to become informed and to act.

Sampling issue networks

Before commencing the public engagement analysis, we first drew issue networks in the two areas at the national and European levels for both countries. As noted previously, issue networks are defined by the ways that actors hyperlink to other actors – along with various other digital mechanisms in their public communication – to signal who they are and how they define the matter at hand (boyd and Heer 2006; Foot and Schneider 2006). Linking is intentional; therefore, the way that organizations link or fail to link back to one another suggests much about the network relationships, such as the centrality of the various actors and their shared orientations to issues. Inlinks received by organizations indicate measures of recognition or prestige from other organizations in the network. Outlinks to other organizations reflect (1) efforts to influence or support other members of the network, or (2) recognition of an actor's importance to the issue (e.g., as a target of claims or source of information). It is important that the issue network is not a simple reflection of the strategic agreements among specific actors: some actors may not be visible and others may be included as targets of criticism. The network map is more like a satellite picture of a civil society public communication sphere that identifies the network players and their spatial relationships, which may be used to identify the organizations on which to focus the finer-grained investigation of engagement opportunities.

Mapping these networks involves following links out from a set of organizational websites that we determined to be important to a network. (This may be understood as corresponding to the selection of representative newspapers in mass media studies.) The relationships among these starting-point sites – and the others that they link to and receive links from – provide the basic membership of an issue network. Some networks, of course, do not develop dense interlinking and that alone is an interesting indicator of their lack of public engagement capacity.

Our two selected issues present different sampling challenges at the national level. Because fair trade operates nationally with gate-keeping organizations that control the international fair trade label, it makes sense to see how networks emanate from those organizations. Although these organizations are constituted rather differently from country to country, they offer starting points for network "crawls" (see the explanation in the next section) to establish issue networks on trade and development. We conducted network crawls using the member lists of the UK and German national fair trade organizations: the Fairtrade Foundation and TransFair, respectively.[3]

In the case of the environmental and climate change networks, there was no such obvious starting point. However, the December 2009 UN Climate Conference in Copenhagen served as a catalyst for increased movement activity and, at the time of our sampling in the spring of 2010, the collective organizing around this activity was still clearly visible. We located national coalition websites in both countries and initiated network crawls from the coalition member lists. This difference in starting points for generating the network maps offers a useful contrast between two steady-state issue networks (on fair trade) and two networks in the process of mobilizing for protest actions (on the environment).[4]

The EU-level networks were drawn from German and UK members of the Green Ten and Concord platforms as identified on the EU civil society contact group website.[5] Although we extracted national slices, each platform – in principle – coordinates organizations from across all EU countries.[6]

---

[3] In the UK national sample, the web crawl starting points were the fifteen "charity stakeholders" named on the website of the UK Fairtrade Foundation website (www.fairtrade.org.uk), plus the foundation itself. The German national sample began with the thirty-six members of the gatekeeping organization Transfair (www.transfair.org), plus Transfair itself.

[4] The UK national sample was taken from the Stop Climate Chaos Coalition, a broad NGO umbrella coalition that organized the largest protest in the United Kingdom on the eve of the UN Climate Conference (available at www. stopclimatechaos.org). The crawl was initiated from a list of 104 organizations that joined this coalition. The German sample was drawn from the Copenhagen protest coalition *Die Klima Allianz* (available at www.klimagipfel2009.de/ cop15/organisationen) as a starting point. We gathered all fifty-six member organizations of klimagipfel2009.de.

[5] Available at www.act4europe.org/code/en/default.asp.

[6] The EU-level fair-trade networks were drawn as follows. The UK sample began from the UK national coordinating organization in the EU Concord platform, Bond (available at www.bond.org.uk/index.php). Bond is a broad coalition of development, relief, and trade organizations that ranges beyond fair-trade issues to include disaster relief, clean drinking water, and other issues. We screened this list for organizations that focus on trade and economic justice. A sample was created by selecting 10 percent of the 360 Bond UK member organizations. We selected every tenth organization from the members list on

The starting points established for each network were analyzed in terms of how they linked out to other organizations to reveal larger issue networks. We conducted an automated network crawl to search for links from the starting-point organizations to other sites to produce network maps for each country, issue, and level.[7] These networks became the populations from which we drew our network samples for measuring public engagement orientation.

Evaluating the networking profile

Mapping the issue networks allowed us to assess the first dimension of the networks' engagement capacity as issue publics: that is, their networking profile. Patterns of interlinking reveal the closeness, density,

---

the Bond website, which resulted in thirty-six organizations. The German sample started from the German national coordinating organization in the Concord platform, Venro. We selected every fourth member from the list of 118 members (available at www.venro.org/mitglieder.html). We gathered thirty organizations, which we then screened for focus on trade and economic justice.

In the EU-level environmental networks, both samples were drawn from the Green Ten platform member organizations and networks. The UK sample consisted of the UK members or partners of each of the ten organizations and networks, which resulted in a sample of forty-eight. The German sample started with the twenty-five German affiliate organizations from the same Green Ten member organizations and networks. We screened all organizations for a general focus on climate issues, following the same procedures as for the fair-trade sample.

[7] The organization URLs were used as starting points in Issue Crawler, a tool made available by Richard Rogers at the University of Amsterdam. The Issue Crawler identifies networks of URLs and locates them in a relational space (which we refer to as a "network map") on the basis of co-link analysis. A co-link is a URL that receives links from at least two of the starting points for each iteration (or "click") as the crawler moves out from the starting points. Using co-link analysis thereby sets a higher bar for network inclusion than other mapping methods (e.g., snowball analysis) that include more weakly tied organizations. The co-linking criterion highlights actors that emerge in more tightly connected networks. It is an appropriate approach in this case in which we are interested in comparing networks in terms of density of linking and structural stability that gives their engagement efforts some coherence. We set the reach of the crawl at one iteration from the starting points. Rogers (2004) recommends this procedure to derive a network that includes organizations concerned with the same issue (as opposed to reaching the support networks for larger categories of concern). We set the crawler to a crawl depth of three, which instructs it to drill two pages beyond the home page to follow any outlinks on those pages. In our experience, this captures most network links that matter to the mission of organizations (see also Bennett and Segerberg 2011, 2013).

Figure 5.1. UK national-level fair trade network showing dense co-linking among organizations.
Source: Map by issuecrawler.net, courtesy of the Govcom.org Foundation, Amsterdam. Used with permission.

and centrality of organizational relationships across networks and create pathways for users to find sites of information, action, and other organizations. Space prevents us from describing all of the relevant issue network maps, so we illustrate this step with one national-level and one EU-level map.

Figure 5.1 shows the national level fair trade issue network in the United Kingdom (in 2010). It is a highly interconnected network, in which many organizations link to one another. We followed this network for several years and note that it is remarkably stable, with a stable set of densely linked organizations at the core (Bennett and Segerberg 2013). By contrast, the EU-level fair-trade network in the United Kingdom had minimal density or cross-linking among organizations. We employed two different crawl methods to determine this result. The initial co-link crawl produced a cluster map that is remarkably similar to Figure 5.1, which means that the network was populated largely by the outreach efforts of the relatively small number of organizations active at the national level that also appear in the European-level issue network. As the overlapping organizations reconstituted their initial network, most of the unique EU-level UK organizations disappeared from the network. Thus, the co-link crawl indicated that although there was a certain degree of "Europeanization" as organizations from the national level moved into the network associated with the EU civil society platform, the national and EU civil-society actors did not cooperate well together at the EU level.

To understand whether the unique EU-level actors formed any type of network, we undertook an interactor crawl on the members of the Concord platform of trade and development organizations affiliated with the UK coordinating organization (i.e., Bond). Interactor crawls relax the criteria for network inclusion by mapping only single links between any two organizations. Figure 5.2 reveals the resulting "star" network centered on Bond. This indicates that the EU-level development organizations are organized rather hierarchically and do not share many close, cross-linking relationships – at least insofar as their public façade is concerned. A subsequent interactor analysis was based on the set of UK organizations more narrowly defined around fair-trade initiatives (e.g., excluding relief and health organizations). That map revealed that the star formation around Bond was joined by a second, more densely linked cluster of the overlapping national-level organizations shown in Figure 5.1, which again suggests that the national- and European-level issue networks are structured differently and remain distinct in the network around the platform.

The notable differences between the EU- and national-level networks led us to choose different methods for selecting the sites to be coded for public interaction in the second step of the analysis. For the national-level networks, we screened the core organizations to select those that, respectively, focused on trade or development policy (excluding organizations that clearly operate in other areas, such as disaster relief), or environmental protection or climate change (excluding organizations focusing on, for example, workplace environment or environmental health policy). The same screening was conducted for the samples drawn from the corresponding EU platforms. However, as previously noted, when we attempted to generate samples based on co-link maps

Figure 5.2. EU-level fair trade network in the United Kingdom, showing a hierarchical or "star" structure with little co-linking among organizations.
Source: Map by issuecrawler.net, courtesy of the Govcom.org Foundation, Amsterdam. Used with permission.

of the EU-level networks, we found that unique EU-level organizations tended to disappear because they were not linked to or from multiple other organizations. Thus, for the EU level, we sampled directly from lists of UK and German member organizations in the civil society platforms. These samples also were screened for a focus on climate change/natural environment and fair trade/economic justice, respectively. Organizations that did not fit these classifications were replaced randomly and screened until the original sample sizes were met. The resulting sample sizes that we used to code public interaction opportunities among organizations ranged from fifty-eight organizations (i.e., the UK national-level environmental network) to twenty-three (i.e., the EU-level German environmental network). The differences in numbers of organizations for the EU-level networks reflect the fact that although those networks spanned broader ranges of policy issues within the

general civil society platform categories, they had fewer unique organizations in the relevant categories of our study.[8] The differences in
numbers of organizations were standardized by reporting the percentages of organizations in each network that displayed each measure of
public interaction.

Evaluating the public interaction profile

After mapping the issue networks, we analyzed each network's public
interaction profile, which indicates to what extent organizations across
a network offer opportunities for citizens to engage as well as the type
of engagement they offer.

Issue publics develop around three broad facets of citizen engagement: attention, discussion, and participation in collective action. The
first element of public attention organized by networks is in some
ways similar to how mass media audiences may selectively attend to
information about an issue in the news. However, the opportunities
for discussion and direct action make the issue publics rather different than their mass media counterparts. The mass-mediated model
puts discussion (i.e., the heart of Habermas's original model) in a passive or vicarious mode, leaving individuals in the "gallery public" to

---

[8] The sample characteristics are as follows. In the environmental networks, the
UK national network included ninety-six sites in the crawled network, leaving
a codable sample of fifty-eight after screening for relevance of policy focus (the
crawl was conducted on May 9, 2010). The German national network included
one hundred sites in the network crawl and fifty-seven codable sites following the
screening (the crawl was conducted on May 9, 2010). The UK EU-level network
began with forty-eight Green Ten partners, of which twenty-four remained after
screening (the sample was drawn on May 25, 2010). The German EU-level network began with twenty-five German Green Ten partners, with twenty-three left
after screening (the sample was drawn on June 6, 2010). In the fair-trade networks, the UK national-level network included ninety-six organizations in the
crawled network, leaving a codable sample of forty-six organizations after screening (the crawl was conducted on April 16, 2010). The German national-level
network included ninety-three organizations, of which thirty-seven were coded
following screening (the crawl was conducted on April 20, 2010). In the UK
EU-level network, nineteen of the thirty-six Bond members were excluded after
screening. The disqualified organizations were replaced by random selection of
new members from the Bond list until the original number of thirty-six relevant
organizations was reached (April 30, 2010). When the German EU-level network was screened, sixteen of the original sample of thirty Venro members were
excluded and randomly replaced with relevant organizations (May 9, 2010).

imitate or mime the discussions held among mostly elite news or editorial sources, which may not resonate with citizens' actual discussion preferences and repertoires (Gamson 1992). The range of participation experiences offered to mass-mediated "gallery publics" is even more abstracted and deferred. Because the discourses are elite-dominated, it is not surprising that civil society action and calls to action are seldom reported or that, when reported, they are marginalized or framed as illegitimate (Gitlin 1980). In the issue public, by contrast, citizens may encounter discussion and participation opportunities that are more directly possible to engage with and to customize. Whereas there are many locations along issue networks where various forms of engagement can occur, the organization website is one unit of analysis that permits measurement and comparison on a scale comparable to mass media analysis. (Other important locations of engagement exist but require close-to-the-ground ethnographic observation; cf. Doerr 2008.)

The three facets of citizen engagement are interesting in the sense that attention is largely an information-oriented process and action involves political performance, whereas discussion serves a bridging function between the two modes of engagement that is inherently interactive. Thus, we inventoried the engagement mechanisms on organization websites in two broad categories of whether they are information- or action-oriented and then, within each category, whether they are interactive (i.e., inviting input from publics) or primarily one-way (i.e., heavily managed by the organization). This framework yielded four key measures that combine to constitute the public interaction quality of the issue public, as follows:

- The first key measure concerns the one-way communication of information. An example of this is when an organization uses its website to inform the general public about itself and what it does.
- The second key measure concerns the potential for information to be contributed in public by actors other than the organization in question. An example includes the opportunity to post a photograph or a comment.
- The third key measure concerns the degree to which an organization seeks to mobilize site visitors in unilaterally decided forms of action. Donating money, joining the organization, and signing a petition are examples of this form of engagement.

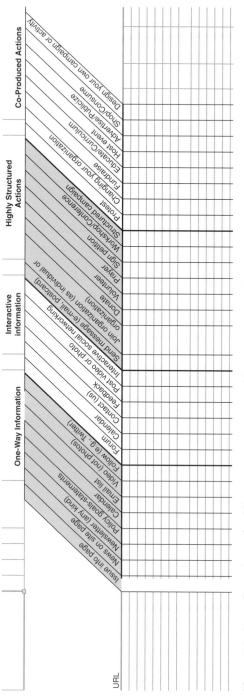

Figure 5.3. Four dimensions of public engagement measured by component indicators across organizations in issue networks.

- The fourth key measure concerns the potential for actors other than the site owner to coordinate an action through public communication on the site or by working offsite to design actions that fit local realities. An example is inviting citizens to organize their friends, workplaces, churches, and schools around a cause.

Each respective measure entails increasingly intense engagement that reflects both rising levels of individual commitment and greater sharing of the definition of issues among organizations and others. When summed, the measurement of engagement mechanisms in organizations throughout a network indicates the network's public interaction profile. Combining the networking and public interaction profiles provides a way to assess engagement depth not just in the singular organization but also across the wider issue network as a whole. This analysis misses various elements – such as organizations too small or poor to have resource-rich websites or that engage people largely offline – and it is less suited to analyzing how networks around covert or illicit issues engage publics. However, it is a reliable method for the purpose of analyzing public advocacy communication in policy-oriented issue spheres.

We inventoried public engagement mechanisms on the websites of all organizations in each network. We identified approximately the same number of measures (i.e., eight) for each dimension of engagement (i.e., we lost two interactive information measures due to poor coder reliability). The resulting scheme for measuring public interaction is shown in Figure 5.3 in the form of the website coding template used by coders.[9] In the next section, we describe one illustration of the entire coding results for an issue network. To reduce the length of the analysis, we thereafter report only summary scores for the four engagement dimensions, along with a score for the sum of the four engagement dimensions across all coded organizations in the network. Thus, the end result of coding the engagement levels for each organization in an issue network is the ability to state the percentage of organizations in the network that offers each form of engagement to the public. In this approach, the websites serve as both proxies for the organizations that created them and communication and structuring

---

[9] The coder reliability coefficients (i.e., a simple percentage agreement, given the use of a "presence or absence" coding protocol) ranged from 0.98 to 0.7 on individual items, and the average for each of the four dimensions was above 0.8.

elements of networks through which information flows, actions are coordinated, and individuals engage.

Comparing public engagement in civil society issue publics

To establish how national- and EU-level issue networks compare in their uses of digital communication to structure public involvement, we considered engagement differences at the two levels for the same issues. We were also able to analyze the degree of engagement that is contributed by the national civil society NGOs that overlap with EU networks, within-nation public engagement differences across different issues, and cross-national engagement differences for the same issues. In general, the national-level networks were richer across all four engagement dimensions compared to the EU-level networks. This pattern holds true for both issues in the United Kingdom and for fair trade in Germany. However, the German climate change/environmental network presents an interesting contrast.

We began by establishing a baseline measure using the UK national-level issue networks. Here, the networks on environment and fair trade are roughly comparable in terms of engagement patterns: both offer a broad array of engagement opportunities, and they are not significantly different on the five summary measures that we used for the remainder of the analysis (i.e., the four engagement dimensions and the overall total engagement score).

As Table 5.1 illustrates, there are no systematic differences in the public interaction levels of the two networks. There are, of course, item differences, which may be due to various externalities in the environment at the time of the analysis (e.g., because the climate network was mapped shortly after the Copenhagen climate summit, protest activities may have been high on environmental organization websites). This suggests interesting possibilities for mapping and assessing networks over time and in response to events. In one-time analyses such as this, we recommend using the summary scores of all the items in a given category of engagement mechanisms to reduce the dominance of any single item (e.g., protests). In addition to the four dimensions of engagement, we created an overall public engagement score by summing the engagement levels across the four dimensions. These scales enable statistical comparisons between issues, between nations, and between national- and EU-level issue networks.

Table 5.1. *A comparison of public engagement mechanisms of UK national-level environment and fair trade networks*

INFORMATION VARIABLES (ONE WAY, INTERACTIVE)	UK national-level fair trade net (N = 46)	UK national-level environment net (N = 58)
SITE: Recently updated?	87%	98%
ONE WAY: Issue info page	93%	93%
ONE WAY: News on site page	89%	94%
ONE WAY: Newsletter (any kind)	61%	63%
ONE WAY: Policy-goal statements	89%	70%
ONE WAY: Calendar	52%	54%
ONE WAY: Email list	63%	44%
ONE WAY: Video (not photographs)	59%	63%
ONE WAY: Follow (e.g., Twitter)	48%	59%
INTERACTIVE: Forum	37%	37%
INTERACTIVE: Calendar	20%	15%
INTERACTIVE: Contact (us)	98%	94%
INTERACTIVE: Feedback	20%	44%
INTERACTIVE: Post video or photograph	24%	15%
INTERACTIVE: Interactive social networking	52%	67%
ACTION VARIABLES (HIGHLY STRUCTURED, CO-PRODUCED)	UK national-level fair trade	UK national-level environment
HS: Send message	61%	52%
HS: Join organization	67%	50%
HS: Donate	52%	59%
HS: Volunteer	52%	43%
HS: Prayer	20%	9%
HS: Sign petition	30%	24%
HS: Workshop/Conference	26%	37%
HS: Structured campaign	57%	76%
CP: Protest	11%	22%
CP: Changing your organization	17%	48%
CP: Fundraise	39%	26%
CP: Educate/curriculum	46%	35%
CP: Host event	35%	22%
CP: Advertise/publicize	54%	46%
CP: Shop/consume	46%	46%
CP: Design your own campaign or activity	30%	35%

(cont.)

Table 5.1. *(cont.)*

OVERALL RESULTS	UK national-level fair trade	UK national-level environment
One-way information (summary score)	0.69	0.68
Interactive information (summary score)	0.42	0.45
Highly structured actions (summary score)	0.46	0.44
Co-produced actions (summary score)	0.35	0.35
Overall public engagement score (sum of four component scores)	1.91	1.92
T-test	one-tailed	
UK national-level fair trade – UK national-level environment	Difference in means	p
One-way information score	*0.02*	*0.35*
Interactive information score	*–0.04*	*0.21*
Highly structured actions score	*0.02*	*0.35*
Co-produced actions score	*0.00*	*0.47*
Overall public engagement score	*–0.01*	*0.49*

Note: Item scores represent the percentage of organizations in each network displaying each engagement mechanism. Summary scores represent averages of item scores for each engagement dimension.

When we compared these national-level UK networks with their EU-level counterparts, we discovered significant engagement differences: the European-level network offers far lower engagement levels than the national networks for both issues and both nations. Table 5.2 compares the national- and EU-level fair trade networks, including and excluding the overlapping organizations in both networks.

To assess the effects of highly visible national-level NGOs that also have joined issue networks in Brussels, we removed the overlapping organizations (e.g., Oxfam and the Fairtrade Foundation) from the EU-level network for the comparison in Table 5.2. To create an even more rigorous test, we removed the overlapping organizations from both networks and still found significant engagement differences in

Table 5.2. *Engagement levels in UK fair trade networks comparing national- and EU-level networks (with and without overlapping organizations)*

	UK national level vs. EU-level (with overlapping organizations)		UK national level (with overlapping organizations) vs. EU-level (without overlapping organizations)	
	Difference in means	p	Difference in means	p
One-way information score	0.12	0.01	0.18	0.00
Interactive information score	0.10	0.02	0.14	0.00
Highly structured actions score	0.10	0.04	0.17	0.00
Co-produced actions score	0.09	0.06	0.13	0.01
Overall public engagement score	0.40	0.01	0.62	0.00

every category, although weaker. Through a process of removing over-lapping organizations from the different networks, we are confident that most of the engagement focus in EU-level networks is from organizations that are central to the national-level networks and, at the same time, seek representation in Brussels. Even with these organizations retained (see Table 5.2), the engagement focus of most EU-level networks is lower.

The environmental networks in the United Kingdom follow this pattern, with the national-level network displaying significantly higher public engagement profiles than the EU-level network for all four categories of engagement (i.e., p ranges from 0.00 to 0.05 for one-tailed tests) and for the overall engagement score ($p < 0.00$). The pattern holds true also for the German fair trade networks, as shown in Table 5.3 (with the exception of one engagement measure: "highly structured actions").

There is an interesting exception to this overall pattern of similar engagement levels between national issue networks and different engagement levels between the national and EU-levels within issues: that is, the German environmental networks, which displayed no significant public interaction differences between the national and the

Table 5.3. *Engagement levels in German fair trade networks comparing national- and EU-level networks (without overlapping organizations)*

	German national level (with overlapping organizations) vs. EU-level (without overlaps)	
	Difference in means	*p*
One-way information score	0.17	0.00
Interactive information score	0.09	0.01
Highly structured actions score	0.02	0.39
Co-produced actions score	0.18	0.00
Overall public engagement score	0.45	0.00

EU-levels. In the German environmental case, the national-level network operated at about the same (low) level of engagement offerings as the EU-level network. In part, this is because there was a surprising level of overlap in the two networks, with fully fourteen of the twenty-three sites appearing in both networks (which we considered to be a sign of greater institutionalization of these networks). However, even with the overlapping sites removed from the EU-level network comparison, the engagement levels were not significantly different (although the number of sites was small at that point).

We attribute this to the long-standing efforts of the Green Party to bring public engagement into government through voting and drawing the social movement community and political institutions closer together. Thus, the engagement patterns of the German NGO advocacy networks are more fully harmonized at both network levels, albeit at the expense of everyday public engagement with the issues. The decrease in public engagement is reflected in the comparison of the UK national environmental network with the German national network in Table 5.4.

The lack of significant differences between the two German networks (with and without overlapping members) is shown in Table 5.5. The one measure of engagement that approaches significance is the highly structured action category, which is dominated by a greater outreach from the European-level issue networks for limited forms of civic engagement (e.g., membership and donations).

Table 5.4. *Comparison of German and UK national-level environmental advocacy networks showing lower levels of engagement in the German network*

	UK national	German national
One-way information score	0.68	0.57
Interactive information score	0.45	0.27
Highly structured actions score	0.44	0.25
Co-produced actions score	0.35	0.23
Overall public sphere score	1.92	1.32

Note: All t-tests $p < 0.00$ (one-tailed in predicted direction of UK scoring higher on public engagement).

Table 5.5. *Comparison of engagement scores in German environmental advocacy networks at national- and EU-levels (with and without overlapping members)*

	German national vs. European-level with overlapping members		German national vs. European-level (European without overlaps)	
	Difference in means	p	Difference in means	p
One-way information score	−0.04	0.15	−0.03	0.30
Interactive information score	0.04	0.13	0.03	0.30
Highly structured actions score	−0.07	0.08	−0.10	0.06
Co-produced actions score	0.03	0.22	0.02	0.36
Overall public sphere score	−0.03	0.41	−0.08	0.33

This finding poses an interesting puzzle pertaining to the institution-alization of environmental politics, suggesting that the rise to power of the German Green Party was accompanied by diminished public engagement by green NGOs. This does not mean that environmental politics in Germany is dead – on the contrary, as the recent decision by the German government to phase out nuclear energy shows. However, the finding does suggest that the issue publics in this area are weak from a public sphere perspective on both the national and EU levels.

The problems of European issue publics

This chapter argues for the importance of examining civil society dimensions of European public spheres through the public communication that civil society actors use and the particular public spheres they help to create. This entails looking beyond mass media spheres to the relatively stable, digitally mediated issue publics developed by organized civil society actors and others. It also entails examining the public engagement quality of European issue publics by measuring and evaluating an issue network's public interaction and networking profiles. Our analysis sheds light on a set of civil society-centered public communication spheres that have the potential to engage citizens while connecting them to governmental institutions and the coordination of action across national borders. However, not all NGO-centered issue networks develop public engagement to the same extent. Using the national issue publics as a baseline to evaluate the corresponding EU-level issue publics revealed a somber picture, reinforcing concerns about the democratic deficit related to civil society involvement in European public spheres.

The most apparent problem that is highlighted when taking stock from this perspective is that the European-level issue networks in our study are comparatively weak – and possibly not even issue publics at all. In an outcome that seems similar to Koopmans' findings (see Chapter 3), the analysis of the network capacity of the EU-level issue networks suggested that there is a certain amount of Europeanization in the sense that nation-based advocacy organizations are moving into the European-level networks. However, Europeanization – in the sense of fellow European advocacy actors and citizens connecting – remains limited. As discussed previously, the advocacy organizations active in both the national and EU networks remained separate from those specializing in work around the EU platform. Furthermore, the issue networks surrounding the national actors that we sliced out of each EU platform also remained separate: there was little or no linking between the national slices at either level.

The lower engagement capacity scores in the EU-level issue networks' public interaction profiles suggest that organized advocacy at that level is weakly committed to engaging citizens. The EU issue networks are not bereft of engagement opportunities, but many stem from national organizations that enter the EU policy arena, bringing engaged citizens with them, and then remain distinct from more professionalized policy counterparts. The organizations that primarily affiliate with the EU civil society platforms are low in public interaction, and they dampen the interaction profile of the network as a whole. This suggests that the EU-level issue networks may have a tendency to "become the public" in a manner similar to that observed in mass media in which dominant news content primarily mirrors elite discourse back to the elites (Statham 2010a, 295–6). This charge has been directed at advocacy organizations before, as when the shift to soft-law policy making increases the willingness of EU institutions to consult with NGOs (Checkel 1999; Warleigh 2003; Locher 2007). Critics argue that civil society organizations in the Brussels arena often serve as substitutes for the voices of European citizens, creating a civic order without credible levels of public engagement, and thereby deepening the EU's democratic deficit (Kroeger 2008; Steffek and Nanz 2008; Haug 2010; Kohler-Koch 2011; Lang 2012). The present analysis suggests that NGO-centered issue networks at the European-level may also be vulnerable to this charge. That said, it is possible that advocacy actors do not always take this route: early results from a similar study of Swedish networks in the same issue areas do not follow the pattern of weaker engagement at the EU-level. Thus, a central question about organized civil society in European public spheres is whether and under what conditions NGO-centered networks engage citizens instead of simply making vague representational claims.

Following on this point, a second problem regarding issue networks from the public sphere perspective is the degree to which incorporation in governance structures may tend to undermine civil society issue publics. We submit that differences in the vibrancy of issue publics can be traced in part to the political relationships between organizations and governance. Our analysis suggests that the public engagement capacities of the issue networks vary strikingly depending on how the core organizations are incorporated into the institutional apparatus of government. As discussed herein, we found richer profiles among nationally rooted issue networks than among the networks centered on the EU platforms working on the same issues. The exception to this pattern was found in the German environmental networks, which displayed little difference between the public interaction profiles at either level and which were far lower than in their UK counterpart. This suggests that when an issue becomes incorporated into governing institutions at either level (e.g., via the Green Party in the national case), NGOs may become more closely aligned with governing processes and less oriented to directly mobilizing citizens. These findings do not necessarily signal a democratic deficit – in fact, on this issue, voting may be a meaningful engagement mechanism in Germany. However, it does indicate that an engagement drain occurred in the related civil society issue networks, weakening the civil society elements of the public sphere in this area. The fact that engagement levels were similar in the fair trade networks in both countries suggests that the effects are not broadly due to country differences but rather are related to particular issues in political context.

The suggested connection between issue and political context makes it intriguing to expand the scope of our inquiry to encompass civil society issue publics in other parts of the EU and around other issues. Furthermore, it is interesting to consider whether the mobilizations around Europe in the wake of the financial crisis dramatically change the patterns discussed here. It is not clear that they do so in all cases. Several post-crisis mobilizations about economic justice that were anchored in organized civil society have traveled to the European level through national issue networks in ways similar to those traced in this chapter. An example is the UK-based Robin Hood Tax campaign that was launched in 2010, the issue network of which (related to the UK national fair trade network analyzed herein) is strong in public engagement (Bennett and Segerberg 2013). The campaign's idea of a financial transaction tax spread across national contexts to gain support in more than ten other EU member states and also traveled up to the Concord platform. A proposal based on the idea finally gained recognition by the European Commission and the European Parliament. In other cases, however, as in the *indignados* protests in Spain (and now Italy), the mobilizations have been resplendent with crowd- and technology-enabled action in which conventional organizations are kept at the periphery (Bennett and Segerberg 2013; cf. Anduiza, Cristancho, and Sabucedo 2014). This development raises challenging questions about (1) how to trace and evaluate the issue publics that emerge in less organization-centered cases, and (2) how the strong domestic mobilizations in which citizens are demanding voice in these forms carry over into efforts to ground civil society issue publics at the EU level.

In summary, our findings illuminate a structural problem for the civil society development of European public spheres: that NGOs specialized in lobbying at the EU-level do not seek to engage publics (perhaps because they are not encouraged to do so). This may not seem surprising, but it does not bode well for developing rich public spheres with a voluble civil society. Future work should address the implications of the finding that overlapping national-level organizations that are not institutionally incorporated boost the engagement capacity of the EU networks. Observers such as Sidney Tarrow condition the rise of European democracy to "the capacity of social movements, public interest groups, and other non-state actors to make alliances with other combinations of national government actors, supranational institutions, and with each other" (Tarrow 2001, 250). In line with this observation, rather than making structural changes in the professional organizations – many of which are not set up to run campaigns or offer menus of public activities – perhaps these instead can develop partnerships with organizations that regard public engagement as more central to their mission. This suggests the desirability of closer relationships between professionalized NGOs that cluster in Brussels and actors working closer to the ground to support the development of a rich European public sphere anchored in a more vibrant civil society.

PART II

Consequences: does the Europeanization of public spheres matter?

6 | European public spheres, the politicization of EU affairs, and its consequences

THOMAS RISSE

At first glance, the euro crisis has brought out the worst stereotypes in the public spheres that Europeans might imagine about one another.[1] Greek street posters depicted German Chancellor Angela Merkel in a Nazi uniform with the European Union (EU) stars around the swastika. A German news magazine portrayed Aphrodite giving the finger with the title "Crooks in the Euro-Family" (note, however, that the Eurozone is still portrayed as a "family").[2] Europeans appear to fall back into nationalism and to advocate nationalist responses to the worst crisis the EU has ever faced. It is no wonder, then, that former Italian Prime Minister Mario Monti warned about the "psychological breakup of Europe."[3] Yet, his warnings represented transnational communication because he made his comments in the German magazine *Der Spiegel*.

---

[1] Drafts of this chapter were discussed at the workshops of the European Public Spheres project in the framework of the *Kolleg-Forschergruppe* "Transformative Power of Europe?" in April 2011 and January 2012. Funding by the German Research Foundation (DFG) is gratefully acknowledged. For detailed comments on the draft, I thank the participants in the workshops, particularly Stephanie Anderson, Tanja Börzel, and Marianne Van de Steeg. I also learned much from a workshop on politicization of supranational governance at the Social Science Center in Berlin, February 7–8, 2013, organized by Pieter de Wilde and Michael Zürn.

[2] See www.dailymail.co.uk/news/article-2054406/Furious-Greeks-lampoon-German-overlords-Nazis-picture-Merkel-dressed-SS-guard.html?ITO=1490 (accessed August 6, 2013); http://p4.focus.de/img/gen/Z/r/HBZrzUeA_Pxgen_r_Ax480.jpg?http://p4.focus.de/img/gen/Z/r/HBZrzUeA_Pxgen_r_Ax480.jpg? http://p4.focus.de/img/gen/Z/r/HBZrzUeA_Pxgen_r_Ax480.jpg (accessed August 6, 2013). It is interesting that the editorial offices of *Focus* magazine denied copyright permission to reproduce the front cover in this book.

[3] Available at www.spiegel.de/politik/ausland/italiens-premier-monti-warnt-im-spiegel-vor-auseinanderbrechen-europas-a-848280.html (accessed August 6, 2013).

There is no doubt that the euro crisis has politicized European affairs and the EU, probably like no other previous event in the history of European integration. How to respond to the euro crisis is being hotly debated across borders. Austerity programs and stringent budget cuts are being proposed (and imposed on the EU's southern tier), and others advocate (Keynesian) economic-growth strategies to avoid long-lasting recessions and growing unemployment in the Eurozone. At the same time, public-opinion polls reveal that majorities of Europeans agree that European rather than national solutions to the crisis are the best way and that European integration will increase rather than decrease as a result (European Commission 2011).

Part I of this book argues that we are witnessing the emergence of Europeanized public spheres entailing transnational cross-border communication on questions of common European concern. The empirical evidence appears to be consistent with an account according to which reporting about the EU increased over time following the growing domestic salience of EU policies. The more salient and visible that EU institutions and the rules and policies emanating from them became in the domestic politics of the member states, the more that news coverage of the EU increased, which led to the emergence of Europeanized public spheres. As a result, a European-wide "communicative space [is] in the making" (cf. the titles of Fossum and Schlesinger 2007 and Koopmans and Statham 2010a).

Part II asks whether the Europeanization of public spheres actually matters. This chapter discusses the relationship between the Europeanization of public spheres and the politicization of EU-related issues, as well as its likely consequences.

I argue, first, that the observable Europeanization of public spheres is linked to the growing politicization of EU affairs. The Europeanization of public spheres emerges through crises, conflicts, and contestation (see Chapter 4). It both constitutes and reflects the emergence of an EU polity and the progress in European integration during the past twenty years. There is an emerging consensus in the scholarly literature that politicization finally has arrived in the EU (see Chapter 8). The politicization of EU affairs is now in full swing and is probably irrevocable. The more Europe "hits home" in the domestic politics of the member states and beyond, the more EU affairs – both constitutional questions and policy issues – become salient in the various national public spheres. At the same time, as "news value" theories suggest (e.g., McCombs and Shaw 1972; Venables 2005), issue salience is directly linked to politicization because newsworthiness and issue cycles in the media are strongly correlated with polarization and political controversy. It does not matter for my argument whether politicization leads to greater issue salience and, thus, to a greater presence of the EU in the media or whether it is the reverse and increasing issue salience leads to growing politicization.

Second, however, politicization and Europeanization are not the same and must be distinguished conceptually. The increased polarization over EU affairs must not necessarily lead to more Europeanization with regard to actors and frames of references (see Chapter 1). Politicization also might entail a renationalization of EU-related discourses (see Chapter 8). In this case, politicization would lead to further gridlock and eventually to a breakup of the EU – as some have argued (e.g., Bartolini 2006) – rather than greater European democracy and, ultimately, to a strengthening of the EU, as others have hoped (Hix 2006).

Third, I claim, therefore, that the consequences of politicization are highly contingent on scope conditions. In particular, the more politicization takes place in Europeanized public spheres and the more issues are framed as matters of common European concern, the more a renationalization of EU politics can be avoided and the more the optimistic view about European democracy is likely to carry the day. The euro crisis provides a crucial test here.

Finally, the evidence is rather vague about how the euro crisis is represented in the various public spheres. The available data seem to reveal, however, that the politicization of the euro crisis has led to high levels of Europeanization concerning the actor dimension (see Chapter 1 in this volume for these distinctions; and see Chapters 3 and 8 for evidence). EU and actors from other EU member states are routinely present in various public spheres. Unfortunately, we know less with regard to whether the euro crisis has been framed as a national or as a common European problem in the public spheres.

However, we do know how ordinary citizens react to the euro crisis and to its representations in the media. These data seem to confirm the more optimistic view. I use data from public opinion polls pertaining to the euro crisis to argue that politicization has not led to decreased European "solidarity among strangers" (Habermas 1996d), as many fear. Quite the contrary, European identity increased rather than decreased during the crisis, and many Europeans are prepared to pay a price for their Europeanness. Ultimately, I claim that the emerging transnational communities of communication in the EU, as well as citizen attitudes with regard to the euro crisis, demonstrate a rather mature European polity.

This chapter proceeds in the following steps. First, I begin with conceptual remarks about politicization. Second, I discuss the emerging consensus that EU affairs are increasingly politicized in the public arenas. Third, I analyze the consequences of politicization and the Europeanization of public spheres for transnational European identities.

Politicization and Europeanization: conceptual clarifications

"Politicization" has become such a buzzword in EU studies (e.g., Beyers and Kerremans 2004; Hooghe and Marks 2009; overview in De Wilde 2011; De Wilde and Zürn 2012; Statham and Trenz 2013b; Zürn and Ecker-Ehrhardt 2013) that the term requires clarification. With regard to the EU, politicization could mean, for example, that the party affiliation of European Commissioners becomes the subject of political controversy. It also could mean that the EU's institutional setting or European integration as such is being debated in various arenas. Most important, politicization could entail EU policies in various issue areas being hotly contested in transnational public spheres or in the domestic settings of various member states.

What these various meanings have in common is that politicization is inevitably about controversy, contestation, and political conflict. Politicization is directly related to politics, the process dimension of political affairs. Thus, and following De Wilde, I define "politicization" as "an increase in polarization of opinions, interests, or values and the extent to which they are publicly advanced towards the process of policy formulation within the EU" (De Wilde 2011, 566–7; see also Chapter 1 in this volume).

With regard to the politicization of EU affairs, we must distinguish among the issues being debated.[4] On the most general level, politicization might concern *constitutive* issues of the EU – for example, the very principle of European integration including the question of who should be(come) a member of the EU. The debate over Turkish

---

[4] I thank participants of the European Public Spheres workshop in April 2011 for their input on the following. See also Kriesi et al. 2008; De Wilde 2011.

membership constitutes a prominent example of the latter, or the British controversy of whether the United Kingdom should stay in the EU. In contrast, Eastern enlargement of the EU has never been as politicized (Schimmelfennig 2003). Constitutive issues ultimately concern the very identity of a polity – that is, answers to the questions "Who are we?" and "Who belongs to us?"

Politicization also might involve *constitutional* issues pertaining to the institutional framework of a polity. The old controversy between supranationalism and intergovernmentalism concerns these constitutional issues as well as the balance of power among the European Commission, the European Parliament (EP), and the Council of Ministers or the competences of the EU as compared to the member states (Bartolini 2006). In the context of the euro crisis, for example, whether the European Central Bank should be entitled to buy up state bonds on secondary markets from member states facing a soveign-debt crisis has been hotly debated. In Germany, the competencies of the national parliament with regard to the European Financial Stability Facility (EFSF) and the European Stability Mechanism (ESM) have been subject to much controversy as well.

Finally, politicization might involve the *policy issues* on the EU agenda itself. It even could be argued that the EU has become a "normal polity" as specific EU policies, rules, and decisions are scrutinized and debated controversially in the various and interlinked public spheres. A prominent example of issue politicization during the euro crisis concerns the controversy over how budget discipline and growth-inducing economic policies can or cannot be combined. Another policy example is related to the issue of whether and to what extent private-capital owners should contribute to bailing out banks and other financial institutions.

How do we know politicization when we see it? The following dimensions serve as empirical indicators of politicization (Hutter and Grande 2012; Kriesi and Grande 2012):

- substantial increase in the issue salience of European questions in the various public spheres
- growing polarization on EU-related issues among elites in the various public spheres[5]

---

[5] Grande and Kriesi (see Chapter 8 in this volume) add a third dimension: the increased resonance of these conflicts among the citizens leading to cleavages in

Europeanization of Public Spheres/ Politicization of EU Issues	Low	High
Low	• Low issue salience • Few controversies • Few European actors in national public spheres • Few transnational claims and/or dissimilar frames of reference across national public spheres	• High issue salience • Few controversies • European actors present and involved in national public spheres • Many transnational claims and/or similar frames of reference across national public spheres
High	• High issue salience • Strong polarization • Few European actors in national public spheres • Few transnational claims and/or dissimilar frames of reference across national public spheres	• High issue salience • Strong polarization • European actors present and involved in national public spheres • Many transnational claims and/or similar frames of reference across national public spheres

Figure 6.1. Politicization and Europeanization of public spheres.

These first two dimensions of politicization are directly linked to public spheres, whether national or transnational. Polarization means that issues become subject to public debates and controversies among interest groups and political parties, as well as in the various public spheres. It implies political conflict as well as publicity; there can be no politicization behind closed doors and outside of public spheres. In addition, politicization is about the intensification of political debates in the public spheres. EU policies are politicized when they are debated in much the same way as domestic or other issues are discussed in the member states (e.g., health care or the intervention in Afghanistan). In short, EU affairs become part of "normal politics."

However, the politicization of EU affairs and the Europeanization of public spheres are not necessarily the same, if we follow the conceptualizations in the introduction to this book (Figure 6.1). Only the first dimension of politicization (i.e., issue salience) is also a defining dimension of Europeanization. The other dimensions of politicization and of Europeanization are orthogonal to one another. There can be

public opinion (Schattschneider 1960). I would argue, however, that it constitutes one of the possible consequences of politicization whether or not it resonates with the citizens.

a high degree of Europeanization with regard to issue salience, presence of transnational actors in national public spheres, and transnational claims making or similarity of frames, but there is little politicization in terms of polarization (see the upper-right quadrant in Figure 6.1).

However, there also might be strong politicization but little Europeanization (see the lower-left quadrant in Figure 6.1). Politicization can take place exclusively in the domestic realm of some member states without much transnational influence. For example, the EU is highly controversial and, thus, politicized in the British public spheres, but a transnational dimension to these debates is mostly lacking – at least when compared to other member states. In this case, we have politicization without Europeanization, whether vertical (i.e., communicative linkages between the national and the European levels) or horizontal (i.e., linkages between various national levels; on these distinctions, see Koopmans and Erbe 2004 and Koopmans and Statham 2010b, 38). Moreover, framing can be completely different and hardly Europeanized despite strong politicization of EU issues in national public spheres. For example, the national media in Greece might frame the euro crisis as a German attack on the well-being and welfare of Southern Europeans, whereas the German media could portray it as resulting from the "lazy Greeks" piling up public-debt levels. This indicates strong politicization but, again, little Europeanization.

However, politicization also can involve transnational arenas as the Europeanization of EU politics in the various and transnationally interconnected public spheres. The more we observe controversies connecting the various national public spheres or involving national public spheres and the European level, the more we witness truly transnationalized and politicized debates. I argue in the next section that it makes a significant difference whether or not politicization goes together with the Europeanization of public spheres (see the lower-right and lower-left quadrants in Figure 6.1). We are likely to see different consequences with regard to identification levels with Europe and the EU and concerning policy consequences.

The increasing politicization of EU affairs: empirical findings

Before discussing the likely consequences of politicization, we must establish that we actually can observe increased public controversies about EU affairs. Indeed, there is an emerging scholarly consensus that the "sleeping giant" (Franklin and Van der Eijk 2006) has finally awakened and that EU issues are now being politicized across national and transnational public spheres.

It must be pointed out, however, that politicization of EU affairs is not a new phenomenon (Meyer 2009, 2010). During the 1950s, for example, constitutive issues such as the institutional form and composition of the European Economic Community were heavily debated in both various domestic public spheres and transnational arenas. Whereas Eastern enlargement as such was not controversial, British membership was subject to debates from the very beginning – not only in the United Kingdom but also in member states such as France. Most recently, the question of Turkish EU membership has become a constitutive issue that is heavily politicized in the various public spheres across Europe (as well as in Turkey; see Risse 2010, 213–20; see also Wimmel 2006; Madeker 2008). The controversy is not only about the borders of Europe and who, as a result, has a legitimate claim to EU membership. Rather, it is mostly about the EU's own identity. If Europe and the EU are conceptualized as modern, inclusive, and liberal communities, then Turkey can become a member in principle as long as it respects the Copenhagen criteria. At least the door remains open for Turkish membership. However, right-wing populist parties across Europe as well center-right parties – including the German Christian Democrats and the French post-Gaullist *Union pour un Mouvement Populaire* – also have used identity-based arguments to claim that Turkey does not belong to "Europe" because it does not share its Christian and cultural heritage and, thus, European values. In this case, then, the content of European identity – of "who we are" – is at stake and heavily contested. In other words, the politicization of Turkish EU membership takes place along the "cosmopolitan–nationalist" cultural cleavage that has been emerging in Europe following globalization, as Grande and Kriesi argue in Chapter 8.

However, politicization has involved not only constitutive issues in the past but also constitutional questions pertaining to the EU's institutional structure, mostly in conjunction with decision-making processes concerning treaty reforms. In their study of mass-media reporting in France, Germany, and Great Britain on the EU constitutional reforms in the early 2000s, Paul Statham and Hans-Jörg Trenz showed how national public spheres served as a conduit for the gradual politicization of institutional questions in the EU (Statham and Trenz 2013a, 2013b). First, their claims-making analysis (see Chapter 2 in this volume) demonstrated that governmental and executive actors dominated the debate during the preconvention and drafting phases of the Constitutional Treaty. This is not surprising given that national governments are institutionally the "masters of the treaties" and, therefore, heavily involved in the treaty making. However, their analysis also shows that the Constitutional Convention with its majority of parliamentarians (national and European) did not leave much of a mark in the national public spheres. Second, the latter came to the fore – together with political parties and civil society – during the ratification phase of the treaty, particularly during the referendum debate in France (see also Rauh 2013). At the same time, the issues involving the constitutional reforms became more controversial and politicized, once again predominantly in France (the British and German media merely took observer positions during the referendum debates; see Jentges, Trenz, and Vetters 2007). Moreover, the polarization did not occur only along the cosmopolitan–nationalist cleavage in terms of pro- versus anti-European integration; it also took place along the more traditional socioeconomic cleavage. For example, the French Socialists opposed the Constitutional Treaty and denounced it as a "neoliberal project," favoring a more "social Europe." This would exemplify what Grande and Kriesi call the "interventionist–cosmopolitan cleavage coalition" (see Chapter 8 in this volume).

Finally, specific EU policies always have been controversial on occasion and in various member states. Examples include the EU regulations concerning genetically modified organisms (Everson and Vos 2009); the controversies about the Fauna Flora Habitat directive protecting biodiversity (Laffan and O'Mahony 2004; Börzel 2009); and the so-called Bolkestein directive on services in the internal market (Crespy 2010; Grossman and Woll 2011). A regular issue of contestation over policies concerns the EU budget negotiations (De Wilde 2012). During the euro crisis, politicization of EU issues involved the bailout of debtor countries as well as the austerity conditionality attached to it.

Thus, politicization as such is not new in the EU, but it used to be sporadic and confined to specific constitutive, constitutional, or policy issues, or even to specific member states. In general and until the early 1990s, there were few transnational controversies about the EU giving rise to a "permissive consensus" with regard to EU policies and institutions (Hooghe and Marks 2009). This has changed profoundly. A significantly more widespread politicization of EU affairs in the domestic politics of various member states that are interconnected through transnational public spheres has been underway since the end of the 1990s. Indicators are, for example, as follows:

- the increasing salience of European issues in the various public spheres (Risse 2010, 128–39)
- the growing importance of identity politics in the debates about EU enlargement as well as constitutional issues (Checkel and Katzenstein 2009b)
- the emergence of Euroskepticism as a force to be reckoned with across Europe[6]
- the increasing conflicts and intense debates over specific policy issues, such as the rescue of the euro and the prevention of sovereign default in the Eurozone.

Unfortunately, there are only a few longitudinal studies available that measure whether we indeed can observe a long-term trend of increased politicization of EU affairs as defined previously. To my knowledge, the project by Edgar Grande and Hanspeter Kriesi is the only one so far that traces the degrees of politicization over European issues in various national public spheres since the 1970s (covering Austria, Great Britain, France, Germany, and Switzerland; unfortunately, no Scandinavian or Eastern European country is included; for details, see Hutter and Grande 2012; Kriesi and Grande 2012; see also Chapter 8 in this volume). A longitudinal study investigated the six original EU member states (i.e., Germany, France, Italy, and the Benelux countries) covering the years 1990–2012 (Rauh 2013).

These studies use different measurements to assess the polarization component of politicization (see previous discussion). Whereas Grande and Kriesi used the distance of party positions from the weighted-average position of all parties to determine polarization, Rauh used the degree of public resonance to measure the degree to which public opinion is polarized over European issues.

---

[6] See, e.g., Marks and Steenbergen 2004; Taggart and Szczerbiak 2005, 2008; Hooghe and Marks 2007a.

Despite these different measurements, however, both studies conclude that the politicization of EU-related issues has intensified. This trend includes Switzerland but not the United Kingdom, where EU affairs have been politicized on a higher level than in the other member states for a long time (Hutter and Grande 2012, 22–30). With regard to salience – the first indicator of politicization (see the previous discussion) – a "post-Maastricht" effect is observable in France, Austria, and Germany. In addition, Rauh shows politicization peaks during EP elections (Rauh 2013). It is interesting that Hutter and Grande report that the share of non-executive actors (mostly opposition parties) in the political debates increases substantially in all five countries. They conclude that "by the end of the 2000s, European integration has become a salient issue of political contestation between government and opposition parties in election contests, comparable to domestic policy issues" (Hutter and Grande 2012, 27). This constitutes a significant departure from earlier findings that the European public sphere is dominated by executive actors (i.e., national governments and the European Commission; see Koopmans and Statham 2010a; see also Chapter 3 in this volume). If this trend can be confirmed, it would indicate that the more EU issues become the subject of domestic political debates in the member states, the less the discourses can be dominated by executive actors and the more other actors – political parties and civil society – come into play. However, we also should note the institutional context of these debates. It is to be expected that political parties, including opposition parties, become involved in the politicization of European issues during election campaigns – whether national or European – and with regard to the ratification of EU treaties.

The politicization of EU affairs is still unevenly distributed among the member states. It seems to be most pronounced in the Eurozone and, thus, in Continental Europe, whereas for lack of data, we can only speculate about Scandinavia and Eastern Europe. Great Britain is a special case. On the one hand, EU affairs have been politicized in the British public sphere for a long time. On the other hand, the British public sphere is also the least Europeanized, with few transnational linkages (Koopmans and Statham 2010a).

However, to what extent are the increasingly politicized debates on European issues also Europeanized in the various public spheres? In other words, are these growing controversies about EU-related questions located in the lower-left quadrant in Figure 6.1 (i.e., politicized but not Europeanized), or can we observe movements toward the lower-right quadrant (i.e., politicized and Europeanized)? Regarding issue salience – an indicator of both politicization and Europeanization – all available data confirm the trend toward the increased significance of EU questions in national public spheres (see also Meijers 2013 for television news in Germany and the Netherlands). Regarding the actor dimension of Europeanization ("horizontal" and "vertical"; see Chapter 1 in this volume; see also Koopmans and Statham 2010b), Grande and Kriesi show in Chapter 8 the extraordinary presence of supranational EU actors, as well as executive actors from other countries, in the debates surrounding the euro crisis (see also Kriesi and Grande 2012, and Chapter 3). However, it is Germany and Chancellor Merkel that dominate "horizontal Europeanization" – that is, the contribution of foreign actors to national debates in the various public spheres. Kriesi and Grande also demonstrate that – in contrast to the discussions about the Constitutional Treaty – the politicization of the euro crisis again is dominated by executive actors, whether national or European. Only in Germany are national parties clearly visible, which reflects the domestic controversies over how to deal with the crisis (both within and between the major parties). However, the Kriesi and Grande data are confined to "creditor" countries in the euro crisis. I am fairly certain that the picture would change if "debtor" countries such as Portugal, Spain, Italy, and Greece had been included in the analysis – given the degree of domestic politicization of the crisis in these countries.

Unfortunately, we lack data on the third indicator for Europeanization: the degree to which claims are directed toward international, supranational, or transnational actors and the degree to which similar frames and meaning structures characterize the debates in the various public spheres. Kriesi and Grande show that executive actors – both national and European – tend to frame the euro crisis predominantly in economic terms, whereas parties – both national and in the EU – also use cultural frames (Kriesi and Grande 2012, 35). They also argue that the crisis pitched the German–French "couple" (i.e., Chancellor Merkel and President Sarkozy, in this case) against the rest of Europe – both EU institutions and national governments – particularly in Southern Europe (Kriesi and Grande 2012, 18, 34). Thus, the conflict lines in the euro crisis are clearly Europeanized. Sonja Puntscher Riekmann and Doris Wydra (2013) analyzed public debates on the euro crisis in the German and Austrian parliaments and confirmed this point. They also showed that parliamentarians support solidarity with the debtor countries but that this solidarity is strictly conditional and framed in terms of economic and political self-interest.

What we do not know, however, is whether similar meaning structures have emerged during the crises, particularly between the creditor and the debtor countries. For example, is the crisis perceived in Spain, Italy, and Greece as a fundamental attack of Northern Europeans on their way of life, whereas Germans, Dutch, and Finns blame Southern European laziness or incompetence for it? Or is the crisis framed as an issue of common European concern, as a conflict between those favoring balanced budgets and austerity, on the one hand, and those promoting economic growth and measures to boost employment, on the other? The latter would constitute strong politicization, but it would be clearly Europeanized politicization (see the lower-right quadrant in Figure 6.1) rather than giving rise to nationalist reactions, as Grande and Kriesi suggest (see Chapter 8). I return to this point in the next section by using data on the resonance of these debates in public opinion.

To summarize the discussion in this section, we are witnessing the politicization of EU affairs across the board and, therefore, a turning point in the history of the EU. Moreover, most indicators suggest that the politicization of EU-related questions – constitutive, constitutional, and pertaining to specific policies – takes place in Europeanized public spheres, at least with regard to the actor dimension. In this sense, the "genie is out of the bottle." As De Wilde and Zürn (2012) argue the politicization of European integration cannot be reversed, but national and supranational policy makers must address it. The question is no longer whether or not politicization should be promoted (see, e.g., the controversy between Hix 2006 and Bartolini 2006) but rather how it will evolve and what the likely consequences are for the European polity. The discussion now turns to these consequences.

The consequences of politicization: nationalist backlash or "solidarity among strangers"?

If politicization of EU affairs is here to stay and the euro crisis has simply reinforced trends that have already been in motion, the question nevertheless arises about what the likely consequences are for the

European polity. Two positions can be discerned in this context. First, there are those who have argued for a long time that the politicization of the EU and its policies will lead inevitably to more gridlock in the EU, given the consensus requirements of European policy making. Although it may or may not improve the input legitimacy of the EU, it is certain to undermine its remaining output legitimacy, as Stefano Bartolini and Fritz W. Scharpf suggest (Bartolini 2006; Scharpf 2009; see also Risse 2010, chap. 10). According to Scharpf, the euro crisis has exacerbated the problem: the politicization of the EU challenges the input legitimacy of the EU (i.e., the "democratic deficit"; Follesdal and Hix 2006; see also Chapter 10 in this volume), but the measures to rescue the euro, including neoliberal austerity policies, are likely to further reduce the EU's output legitimacy (Scharpf 2013, 1–2).

Grande and Kriesi (Chapter 8 in this volume; see also Kriesi and Grande 2012) also point to the negative consequences of politicization in the euro crisis. According to them, the politicization of EU issues takes place along the cultural cosmopolitan–nationalist cleavage and has been driven primarily by actors located at the nationalist end of this cleavage (e.g., right-wing populist parties promoting principled Euroskepticism).[7] Grande and Kriesi argue that the cleavage coalitions at the cosmopolitan end of the cultural cleavage are simply too weak or too divided to put forward a viable alternative to the nationalist politicization in the public sphere. Moreover, there are few civil-society organizations and social movements promoting further European integration (Chapter 5 in this volume; see also Rauh 2013). In conjunction with an increasing nationalist framing of the euro crisis pitting Northern Europe against Southern Europe or even "Germany versus the rest," Grande and Kriesi suggest that politicization probably will lead to a nationalist backlash and the strengthening of Euroskepticism across the board – which might even endanger European integration in the long run.

Second, however, there also is a more positive evaluation of the likely consequences of politicization. From a normatively oriented point of view, politicization is a necessary ingredient of a viable democracy, which holds true for both the deliberative and the competitive

---

[7] "Euroskepticism" does not denote critical attitudes toward EU policies but rather principled opposition to European integration (see Chapter 1). Euroskeptical parties primarily politicize constitutive and constitutional questions in the EU.

variants of democratic theory (see Chapter 10 in this volume). If lively public spheres are constitutive parts of any democratic polity, then politicization almost inevitably would strengthen European democracy. Moreover, politicization of Europeanized public spheres would go a long way to remedying the incongruence in the EU multilevel governance system between where decisions are made (in Brussels) and where politics plays out (in the national capitals; on this argument, see Schmidt 2006). Some scholars go even further and regard the politicization of EU affairs during the euro crisis as a window of opportunity to promote a European federal union or even a state (Habermas 2013).

However, there also is a more analytical version of this more positive view (see, e.g., Zürn 2014). Regarding the consequences of politicization and Europeanization for European identity and the attitudes of citizens toward the EU, it crucially depends on whether or not politicization and Europeanization of public spheres go together in the euro crisis (see the lower-left quadrant in Figure 6.1). I have argued in this chapter that the current politicization of EU affairs satisfies at least two of the three indicators for Europeanization as specified in the introduction of this book (i.e., issue salience and actor dimension; see Chapter 1), whereas we lack data to reach firm conclusions on framing and meaning structures. On the one hand, the euro crisis has been framed as an existential challenge for the EU that must be dealt with collectively (see the quote by former Italian Prime Minister Mario Monti at the beginning of this chapter).

On the other hand, depicting Angela Merkel as a Nazi and the Greeks as crooks is unlikely to increase the sense of community among Europeans. Nationalist stereotypes abound during the euro crisis, particularly in various tabloids. These stereotypes serve to exclude the other from the community and to deny their trustworthiness in a public arena.

These considerations lead to two scope conditions under which the politicization of public spheres is likely to increase the sense of community among Europeans. First, as Bruter shows (Bruter 2005, 127–8), good news about the EU is good news for identity. Positive reporting as compared to "bad news" about the EU increases political identification levels with the EU by more than 20 percent (see also Chapter 7 in this volume). Meijers shows, however, that television news in Germany and the Netherlands has increasingly presented the

EU in negative terms during the euro crisis (Meijers 2013). Stoeckel presents an interesting finding in this regard (Stoeckel 2009): on the one hand, greater issue salience of the EU in the media leads to higher identification levels with the EU. On the other hand, greater visibility also increases critical attitudes of citizens toward EU policies and European integration in general. In other words, people do not seem to like what they see, even though they increasingly identify with Europe and the EU. I argue herein that this is exactly what has been happening so far during the euro crisis.

Second, and probably more important, framing is likely to matter for identification levels not only in terms of whether the EU is portrayed in positive or negative ways. It makes a huge difference whether a political issue is discussed as a matter of common European concern or as one driving Europeans apart. Debating European issues as *European* questions, then, not only constitutes the EU as a polity and a community of communication. It is also likely to increase political identification levels with the EU. Such a common European viewpoint does not imply that the EU is portrayed in a harmonious way. In fact, contestation and polarization are necessary for the emergence of a common European perspective (see Chapter 4 in this volume). What should matter for identification levels is whether the conflict pitches Europeans *as Europeans* against one another rather than Germans against Greeks.

Briefly, issue framing is crucial for whether the politicization, the Europeanization of public spheres, and the emergence of collective European identities are linked in a virtuous or in a vicious circle. Politicization can lead to a transnational community of communication, but it also can result in the de-Europeanization of public spheres and their renationalization.

As stated previously, we lack data with which to discern with certainty whether similar frames of reference have emerged during the euro crisis – in particular, whether the public spheres in the Northern European creditor countries have been discussing the issues in similar ways as the (mostly) Southern European debtor countries. However, several years into the crisis, we do know more about how the crisis has played out in mass public opinion. The results give rise to cautious optimism supporting the second position with regard to the likely consequences of politicization (Risse 2013).

First, the polarization of public opinion with regard to European integration has increased strongly during the euro crisis (Rauh 2013,

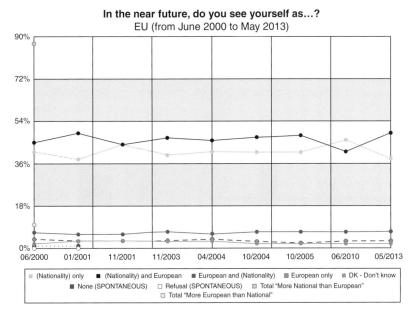

In the near future, do you see yourself as...?
EU (from June 2000 to May 2013)

Legend: (Nationality) only · (Nationality) and European · European and (Nationality) · European only · DK - Don't know · None (SPONTANEOUS) · Refusal (SPONTANEOUS) · Total "More National than European" · Total "More European than National"

Figure 6.2. Identification with the EU: EU average 2000–2013. Available at http://ec.europa.eu/public_opinion/cf/showchart_line.cfm?keyID=266&nation ID=16,&startdate=2000.06&enddate=2013.05 (accessed August 9, 2013).

25). The overall positive image of the EU declined and trust levels in EU institutions have reached all-time lows, even though citizens continue to trust the EU more than their national institutions (European Commission 2012, 15; 2013, 9). However, support for EU membership has not suffered much on average, particularly not in the Eurozone (Directorate-General for Communication 2012, 14–16).

Second, however, identification levels with the EU actually increased rather than decreased during the crisis. The graph in Figure 6.2 depicts answers to a question regularly asked by the Eurobarometer polls, which has served as a strong indicator for European identity in the literature (see, e.g., Hooghe and Marks 2005; overview in Risse 2010, chap. 2; Fligstein, Polyakova, and Sandholtz 2012). In particular, it has been shown repeatedly that the major demarcation line is between those who exclusively identify with their nation-state (i.e., "exclusive nationalists"; see the dark line in Figure 6.2 between the 36 and 54 percentage lines) and those who hold Europe as a secondary identity (i.e., "inclusive nationalists"; see the grey line in Figure 6.2 between

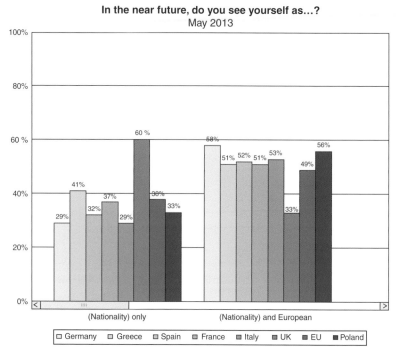

Figure 6.3. Exclusive versus inclusive nationalists in selected EU member states, 2013. Available at http://ec.europa.eu/public_opinion/cf/showchart_column.cfm?keyID=266&nationID=16,6,3,4,8,24,5,15,&startdate=2013.05&enddate=2013.05 (accessed August 9, 2013).

the 36 and 54 percentage lines). The latter have an overall positive view of the EU and of EU membership, and they also hold "cosmopolitan" values in the Grande and Kriesi sense (see Chapter 8 in this volume).

In spring 2013, 59 percent of polled citizens showed at least some degree of identification with the EU (i.e., the "inclusive nationalists" plus those who identify more with Europe than with their nation-state, see Figure 6.2) compared to only 38 percent who identified exclusively with their nation-state. Although the number of inclusive nationalists decreased in 2010, it had reached the pre-crisis levels of the 2000s again in 2013. More important, higher numbers of German, French, Italian, Spanish, Greek, and Polish citizens identify with Europe than the EU average, and Great Britain remains the outlier with 60 percent exclusive nationalists (see Figure 6.3). A closer look at the Eurozone countries does not reveal divisions between creditor and debtor countries with regard to identification levels.[8] German identification with Europe, which has increased gradually in the past decade and reached an all-time high in 2013 with 69 percent showing some degree of European identity (the 58 percent "inclusive nationalists" in Figure 6.3 plus those identifying with Europe more than with their nation-state). With regard to the major countries in crisis, the results also are interesting: a majority of Italian and Spanish citizens had always identified with Europe (at least as a secondary identity), but there had been some decline in both countries. By 2013, the identification levels again had reached pre-crisis levels. The case of Greece also is significant because it has always been a country with lower-than-average identification levels with Europe. This trend reversed in 2013: 51 percent showed some degree of identification with Europe for the first time since the early 1990s (see Figure 6.3).

I do not claim that these figures result directly from the politicization of the euro crisis in various public spheres. However, they disconfirm that (exclusive) nationalism is growing in the EU and the Eurozone as a result of the crisis.

Third, the data also demonstrate that citizens are prepared to pay a price for their European identity. Proclaiming some identification with the EU is easy, but what about "solidarity among strangers" (Habermas 1996d) in times of crisis when European identity becomes costly? Gerhards and Lengfeld (2013) show that social integration in the EU is on the rise. Time-series data from Poland, Germany, and Spain demonstrate that EU citizens grant one another equal political and social rights, which include access to social benefits and the welfare state. Kuhn and Stoeckel (2014) found that the distinction between exclusive and inclusive nationalism is salient with regard to support for economic governance in the EU. The more people identify with Europe, the more they are prepared to support economic governance with redistributive consequences. Regarding the Eurozone, majorities of citizens support giving financial help to another EU member state facing economic and financial difficulties (European Parliament 2011, 20; there are no differences between Northern and Southern Europe except for

---

[8] The following is based on calculations from the EU Eurobarometer website: http://ec.europa.eu/public_opinion/cf/showchart_line.cfm?keyID=266& nationID=16,6,3,4,8,24,5,15,&startdate=1992.04&enddate=2013.05 (accessed August 9, 2013).

the United Kingdom). However, more detailed surveys among German citizens show that their solidarity with Southern Europe is conditional (Bechtel, Hainmueller, and Margalit 2012a, 2012b; Lengfeld, Schmidt, and Häuberer 2012): more than 80 percent support reciprocal financial help and large majorities are in favor of bailing out debtor countries if and when measures are taken to ensure budgetary discipline. Moreover, Germans are more inclined to help the Irish, the Italians, and the Spanish than to bail out Portugal or Greece. It is interesting, however, that the preparedness of German public opinion to support financial assistance to crisis countries increased rather than decreased during the euro crisis.

In summary, these data show that European identity has not declined during the euro crisis and that the majority of Europeans is prepared to pay a price for their European identity and to show solidarity with their fellow EU citizens. Although the cosmopolitan end of the cultural cleavage might not be populated by many parties in the political space (see Chapter 8 in this volume), there are numerous citizens in both Northern and Southern Europe who can be mobilized around these causes. I am not arguing that this results from the increasing politicization and Europeanization of EU affairs in the public spheres because it would be premature to draw any firm causal connections. However, the European polity seems to be more mature than the pessimists quoted herein assume. As a consequence, politicization might strengthen rather than weaken the European polity.

Conclusions

This chapter has addressed the relationship between politicization and the Europeanization of public spheres, on the one hand, and its likely consequences for the European polity, on the other. I define "politicization" as growing issue salience of EU-related issues and increasing polarization of positions in the public spheres.

The results can be summarized as follows. First, we are witnessing the increasing politicization of EU affairs with regard to both policies and constitutional issues, with some spillover to constitutive questions. The euro crisis has further exacerbated this trend. Thus, the question is no longer whether politicization is desirable but rather how to deal with it and its likely consequences. Second, politicization and the Europeanization of public spheres are strongly interconnected insofar as increasing controversies about the EU take place in the various public arenas, but they are not the same (see Chapter 8 in this volume). However, the politicization of EU affairs satisfies two of the three conditions for Europeanization – namely, the increase in issue salience of EU issues and the growing presence of European actors – from other EU countries (horizontally) as well as from the EU (vertically) – in the various public spheres, as speakers and as targets of communication. Regarding the third component of Europeanized public spheres – the similarity of meaning structures and frames of reference – the jury is still out, and it depends on how we interpret the evidence (see Chapters 2 and 4 in this volume). However, framing EU issues as questions of common European concern about which Europeans debate *as Europeans* is crucial for a transnational community of communication to emerge and for the ensuing identification processes.

Third, regarding the likely consequences of politicization, the scholarly literature is divided between those who fear increasing nationalist backlashes and those who are generally optimistic with regard to the effects for European democracy and the polity in general. Whereas Grande and Kriesi are more skeptical (see Chapter 8 in this volume), I agree with those who offer a more positive evaluation. I use the euro crisis to demonstrate that public opinion in Europe has not reacted to the politicization of EU affairs with increased nationalism. Whereas the polarization in public opinion with regard to EU policies and – to some degree – EU institutions has increased, identification levels with Europe have grown as well. Moreover, the euro crisis has brought about a sense of "solidarity among strangers," at least in the Eurozone.

In conclusion, I discuss some of the policy consequences. First, the euro crisis demonstrates that politicization is here to stay. The EU will remain visible in the national public spheres given the salience of its policies in the domestic realms. The Eurozone bargain in the current crisis – that is, strict austerity policies in countries threatened by sovereign default against financial bailout and European financial solidarity – has real and serious consequences for people in terms of employment, pension schemes, and the like. The EU-wide recession further complicates the economic situation. It is no wonder that we are experiencing social mobilization and the continuous politicization of EU economic and financial policies. Moreover, environmental issues, immigration policies, monetary issues, social policies, the future of the welfare state, Turkish EU membership, and military interventions outside of Europe remain hot political topics in most EU member states, and the EU is an integral part of it. The "permissive consensus" has given way to a "constraining dissensus" in the EU, as Hooghe and Marks argue (Hooghe and Marks 2009).

This means that the natural reaction of many European policy makers – whether supranational or national – namely, to silence debates and to ride out politicization is unlikely to be successful (see De Wilde and Zürn 2012). It also means that the tendency of the European Commission to revert to a technocratic policy style in times of crisis will not work. If policy makers and chief executives try to ignore the increasing politicization in the public spheres, they will only strengthen the various Euroskeptical coalitions at the nationalist end of the cultural cleavage (see Chapter 8 in this volume).

Moreover, the tendency of policy makers – whether European or national – to frame EU issues primarily in constitutive and constitutional rather than in policy terms both hinders politicization and might render Europe ungovernable in the long term. I argue herein that politicization is inevitable and, as a result, the only question to be asked is *which* politicization about *which* topics. Most public opinion surveys indicate that voters care about the state of the economy, unemployment, education, health care, and the fate of their pension systems. The question then becomes to what extent EU policies are necessary to cope with these issues. What type of policies should the EU pursue to foster economic growth and reduce (youth) unemployment in the Eurozone? Do we need more budgetary discipline in the Eurozone, or does austerity hamper economic growth? What is the right mix between these two policies? These are major *policy* issues about which European voters care deeply. Politicization of these issues in the various national public spheres – which we currently are witnessing during the euro crisis – is familiar territory for most parties in the various countries. Moreover, these policy issues are situated along the traditional socioeconomic (i.e., left–right) cleavage that structures most European- and national-party families (see Chapter 8 in this volume; see also Kriesi et al. 2008). As a result, conservative and social-democratic parties should have no trouble politicizing most European policy issues.

The situation becomes more complicated as more constitutional or even constitutive issues are politicized in the EU. In some cases, this is unavoidable. Whether Turkey should become an EU member is a constitutive issue that concerns core questions of what defines European identity. However, European leaders have the tendency to tinker with EU treaties whenever a major policy problem arises and, therefore, to transform policy issues into constitutional issues. This results in reframing political issues into legal ones. For example, by 2013, the euro crisis led to a whole new set of intergovernmental treaties in the EU, among them the Fiscal Stability Treaty, which committed the parties to a balanced budget, and the treaty to set up the ESM, which is based on an amendment to the EU treaties and will replace the EFSF and substitute it with more financial "firepower."

Such a strategy to transform EU policy issues into constitutional questions and then to politicize them might work in those cases in which the major parties share a pro-European integration attitude (i.e., they are closer to the cosmopolitan end of the cultural cleavage). Transforming EU policy into constitutional issues strengthens the power of national governments vis-à-vis their parliaments, as long as they experience large pro-EU majorities. In Germany, for example, the pro-European consensus among all major parties – whether in government or in opposition – allowed Chancellor Merkel to govern with a super-majority in the German Parliament whenever it had to agree to a major policy measure or a treaty change during the euro crisis. In this case, framing the issues in constitutional or even constitutive terms (e.g., "if the euro does not survive, European integration will be finished") in the national public sphere paid off. Social Democrats and Greens supported Chancellor Merkel from 2010 to 2012, despite the fact that she could no longer rely on the majority of her own coalition parties in the German Bundestag, given the internal opposition against her course of action. So far, only a small Euroskeptical party has arisen in Germany, although there is certainly an electoral vote to be gained among the approximate 40 percent German exclusive nationalists.

This is different in countries with major Euroskeptical parties such as France (*Front National*), the Netherlands (*Partij voor de Vrijheid*), and Austria (*Freiheitliche Partei Österreichs*), as well as the United Kingdom (i.e., the majority of the Conservative Party and the UK Independence Party). Framing policy issues in the EU as constitutional or even constitutive questions certainly mobilizes right-wing populist parties at the nationalist end of the cultural cleavage. Kriesi and Grande (2012) argue further that these parties contributed to politicizing EU affairs in most countries. In other words, politicizing constitutional issues in the EU is likely to empower Euroskepticism if there is no counterresponse at the cosmopolitan end of the cultural cleavage and if there is no powerful cleavage coalition (see Chapter 8 in this volume) to respond with a counterframe defending the vision of a modern, liberal, and cosmopolitan Europe.

Thus, if pro-European governments want to retain control over the process, there is no way around proactively dealing with politicization in the various public spheres and contributing to transnational communication in the EU. With regard to gridlock and fears of it, there also is a normative argument to be made in a democratic polity. If politicization leads to more informed choices and votes by the people, so be it. Furthermore, if voters do not like what they see in the EU and in European integration, this is a normal and legitimate outcome in a democracy. Silencing legitimate concerns and debates will only make things worse because doing so creates suspicion among citizens that elites do what they want to anyway. It should come as no surprise in this context that trust levels in European as well as national institutions have reached an all-time low during the euro crisis.

This type of politicization is likely to increase the legitimacy of EU politics because it is about Europeanizing domestic politics in the sense that European policies rather than European integration as such become subject to controversies in the public spheres. Politicization in terms of framing issues as of common European concern and focusing on political rather than constitutional questions are likely to lead to transnational disputes, thereby creating a European community of communication. As I have argued herein, significant majorities of citizens of Europe actually feel European at least to some extent, and majorities also are prepared to pay a price for their loyalty. So, why are European and national policy makers so afraid of public opinion and of politicization?

7 | Media and identity: the paradox of legitimacy and the making of European citizens

SARAH HARRISON AND MICHAEL BRUTER

Ever since research on European public spheres has emerged in the social science and communication literatures, it has rested on implicit links with the question of European identity. With the crisis that emerged since the beginning of the 2010s, questions on whether a European identity would be strong enough to allow the European Union (EU) to survive through unprecedentedly turbulent waters became even more topical. In turn, European public spheres have been perceived as a cause, a consequence, or a symptom of European identity. Always, however, public-sphere researchers have considered European identity as the "bigger picture" that would bring citizens back into the equation. This chapter makes this implicit link somewhat more explicit and provides a direct understanding of how citizens' European identity is potentially affected by news on Europe, thereby reflecting on the causal links that "bring politics back in."

Much of the research on European identity and the European public spheres seems to have been built around a duality of assumptions that is nothing short of paradoxical. First, many have assumed that European identity could emerge only under the condition that a European public sphere in which European issues are debated exists. Second, any criticism of European institutions and policies perceived as "Euroskepticism" is assumed to potentially prove that the European identity does not exist. Although neither assumption is intellectually obvious, it seems to us that they are largely incompatible and, at face value, the public-sphere condition seems more tenable than the "skepticism-less" condition. Indeed, can a political system emerge without political debate? Can a political community emerge without politicization and political dissent? In this chapter, we support the argument that although politicization is not without risk (see, e.g., Hooghe and Marks 2006), it may not be only a necessary cause but also a necessary consequence of the emergence of a European identity. In other words, we suggest that the more European people feel, the more that they appropriate debates on Europe, the more polarized they can become about them, and the more politicized is their perception of "their" – thereby appropriated – system. This contrasts with an older perception – still rife in much of the mass media – that citizens would be either pro-European and like everything European as a result, or Euroskeptic and hate everything European as a matter of principle. To support our argument, we examine the findings of our research about the impact of news on citizens' levels of European identity using a three-wave, two-and-a-half-years-long panel-study experiment that was run in six EU member states. We begin this chapter by highlighting paradoxes of EU legitimacy that point out the apparent compatibility between Euroskepticism and European identity. We then analyze the results of the panel-study design, which show how good and bad news on Europe (and symbols of European integration) affect the identity of citizens over time. We conclude the chapter by highlighting the dangerous but necessary role of politicization in the creation of a political identity.

Down or up?

In June 2009, Europeans voted in the seventh direct European Parliament (EP) elections. On this occasion, the average turnout across the entire EU reached a record low, previously set five years earlier in June 2004. Journalists and politicians alike deduced that the democratic crisis of the EU therefore must be symmetrically reaching an all-time high, and they hastened to conclude that Europeans are not interested in the EU, that they do not trust their European institutions, and that – by and large – they simply do not feel European. The starting point of this argument was rather dubious in the first place. When we compare the turnout in the twenty-five member states that voted in both 2004 and 2009, it was largely stable. Similarly, whereas the overall European turnout seemed to dramatically decline between the 1999 and the 2004 elections, when comparing the fifteen old member states that alone voted on both occasions, turnout had in fact increased.

In the context of studying the relationship between the emergence of a European public sphere and that of a mass European identity, this hasty interpretation of an apparently obvious public-opinion measure (whereby we conveniently ignore that completely different countries are voting in the three elections being compared) has a major symbolic purpose. Journalists largely explain their lack of coverage of European news by the fact that EU citizens would not be interested. Conversely, politicians explain the vastly domestic focus of their EP campaigns by the suggestion that voters would be more interested in them than in European issues. This contrasts with the fact that European Elections Studies show repeatedly that a dominant and increasing proportion of voters want to hear more about Europe (Van der Eijk and Franklin 1996) and that the French 2005 referendum on an EU constitution witnessed – literally – several million citizens effectively reading the incredibly obscure and long document and buying books that described and interpreted its most minute details.

There is, therefore, a triangle of legitimacy crisis associating citizens, the media, and the European project, whereby the media are claiming to not be in a position to force citizens to be interested in something that they do not like (Bain and Holland 2007) – let alone influence them – whereas citizens are claiming that they are poorly and inadequately informed about the EU. This apparently obscure causality between the meager progress of a European public sphere and the lack of democratic engagement of citizens could be sorted out if we better understood the extent to which the media indeed can influence the European identity of citizens by how they inform them about Europe. After outlining the legitimacy paradox of the EU and models of potential influence, this chapter provides the results of a two-and-a-half-year-long panel-study experiment on the impact of news on Europe on citizens' identity.

Paradoxes of popular legitimacy

As discussed, the bulk of popular elite interpretations – from the mass media to many political parties and to EU institutions themselves – is that EU citizens do not feel European and that Euroskepticism is on the rise and has led to a recent string of "no" votes in referenda on EU questions. Moreover, turnout in EP elections allegedly continues to decline[1] and betrays a disaffection of citizens for a EU that is, consequently, supposed to face a widespread and dangerous crisis of legitimacy at the moment. In fact, a significant number of quality academic publications accept this interpretation (Cederman 2001; Hix 2008).

---

[1] However, this overall decline trend seems to have stopped with the 2014 European Parliament elections.

Although not questioning the fact that European integration indeed is facing a crisis of legitimacy in the sense that there is a mismatch between public preferences in terms of European integration and what is actually proposed to them by their elites, the assumption that this must mean a rise in anti-EU sentiment and a lack of European identity of citizens is less than obvious. In fact, there are as many signs pointing to an increase in general support for the European project, civic engagement, and European identity as there are signs of dissatisfaction with specific aspects of integration. Our suggestion is that European identity in fact is growing but that precisely because an increasing number of EU citizens feel European, they now judge the various policies and institutional reforms of the EU "from the inside," as citizens, and thus on their own merits rather than the principle of integration. Therefore, we would not be witnessing a lack of European identity and rise in Euroskepticism but instead an increasing European identity. We also would observe a reversal from an "outside" Euroskepticism that targets the principles of integration to an "inside" Euroskepticism. The latter takes for granted the principle of durable, continuing integration but targets specific institutional processes, policies, and reforms in the same way it could happen in any other polity. This would explain some of the paradoxical evolution in European opinion.

As discussed previously, turnout between 1999 and 2004 among the member states that voted on both occasions increased. Similarly, the overall decline in turnout in EP elections since the 1970s seems in no way sharper or more troublesome than the parallel participation decline in the context of national-level elections in the same countries (Déloye and Bruter 2007).

The argument that the recent victory of the "no" vote in a number of referenda on questions relating to the EU simply would equate to a popular expression of traditional Euroskepticism is equally weak. The most emblematic of these "nos" – that of the French population in May 2005 – occurred at a time when support for European integration was at its peak. Similarly, for the first time in the history of French referenda on EU questions, the dominant argument of the "no" camp, regardless of its (lack of) credibility was based not on a rejection of integration – or a claim for slower integration – but instead on a claim for faster and more generalized integration that would be increasingly social and political.

Finally, the question of popular legitimacy is difficult to disconnect from the question of institutional trust. Again, the evolution of public opinion when it comes to trust in EU institutions since the early 1980s is highly symptomatic. Twenty-five years ago, there was no EU country where EU institutions were more trusted globally than their national equivalent. By the mid-2000s, however, almost all of the old member states and a large majority of the new states trusted the European Commission more than their national government and the EP more than their national parliament (Tables 7.1 and 7.2). The only exceptions tend to be Sweden and, to a lesser extent, Denmark (parliament only) and Finland (where the scores for national parliament and the European Commission are tied). For those claiming widespread Euroskepticism, this is a shocking truth. Who would think that in thirteen of the fifteen old member states, including the United Kingdom, the European Commission is, in fact, significantly more trusted than the national government? How can we reconcile these findings with suspicion of declining popular legitimacy and never-emerging identity?

The argument of this chapter, therefore, is that it is exceedingly simplistic to start from the assumption that Europeans do not care about the EU and do not feel European. It is equally wrong to assume that because of this presumed lack of interest or, indeed, supposed lack of European identity that powerless media would not be in a position to participate in the strengthening of a European public sphere. We use findings from a long-term panel-study experiment about the impact of news on European identity to show that the media – far from simply following the news demands of citizens – actually participate in shaping their identity over time.

Methods

We use an experimental panel-study design instead of traditional "one-shot" experiments.[1] The sample includes 1,197 respondents from six European countries: the United Kingdom, France, Germany, Belgium, Portugal, and Sweden. The two-and-a-half-year-long[2] study included two years of experimental treatment and a final six-month "resting" period before the third questionnaire. The design respects

[2] The study was conducted between 1999 and 2003.

Table 7.1. *Compared trust in the European Commission and national government*

Country	European Commission	National government	Difference
Poland	49	7	+42
Italy	63	26	+37
Slovakia	54	17	+37
Belgium	63	34	+29
Hungary	58	31	+27
Slovenia	52	27	+25
France	52	29	+23
Ireland	61	39	+22
Portugal	56	34	+22
Germany	39	23	+16
Netherlands	54	39	+15
Lithuania	45	31	+14
Spain	53	42	+11
Czech Republic	35	25	+10
Greece	63	55	+8
Austria	47	39	+8
United Kingdom	26	19	+7
Luxembourg	66	61	+5
Latvia	32	28	+4
Denmark	47	44	+3
Malta	50	49	+1
Sweden	48	48	0
Finland	59	59	0
Estonia	44	45	−1
Cyprus	49	75	−26

Figures in the first two columns correspond to the proportion of citizens who tend to trust the institution. Figures in the third column correspond to the trust advantage (+) or disadvantage (−) of the European Commission when compared to the national government.
Source: Compiled by the authors from Eurobarometer 61 (2004) data, Tables 4.1b and 8.4.

two of the three main advantages of experiments: (1) knowing what news participants are exposed to, and (2) being able to treat this news as exogenous because it is not due to self-selection. However, it relaxes the last traditional experimental assumption: obviously, respondents

Table 7.2. *Compared trust in the European Parliament and national parliament*

Country	European Parliament	National parliament	Difference
Poland	53	8	+45
Slovakia	59	19	+40
Italy	68	32	+36
Hungary	64	29	+35
Slovenia	59	25	+34
Lithuania	52	19	+33
Belgium	64	38	+26
Czech Republic	44	18	+26
Ireland	64	40	+24
France	57	35	+22
Germany	51	29	+22
Portugal	58	37	+21
Spain	62	42	+20
Latvia	40	20	+20
Netherlands	57	43	+14
Estonia	49	35	+14
Luxembourg	67	56	+11
Malta	55	47	+8
Greece	70	63	+7
United Kingdom	30	25	+5
Finland	61	58	+3
Austria	43	41	+2
Sweden	55	58	−3
Denmark	55	63	−8
Cyprus	55	74	−19

Figures in the first two columns correspond to the proportion of citizens who tend to trust the institution. Figures in the third column correspond to the trust advantage (+) or disadvantage (−) of the European Commission when compared to the national government.
Source: Compiled by the authors from Eurobarometer 61 (2004) data, Tables 4.1b and 8.4.

were exposed to other news during the long experiment.[3] To limit this problem, respondents were randomly allocated into the four

---

[3] In traditional "one-shot" experiments, however, this advantage is always limited to the very short time of the experiment, without prejudice to what the

experimental groups and the sample used was as follows: (1) larger (i.e., 1,197 respondents) than in much of the literature[4]; (2) comparative, with respondents from six countries (i.e., the United Kingdom, France, Germany, Belgium, Portugal, and Sweden); (3) significantly more diverse than in many experiments in terms of geography (i.e., at least four different regions per country), gender, age, and socioprofessional categories[5]; and (4) begun at two different times – two years apart[6] – in each location. All of these safeguards are intended to improve the validity and generalizability of the results. For instance, many experiments (perfectly legitimately) rely on limited locations (Ansolabehere and Iyengar 1995; Sanders and Norris 2005)

respondent might have heard, read, or seen just moments before and that may still influence their attitude (a variation on some of the criticisms of Hovland 1959). Moreover, many recent web-based (rather than laboratory-based) experiments such as those mentioned by Iyengar (2002) also have relaxed this particular assumption while gaining in terms of sample size and design quality.

[4] There are obvious exceptions: for example, Sanders and Norris (2005) used an N of 919 and quota sampling. However, most political science experiments use a small N, between 25 and 250 respondents; for example, Iyengar, Peters, and Kinder 1982; Wittmer 1992; Nelson, Clawson, and Oxley 1997.

[5] The experiment did not aim to use a fully representative sample because this is considered unnecessary in the literature. However, as it turned out, the sample – recruited from professional quota lists – was highly varied in sociodemographic terms. The gender balance is only slightly biased toward women: 58 percent and 42 percent men. The median age of the sample is 40, with a standard deviation of 16.8. The youngest respondent is 18 and the oldest is 89. The sample has a slight over-representation of young people: 27.3 percent were younger than 25 years old at the start of the experiment, 27 percent were between 25 and 39, 31.3 percent were between 40 and 59, and the remaining 14.4 percent were 60 and older. Geographical spread almost reflects census data, with all of the major regions of the six countries included represented, and an almost fair representation of communities of various sizes (with a slight bias toward larger cities). The representation of the various socioeconomic categories also almost mirrors census data but with an over-representation of students and wealthy social categories and an under-representation of unemployed citizens.

[6] The results of the experiments that began two years apart were fully similar; that is, the variable corresponding to the starting year, included as a control, has no statistically significant effect in any of the models tested. In addition to the questionnaires, the study included focus groups on what participants meant by Europe and European identity, their perception of the news they read, and photographs they were shown in the newsletter. The discussion also dealt with their perceptions of news on Europe in real life and EU symbols. They also were invited to react to the experiment, which was conceived as part of the debriefing exercise.

or even student samples.[7] By contrast, with our varied samples and six-country comparison, we can verify that any experimental effect is not an artifact of a microcosmic contextual reality. In other words, as explained herein, whereas numbers are too low to draw firm conclusions about comparative differences, similarities across very different contexts strengthen the value of hypothetical findings by validating them beyond context, as is traditional with most different systems designs (Campbell and Stanley 1963; Przeworski and Teune 1970). Similarly, the division of all experimental groups in each country into two subgroups exposed to the experiment at two different times was important to confirm that any observed effect would not be caused by a systematic impact of the specific news on Europe in a given period, particularly considering the six-month lag between the second and third waves of the survey. Like countries and sociodemographic background, timing can be used as a control variable in all models – and has no statistically significant impact in any of them, suggesting that the effects we identify are general rather than context-specific.

Mostly, this panel-study design – although more costly and more complex to organize than one-shot experiments – aimed to avoid the risk of measuring short-term reactions. Instead, data measure the answers of respondents (1) before the beginning of the experiment, (2) after the end of the twenty-four-month experiment, and (3) six months after the end of the experiment.[8] This also made it possible to distinguish between priming or sleeper effects in the causal links highlighted by the experiment. (See a full discussion of priming and sleeper-effect mechanisms in Bruter 2009 as well as references to the works of Roskos-Ewoldsen et al. 2002 and Hovland, Lumsdaine, and

---

[7] Sears 1986 criticized the dominant use of pure student samples (Nelson, Clawson, and Oxley 1997).

[8] There is no "exact science" behind either the twenty-four-month stimulus or the six-month lag, but it is conceived as (1) sufficient time to develop a consistent stimulus, and (2) comparable to uses in the literature. Indeed, Monroe (1978) conceived a two-year period as a natural basis to expect citizens to fully absorb economic information. Similarly, a six-month lag is rather traditional in panel studies. For instance, it is often used in the National Election Study in the United States (Markus 1982, in reference to the first two waves of the 1980 panel), and the British Election Study (CREST 1998, in reference to the panel waves between 1994 and 1997). It is also the "pivotal" lag used by Milavsky, Kessler, et al. (1997), who tested multiple wave gaps in their study of television and aggression.

Sheffield 1949, among others.) Briefly, priming happens when exposure to a given stimulus has an impact on subsequent perceptions
(Roskos-Ewoldsen et al. 2002) – for example, when buying a specific
car makes us notice the make more when we see another one on the
street. Priming heightens the sensitivity of human beings to a specific
stimulus over time, as if it provided a pair of infrared glasses that made
us see specific objects that would not have been visible otherwise. By
contrast, the sleeper effect is about an unusual effect of news that,
instead of being strong at first and then declining over time, is muted
or minored at first and then kicks in more strongly later. In other
words, instead of having an immediate effect of communication that
then progressively decays over more time elapses between exposure and
reaction measure, the sleeper effect works as if a given stimulus were
first "unripe" and ineffectual but, after a while, started acting strongly.

The experiment

After being randomly assigned to one of four experimental groups,
each respondent received a fortnightly newsletter for twenty-
four months. It was based on articles published in European daily and
weekly newspapers and illustrated with drawings and photographs.
The newsletter was four pages long. The first page focused on non-
European international news (the same for all respondents). The fourth
page included unusual news (again, the same for all respondents), such
as the story of a man facing a camel in his garden in Alaska or the latest
controversy on the real height of Mount Everest. The two intermediary pages represented the experimental stimulus per se. They included
news on Europe and the EU, which was systematically either positive or negative, depending on the experimental group. The choice
of positive or negative news respected a certain balance among economic, political and institutional, social, and other news, and between
news on Europe and news on the EU.[9] Details on the types of news
included are in Bruter (2009), but examples include an article on how
the euro had strengthened against the dollar, which illustrates the good
health of the EU economy (good news), or another article on how the
strong euro was disadvantaging European exports (bad news); how the
European manufacturer Airbus overtook the US Boeing Company as

[9] An additional smaller control group was sent a newsletter without news on
Europe and without any photographs.

the world's leading manufacturer (good news), or how the A380 was suffering further production delays (bad news); and how European children had higher educational levels than their American counterparts (good news), or how they were less accomplished in math (bad news).

In addition to text, each newsletter included three photographs or (occasionally) drawings. Again, the respondents were divided orthogonally into two groups systematically exposed to one of two types of photographs: either symbols of Europe and the EU (e.g., a map of Europe, a European flag, or a passport) or placebo photographs (e.g., people and landscapes). The connotation of every item included in the newsletters (i.e., positive, negative, international and other news, and European and neutral photographs) was assessed blindly by three coders. Only the elements unanimously coded by all three researchers were used in the newsletters.

The questionnaires

The questionnaire was written in each language. It included two measures of general European identity, six measures of civic identity, and four measures of cultural identity (Bruter 2009).[10] The questionnaire also included control variables measuring levels of national, regional, and local identity, and – in the context of the pre-test questionnaire – support for and perceived benefits of EU integration, as well as demographic and political control variables (e.g., age, gender, and party preferences). The civic and cultural-identity variables were computed using factor analysis, the results of which are shown in Table 7.3.

Countries and respondents

The study was conducted before the 2004 enlargement, when the EU consisted of fifteen member states. The panel was conducted in six member states. This was not so much to find differences among the countries as it was to ensure the external validity of the experimental results across contexts. This is why our chapter does not discuss

---

[10] The concepts of civic and cultural identities are defined and discussed fully in Bruter (2005, 2009) and Bruter and Harrison (2012). Briefly, "civic identity" can be defined as our identity as a citizen and relationship to our political system, whereas "cultural identity" is a sense or higher relative closeness to people who belong to the polity than to those who do not.

Table 7.3. *Exploratory factor analysis of civic and cultural components of a European identity*

Extraction Component	Eigenvalue	% Variance	Cumulative% variance
1	4.69	46.9	46.5
2	1.88	18.8	65.8
3	0.84	8.4	74.2
...	...	...	...

Component matrix

Variable	Unrotated solution		Rotated solution	
	Factor 1	Factor 2	Factor 1	Factor 2
Civic 1	0.83	−0.29	0.88	0.05
Civic 2	0.82	−0.11	0.80	0.21
Civic 3	0.87	−0.26	0.90	0.09
Civic 4	0.84	0.02	0.77	0.33
Civic 5	0.76	−0.23	0.79	0.08
Civic 6	0.82	−0.24	0.85	0.09
Cultural 1	0.43	0.52	0.20	0.64
Cultural 2	0.20	0.75	−0.10	0.77
Cultural 3	0.44	0.50	0.22	0.63
Cultural 4	0.43	0.73	0.12	0.85

Notes: Results of an exploratory factor analysis of ten variables (six intended to measure the civic component of European identity and four to measure the cultural component). Results of the unrotated and rotated analyses are from using Varimax.

comparative univariate distributions but instead discusses the extent to which causal relationships are upheld across countries. Given the great variety of EU member states, even pre-2004, the study includes the United Kingdom, France, Germany, Belgium, Portugal, and Sweden. These countries represent various "ages" of European integration: that is, founding members (France, Germany, and Belgium); and the 1973 (United Kingdom), 1986 (Portugal), and 1995 (Sweden) enlargements – as well as East Germany within the German sample.[11] This is important because some models (e.g., Bruter 2005; Hix 2005) claim that when a country joined the EU has an impact on public

---

[11] Tests of differences of causal results between the East and West German subsamples were run and proved insignificant.

attitudes toward integration. Moreover, the countries chosen include large (i.e., France, Germany, and the United Kingdom) and small (i.e., Belgium, Sweden, and Portugal) member states because some authors claim that small states have a different relationship to the EU (Thorhallsson 2000). The study also includes countries that are traditionally pro-European (i.e., Belgium, France, Portugal, and Germany) and Euroskeptic (i.e., the United Kingdom and Sweden). Finally, it includes relatively rich and relatively poor states.[12] In summary, we maximized variance to provide the harshest possible test of the general validity of the model.

The starting samples included approximately 200 respondents per country, for a total of 1,197. The return rates over the three waves were rather high for this type of study: 75.4 percent for wave 2 and 63.8 percent for wave 3, with no significant bias in the categories dropping out, despite a minimal incentive (i.e., a book voucher of about €3–4 [US$4–5], depending on the country). Return rates were slightly lower in Portugal. Despite the limited drop-out rates, country-specific analyses must be considered with extreme caution. The details of the recruitment, sampling, and representativeness of the groups are detailed in Bruter (2009). To summarize, it is well known that for experimental purposes, samples need not be representative (Brannigan 2004); however, this study, although making no exception, used diversified samples that ensured general sample balance in terms of gender, age, education levels, and so on. Full-randomization tests were conducted and showed no significant differences across groups. Tests also were performed that confirmed no significant differences in experimental effects across gender, social, and demographic groups. The only exception is age: younger and older citizens proved slightly more influenceable than other generations. Age and gender are included as control variables in all equations.

The effect of news and symbols on European identity over time

The specificity of our research design is twofold. First, it is related to the sheer length of the experiment. Second, it allows a "cooling-off" period of six months after the end of the experimental treatment, which enabled us to assess the continued effect of systematic exposure to good

[12] Moreover, the study includes three major players of European integration: France, Germany, and the United Kingdom (Van der Eijk and Franklin 1996).

or bad news about Europe on the European identity of citizens well after this exposure ceased. Our overall models included hypotheses regarding the effects of both symbols of European integration (which are expected to have a direct and accelerating effect on citizens' identity because respondents exposed to symbols of integration are primed to notice them in their natural environment) and other hypotheses on the effect of positive and negative news on Europe.

Hypotheses were tested that obeyed a double logic of time (in other words, how the effect of an identity stimulus is likely to apply or decay consciously under stimulation, or unconsciously, once stimulation is over) (see Bruter 2009) and components (i.e., following Bruter's 2005 empirical typology of self-expressed, civic and cultural components of identity, which is likely to be most affected by which type of stimulus). The result consisted of four hypotheses: good and bad news on Europe have an effect on levels of European identity (H1), particularly on its civic component (H1b); symbols of Europe and the EU have an impact of European identity (H2), particularly on its cultural component (H2b); symbols have an immediate effect, which then will amplify over time (H3); and news has a "time-bomb" effect – that is, no immediate effect but a strong effect post-lag (H4).

The hypotheses were tested using a series of ordinary least squares (OLS) regressions. In total, six models were tested in which the dependent variables were general European identity at the end of the twenty-four-month experimental treatment (model 1); general European identity again, after a six-month gap without experimental treatment (model 2); civic European identity after the twenty-four-month experimental treatment (model 3); again after the additional six-month cooling-off period (model 4); and, finally, cultural European identity, again after twenty-four months and again after thirty months (models 5 and 6). OLS was used because it assesses the effects of the stimuli in a straightforward and rigorous way while fully controlling for pre-test levels of European identity, support for European integration, and various social and demographic variables such as gender and age. However, given existing debates in the literature, the models also were run using generalized least squares (GLS)[13] with entirely similar results

---

[13] There is significant debate in the literature about how a panel effect is best measured (e.g., Beck and Katz 1995; Hecock 2006). Here, there is no particular reason to suspect heteroscedastic error, particularly considering the split starting

Table 7.4. *Global impact of news and symbols at the end of the experiment and after the six-month lag*

	General identity				Civic identity				Cultural identity			
	t_{+24}		t_{+30}		t_{+24}		t_{+30}		t_{+24}		t_{+30}	
	b (s.e.)	β	b (s.e.)	β	b (s.e.)	β	b (s.e.)	β	b (s.e.)	β	b (s.e.)	β
News	0.05 (0.05)	0.03	0.79 (0.06)	0.35**	−0.15 (0.04)	−0.07**	0.98 (0.06)	0.49**	0.07 (0.06)	0.03	0.21 (0.06)	0.11*
Symbols	0.14 (0.05)	0.07**	0.28 (0.06)	0.13**	0.05 (0.04)	0.03	0.07 (0.06)	0.04	0.56 (0.06)	0.28**	1.01 (0.06)	0.51**
Age	−0.00 (0.00)	−0.05*	−0.00 (0.00)	−0.01	−0.00 (0.00)	−0.01	−0.00 (0.00)	−0.02	−0.00 (0.00)	−0.00	−0.00 (0.00)	−0.03
Gender	−0.11 (0.05)	−0.02	−0.33 (0.06)	−0.15**	0.09 (0.04)	0.04*	−0.11 (0.06)	−0.05	−0.10 (0.07)	0.05	−0.01 (0.06)	−0.01
Pro-EU	0.17 (0.03)	0.15**	0.29 (0.04)	0.27**	0.10 (0.02)	0.10**	0.26 (0.03)	0.27**	0.11 (0.03)	0.11**	0.17 (0.03)	0.18**
DV at t_0	0.63 (0.02)	0.67**	0.37 (0.03)	0.39**	0.69 (0.02)	0.72**	0.08 (0.03)	0.08	0.29 (0.03)	0.31**	0.18 (0.03)	0.20**
France	n.s.	n.s.	0.35 (0.10)	0.13**	n.s.	n.s.	0.61 (0.10)	0.24**	0.23 (0.11)	0.09*	n.s.	n.s.
Sweden	−0.22 (0.09)	−0.07*	n.s.	n.s.	n.s.	n.s.	−0.40 (0.10)	−0.15**	n.s.	n.s.	−0.23 (0.11)	−0.09*
UK	n.s.	n.s.	0.26 (0.11)	0.09*	n.s.	n.s.	n.s.	n.s.	n.s.	n.s.	n.s.	n.s.
Constant	1.66 (0.15)		2.32 (0.19)		−0.07 (0.10)		−0.48 (0.14)		−0.16 (0.15)		−0.51 (0.15)	
R^2	0.62		0.46		0.67		0.46		0.25		0.37	

Notes: Results are OLS regression coefficients, with standard error in brackets.

* Statistically significant at < 0.05; ** statistically significant at < 0.01.

Country dummies were entered in the equation but only those that are statistically significant at 0.05 or better are shown. n.s. = non-significant. The omitted category for the country dummies is Germany. n = 902 (t_{+24}) and 761 (t_{+30}).

national subsamples (e.g., France and Portugal) show strong effects in the context of the third wave (Table 7.5C).

The more complex and interesting finding, however, is related to the modified sleeper-effect hypothesis, which confirms the subconscious – some would say insidious – effect of news on European identity. "Biased" good or bad news on Europe has virtually no effect on citizens' levels of European identity while they are being exposed to it, as illustrated by Figure 7.1. Instead, the unmistakable news effect becomes apparent only after some distance comes between the participants and the systematically connoted news that they were exposed to for two years. Therefore, it is during the months that follow the reception of the last newsletter that the level of European identity of citizens changes dramatically along the lines of the news to which they were exposed. Moreover, when the news becomes effective after the end of the experimental treatment, it is stronger than that of symbols and that of all the control variables (including the respondent's level of European identity prior to the beginning of the experiment and attitudes toward EU integration). By contrast, when the effect of news on the identity of citizens is measured immediately after the experimental treatment, it is virtually nonexistent overall. In a few countries (e.g., France and Portugal), a mild effect exists, but it is nowhere near the effect at t_{+30}. However, by contrast, when it comes to the British sample (with UK citizens being among the most cynical worldwide overall), the effect of news on European identity even appears to be negative (and statistically significant) at t_{+24}, as if respondents were trying to "counterbalance" the bias that constitutes the news they were exposed to in the newsletter (Tables 7.5A and 7.5B). In this context, we call particularly "cynical" those citizens who have a negative response to the news stimulus immediately after being exposed to it (i.e., those who feel less European at t_{+24} when they have been exposed to positive news or feel more European at t_{+30} when they have been exposed to negative news). For those cynical citizens, it is particularly interesting and relevant to see that the effect then is reversed (in the direction of the stimulus) at t_{+30}.

The three-wave panel-study design proves beyond a doubt that the ability of citizens to discount the bias of news on Europe at the time they are being exposed to it does not in any way mean that European citizens are globally immune to the influence of manipulative mass media. Far from it – by the time the last questionnaire was administered

(a) GENERAL

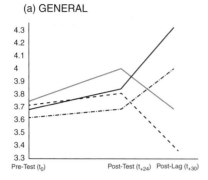

STIMULUS	Pre-Test (t_0)	Post-Test (t_{+24})	Post-Lag (t_{+30})
Negative News Placebo - - - -	3.75 (1.20)	3.80 (1.10)	3.36 (1.28)
Negative News Symbols ————	3.72 (0.96)	3.99 (0.88)	3.71 (1.10)
Positive News Placebo -·—··	3.60 (1.10)	3.65 (1.13)	3.97 (1.02)
Positive News Symbols ————	3.65 (1.25)	3.83 (1.22)	4.28 (0.85)

(b) CIVIC

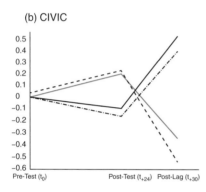

STIMULUS	Pre-Test (t_0)	Post-Test (t_{+24})	Post-Lag (t_{+30})
Negative News Placebo - - - -	0.07 (0.99)	0.24 (1.00)	-0.56 (1.03)
Negative News Symbols ————	0.01 (0.83)	0.15 (0.77)	-0.36 (1.06)
Positive News Placebo -·—··	-0.01 (1.05)	-0.21 (1.07)	0.36 (0.81)
Positive News Symbols ————	-0.01 (1.09)	-0.09 (1.07)	0.47 (0.69)

(c) CULTURAL

STIMULUS	Pre-Test (t_0)	Post-Test (t_{+24})	Post-Lag (t_{+30})
Negative News Placebo - - - -	0.02 (1.14)	0.14 (1.00)	-0.68 (1.11)
Negative News Symbols ————	0.09 (0.97)	0.38 (0.92)	0.56 (0.71)
Positive News Placebo -·—··	-0.05 (0.88)	-0.26 (0.91)	-0.28 (0.85)
Positive News Symbols ————	0.02 (0.95	0.13 (0.85)	0.39 (0.76)

Figure 7.1. Evolution of European identity over time.

Table 7.5. *The impact of news and symbols on European identity by country*

7.5A. General identity

		UK	France	Germany	Belgium	Sweden	Portugal
Wave 2	News	−0.12*	0.20*	−0.10	0.03	−0.12*	0.18**
	Symbols	0.02	0.08	0.24**	0.14	0.11*	0.11
	. . .	. . .	. . .	. . .	. . .	. . .	. . .
	Control t_0	0.79**	0.38**	0.64**	0.35**	0.70**	0.79**
	R^2	0.80	0.40	0.52	0.45	0.84	0.62
Wave 3	News	0.35**	0.25*	0.29*	0.32**	0.75**	0.37**
	Symbols	0.11	0.12	0.22*	0.27**	0.29**	0.06
	. . .	. . .	. . .	. . .	. . .	. . .	. . .
	Control t_0	0.54**	0.32**	0.60**	0.07	0.43**	0.38*
	R^2	0.42	0.44	0.37	0.47	0.58	0.49

7.5B. Civic identity

		UK	France	Germany	Belgium	Sweden	Portugal
Wave 2	News	−0.19**	−0.13	−0.06	−0.11	0.01	−0.02
	Symbols	−0.04	−0.05	0.34**	0.05	0.09	0.05
	. . .	. . .	. . .	. . .	. . .	. . .	. . .
	Control t_0	0.80**	0.34**	0.64**	0.55**	0.92**	0.67**
	R^2	0.78	0.38	0.52	0.20	0.86	0.78
Wave 3	News	0.29*	0.21*	0.61**	0.57**	0.74**	0.49**
	Symbols	0.13	0.20*	0.18	−0.02	−0.12	0.05
	. . .	. . .	. . .	. . .	. . .	. . .	. . .
	Control t_0	0.15	0.15	0.21	0.37**	−0.06	0.21
	R^2	0.16	0.34	0.50	0.61	0.60	0.56

7.5C. Cultural identity

		UK	France	Germany	Belgium	Sweden	Portugal
Wave 2	News	0.14	−0.02	−0.07	0.03	−0.08	0.16
	Symbols	0.21*	0.16	0.25*	0.29*	0.45**	0.21*
	. . .	. . .	. . .	. . .	. . .	. . .	. . .
	Control t_0	0.44**	0.33**	0.36**	0.31**	−0.20	0.61**
	R^2	0.16	0.18	0.35	0.21	0.49	0.51
Wave 3	News	0.26	0.27*	−0.04	−0.10	−0.08	0.28*
	Symbols	0.32*	0.39**	0.57**	0.60**	0.67**	0.33**
	. . .	. . .	. . .	. . .	. . .	. . .	. . .
	Control t_0	0.28	0.31*	0.15	0.37**	−0.24*	0.41**
	R^2	0.13	0.36	0.44	0.71	0.70	0.49

Notes: Results are standardized OLS regression coefficients. * Statistically significant at < 0.05; ** statistically significant at < 0.01. N (first figure for wave 2, second figure for wave 3) for 7.5A, 7.5B, and 7.5C:

– United Kingdom (A: 150, 118; B: 148, 116; C: 147, 116)
– France (A: 181, 154; B: 181, 146; C: 169, 138)
– Germany (A: 146, 118; B: 130, 114; C: 126, 114)
– Belgium (A: 171, 136; B: 147, 132; C: 148, 131)
– Sweden (A: 128, 128; B: 128, 127; C: 128, 127)
– Portugal (A: 124, 108; B: 124, 104; C: 124, 104)

thirty months after the beginning of the experiment (at t_{+30}), good or bad news strongly influenced citizens' identity. This very strong effect – measured after the six-month clearing period that followed the end of the twenty-four months of exposure to the experimental stimulus (t_{+24}) – is, in fact, of a magnitude that only can serve to remind us of the ultimate power of political communication. This communication effect – stronger than ever – radically influences citizens' European identity in a way that sharply contrasts with the limited immediate impact of news that was measured at t_{+24}. Indeed, this effect at t_{+30} is even strong among the British and Swedish samples in which citizens originally showed high levels of resistance to what they read (see Tables 7.5A and 7.5B). In fact, the "time-bomb" finding underlines the fact that there is absolutely no contradiction between knowing that someone is trying to manipulate you and trying to resist such manipulation, on the one hand, and ultimately proving overwhelmingly influenced by it. Increasingly sophisticated and cynical citizens apparently may identify or even resist what they think of as biased news and discount journalistic manipulation while exposed to it. Nevertheless, on the other hand, they still show a genuine and significant subconscious vulnerability to this bias when they stop being directly confronted to the potentially manipulative news source (see Figures 7.1A and 7.1B). In other words, the "time-bomb" effect suggests that although citizens have learned that the media are not objective and may well have their own political agenda, this knowledge, which is efficiently operational at the time news is received, does not prevent the news from having an insidious effect, permeating the heart and mind of citizens over time.

As mentioned previously, the proof that cynicism toward the media does not equate to resistance to manipulation in the long term is shown in the Swedish sample, which proves to be most effective at resisting news effects at t_{+24} (indeed, a statistically significant negative effect) before transforming into the most strongly affected sample by news at t_{+30} (see Tables 7.5A and 7.5B). Even more generally, whereas news on Europe has a strong lagged effect on citizens' identity in every one of the six national groups, the lower the effect at t_{+24}, the higher it seems to be at t_{+30}. It is as if the harder citizens tried to "resist" manipulation, the more vulnerable to it they ultimately proved. Thus, the effect develops far more dramatically postexperimental treatment in the Swedish and British cases than elsewhere. In those cases, news seemed to have a counterproductive effect at first but then a strong positive effect later. In the French sample, however, the barrier of cynicism is weaker at t_{+24}, and good and bad news matter immediately. Whereas it further accelerates later, its final impact is not as strong as in the British and Swedish groups. By and large, however, by t_{+30}, the case remains that the long-term effect of news on civic identity is nothing less than overwhelming. This proves that, ultimately, exposing citizens to regular good news on Europe makes them feel more European over time, whereas exposing them to the type of systematic bad news typically found in the British tabloids is a veritable "identity killer."

Of course, this does not mean that the European Commission simply could send a couple of pages of positive news on the EU every other week and get people to feel overwhelmingly European. Indeed, neither will exposing them to only negative news destroy the Europeanness in anyone. In particular, the most interesting aspect of the translation of our experimental findings into real-life situations is about what will happen to the "immediate cynicism discount" that we observe at t_{+24} for people who are consistently exposed to the same – positive or negative – type of news, and whether the rarity of news on Europe is enough to make this immediate discount irrelevant in real life.

Our strong measures of identity are probably significantly affected only by our experimental stimulus to the extent that, in all likelihood, after two years of intense information on Europe through the experiments, the participants were probably exposed to more news on Europe than the average European throughout an entire lifetime. In this sense, identity is not proven to be more malleable than expected by our findings. What the findings confirm, instead, is the scarcity of news on Europe in the current media landscape and the scope for impact of any potential genuine information on Europe (e.g., through civic education).

Cynicism, politicization, identity, and the public sphere

The "time-bomb" effect highlighted in this chapter poses in an unusual way the question of the relationship among the emergence of a European public sphere, the politicization of European politics, and the emergence of a mass European identity. Clearly, politicization can be dangerous, in that we found that, ultimately, a steady stream of bad news on Europe can negatively affect the European identity of citizens – in particular, their civic identity that is most likely to result in a sense of civic duty and allegiance. Conversely, good news on Europe can significantly reinforce the European identity of citizens (this was not obvious as such because much of the political communication literature suggests that, in many respects, bad news frequently has more effect than good news). Even more important, it is unclear whether in the absence of politicization of Europe – and, therefore, of European news – any sense of identity would survive. Our recent work shows that across the EU, levels of European identity are high (see, e.g., Bruter and Harrison 2012, which presents the results of a three-wave time-series study on European identity with a first wave taking place in all twenty-seven member states of the EU with thirty thousand respondents and additional waves in eight member states). In fact, the levels are significantly higher than what has long been assumed by the discipline in the absence of large-scale ad hoc measures. If this is true, it suggests that the emerging collective identity of Europeans can survive the dangers of repeated negative news and instead use the politicization of Europe to anchor citizens' identity on genuine European areas of political contestation. Moreover, if the politicization of Europe is finally occurring and a genuine European public sphere is partly emerging (see Part I), this may be a consequence rather than a cause of a strengthening European identity. Journalists are not known to willingly sacrifice space to questions that do not interest their readers. So we must think of the full consequences of our findings on the case of Europeanized public spheres. We know that European integration is, by any standard, a regular focus of political discussion across national public spheres and occasionally across a Europeanized public sphere (e.g., in the context of the 2005 referenda on the EU Constitution or in the context of the Greek financial crisis). If our model suggests that discussion of polity-relevant political issues, whether positive or negative, is a sign of appropriation of a political system and therefore a sign of identity consolidation, then this is probably evidence that a European political identity has developed in its own right to create a demand for the treatment of such topics.

The relationship among public sphere, politicization, cynicism, and identity undoubtedly is complex and the ability of any actor – whether institutional, political, or individual – to proactively control any of these factors is extremely theoretical at the very least. There is, and statistically significant variables. The regressions were run for the entire sample, with country dummies, and then within each country. Of course, it was signaled that country-specific regressions in particular had to be considered with caution because of the relatively limited number of cases.

In the context of this chapter, we do not focus on the effect of symbols of Europe on participants' European identity but rather look only at the model of news. However, because the effect of symbols was part of the models, we briefly mention that news on Europe has a strong effect on European identity, particularly on its cultural component (although it also has a statistically significant effect on the spontaneous expression of European identity). This effect occurs during the experimental phase but accelerates further in the six months that follow the end of the experimental treatment, thereby suggesting that respondents who are regularly exposed to EU symbols are effectively primed to notice them more in their natural environment.

The effect of positive and negative news about Europe

As described previously, hypothesis H2 stated that positive and negative news on Europe will affect European identity, particularly its civic component (H2b); whereas H4, which is grounded on a modified sleeper-effect theory (which would not be due to source-specific idiosyncrasies but rather to an attribute of the citizens – namely, cynicism), claimed that this effect will be delayed until after the lag that follows the end of the experiment. This hypothesis has significant implications for our understanding of the impact of political communication on increasingly cynical citizens. First, the panel-study experiment confirmed that, over time, news on Europe has an impact on the European identity of citizens. This effect is predominantly strong on the civic component of European identity, but news on Europe also affects general identity (Table 7.4). Cultural European identity is less influenced by good and bad news about Europe and the EU, although some of the

dates for each group in each country. However, because only three time points are included, to avoid any unnecessary methodological controversy, all of the models also were tested using a generalized estimating equations extension of GLS instead of OLS with full controls. The results were fully comparable with the same variables appearing as statistically significant and important in the two models.

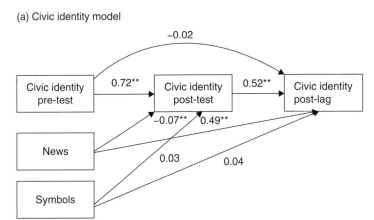

(a) Civic identity model

Valid *N* = 829 (t_{+24}), 740 (t_{+30})
Other controls included in the equation: age, sex, support for EU, country dummies

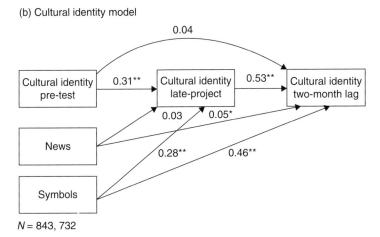

(b) Cultural identity model

N = 843, 732

Figure 7.2. Summary three-wave model.

however, little doubt that some underlying causal links are at stake and that, for instance, the existence of a European public sphere or absence thereof would have an impact on the dynamics of politicization experienced across the various EU member states. The likely shape of this dynamic causality is partly illustrated by the fully developed models of European civic and cultural identities over time (Figure 7.2(a) and 7.2(b)). These models deconstruct and distinguish how the immediate and lagged effects of news on Europe and EU symbols combine to progressively affect identities. They also highlight how cultural identity (i.e., identification with a community) is more volatile than civic identity (i.e., identification with a political system) in the long run, which is a symbol of how entrenched the EU as a political system has become in the political identity maps of Europeans.

Our findings show how the sophistication of citizens and their vulnerability to manipulation paradoxically go hand in hand in our highly critical contemporary polities. When accused of influencing the public, many think that such an accusation is illogical insofar as sophisticated and cynical citizens will treat journalistic messages with a critical eye that immunizes them against manipulation. Instead, we show that even if British citizens effectively know that their mass media (and particularly tabloids) are globally Euroskeptic, this does not undermine the ability of the media to make British citizens feel significantly less European than others. Instead, the "time-bomb" effect suggests that the very sophistication and cynicism of modern-day citizens might well make them even more vulnerable to the influences to which they think they are immune. Moreover, the principle of news self-selection (Zaller 1992) hardly applies to the politicization of European integration because European coverage is most unlikely to constitute a strong basis for news-outlet selection (unlike the general conservative/ liberal stance that Zaller predominantly considers in his work). Bias in European coverage often is nationally entrenched rather than splitting national media lines, which limits the ability of any citizen to select news according to the level of "euro-sympathy" of media sources in most cases.

Politicization is not so much a choice as a fatality and not so much a cause as a consequence. In the context of the current crisis, we are witnessing more debate about EU affairs and input than ever before. This debate, however, is a natural consequence of the European political system being integrated by citizens and being perceived as more relevant and "real" than ever before. The existence of a European public sphere that could channel the shape of European political debates into centrifugal directions – whereas its absence would likely result in an explosion of political fracture lines around communities – is key to the likely nature of the news to which various subcategories of EU citizens will be exposed. Therefore, according to our findings, it is the way this news will shape their identities. As such, in a context of necessary and meaningful politicization, the convergence of national public spheres into a European public pattern will have a significant impact on the expression of political tensions that, in coming years, will continue to oppose determined Euroskeptics to ever-more integrated European citizens.

8 The restructuring of political conflict in Europe and the politicization of European integration

EDGAR GRANDE AND HANSPETER KRIESI

In this chapter, we link the debate on the emergence of a European public sphere (Wessler et al. 2008; Koopmans and Statham 2010a; Risse 2010) to current transformations of political conflict in Europe and the politicization of the European integration process. Our starting point is the assumption that the transnationalization of public spheres is both an "enabling condition" for the politicization of European Union (EU) politics and its product, as the premise of this book argues. The crucial questions, then, are as follows: Who are the driving forces and beneficiaries of this politicization? Which actors make most effective use of these new discursive opportunities? What are the most likely consequences of this politicization of European integration? Most authors agree that an expansion of the European public sphere and a politicization of the integration process are necessary preconditions for the further development of the EU political system. Normative approaches to European integration assume that politicization will have mainly positive effects on the integration process because it gives cosmopolitan supporters of the "European project" better opportunities to articulate their views and to mobilize European citizens (Delanty and Rumford 2005; Beck 2006; Habermas 2006a, 2011; Beck and Grande 2007; Eder and Trenz 2007). In these arguments, the link between politicization and European integration is crucial, although our knowledge on its constitutive factors, causal relationships, and dynamics is still insufficient. Against this background, this chapter explores empirically the link between politicization and European integration. Based on a dynamic framework of political structuring (Grande and Kriesi 2012),[1]

[1] The framework for this chapter is inspired by Stein Rokkan's analyses on political structuring in Europe (Rokkan 1999; see also Kriesi 1998 and Bartolini 2005). It assumes that modern societies can still be characterized by a limited number of widespread and permanent "cleavages," a specific structure of political conflict that integrates social, normative, and institutional elements.

we analyze two factors that have been decisive in shaping this link: (1) the *structure of political conflict* produced by the recent politicization of the European integration process; and (2) the *actors and actor constellations* responsible for this structuring of political conflict.

The chapter advances two arguments. First, it argues that the politicization of the European integration process must be interpreted in the context of a more fundamental transformation of political conflict in Western Europe. The politicization of the European integration process has not produced a "pro- and anti-EU cleavage"; rather, this conflict is a constitutive part of a more fundamental "integration–demarcation" (or "cosmopolitan–nationalist") cleavage, which has been emerging in Western Europe in the past two decades as a consequence of globalization (i.e., societal "denationalization") (Zürn 1998). This new cleavage, in particular, has been transforming the existing cultural-conflict dimension in the political space. Constitutive for this new cleavage have been issues such as immigration and European integration.[2]

Second, we argue that the politicization of the European integration process is highly ambiguous from a normative point of view. The new cleavage has produced several "cleavage coalitions," and it is an empirically open question which of these cleavage coalitions dominates the politicization of the integration process. In the past two decades, it has been the Euroskeptic parties of the new populist right that have exploited the new structural cleavage most successfully in Western Europe. The euro crisis, thus far, has intensified this conflict but it has not transformed its basic structure.

Our empirical analysis is based on data for national elections and public debates collected in two research projects: (1) "National Political Change in a Globalizing World," which was completed in 2009 and covers six Western European countries (i.e., Austria, France, Germany, the Netherlands, Switzerland, and the United Kingdom); and (2) "Politicizing Europe," which was completed in 2013 (i.e., covering Austria, France, Germany, Sweden, Switzerland, and the United Kingdom).[3] The data on national elections include a period from

---

[2] For a detailed empirical analysis of this transformation, see Kriesi et al. 2008 and Kriesi et al. 2012.

[3] Because the focus of this book is on the EU only, we excluded Switzerland from the analysis in this chapter, except in those instances in which we explicitly indicate it.

the mid-1970s to the end of the 2000s; public debates on globalization issues (including European integration) are covered from 2004 to
2006; and the public debate on the euro crisis covers the period from
December 2009 to March 2012. Our data come from daily newspaper
content. For each country, we selected one quality newspaper and, for
national election campaigns, we added the most widely read tabloid
in each country.[4] In coding newspaper data, we used a core-sentence
approach (cf. Kleinnijenhuis et al. 1997; Kleinnijenhuis and Pennings
2001). By means of this method, we were able to measure the position
that actors take on a specific issue as well as the salience they attribute
to this issue. This has important advantages for understanding the
structure and dynamics of political conflict in public spheres.[5]

The chapter is organized in five sections. First, it presents a model
of political conflict that distinguishes three types of globalization conflicts. Second, it shows empirically how these conflicts have been transforming the structure of political conflict in Western Europe. More
specifically, we identify the contribution of European integration issues
in this context. Third, we analyze public debates on European issues in
the mid-2000s and identify the actor constellations in those debates.
Fourth, we identify five "cleavage coalitions" that occupy markedly
different positions in the two-dimensional political space. Most important in our context is the formation of three "nationalist" coalitions
composed of trade unions, radical-right parties, and several Conservative and Christian Democratic parties. Fifth, we analyze actor positions and actor constellations in the public debate on the euro crisis.
Based on this empirical evidence, the chapter concludes by arguing
that the emergence of a European public sphere and the politicization
of EU politics is not good news per se. Controversies about European
integration contribute substantially to the restructuring of political
conflict in Western Europe. However, our knowledge of the political
processes that shape and direct the politicization of EU politics is still
insufficient.

---

[4] The selected newspapers for the content analysis are *Die Presse* and *Kronen-
zeitung* for Austria; *The Times* and *Sun* for the United Kingdom; *Le Monde* and
Le Parisien for France; *Süddeutsche Zeitung* and *Bild* for Germany; and *NRC
Handelsblad* and *Allgemeen Dagblad* for the Netherlands. For the debate on the
euro crisis, we coded only the respective quality newspapers.
[5] For details of the research design and methods, see Dolezal et al. 2012.

The theoretical framework: denationalization and political conflict in Western Europe

Why should we expect a politicization of the European integration process? The most obvious and commonly given answer to this question is that politicization is a response to the major integration steps in the past two decades, particularly the Maastricht Treaty, Economic and Monetary Union, Eastern Enlargement, Constitutional Treaty, and euro crisis. This answer is not completely wrong, but it is certainly incomplete. It shares a major shortcoming of large parts of research on EU politics – namely, that it is too EU-centric. Our research on political conflict in Western Europe reveals that the politicization of European integration must be interpreted as part of a more fundamental transformation of cleavages that has been caused by processes of "denationalization" since the 1980s.

The consequences of globalization are obviously not identical for all members of a national community – and among national communities. There is sufficient empirical evidence that globalization and European integration give rise to new disparities, new oppositions, and new forms of competition. These new forms of economic, cultural, and political competition create new groups of (actual or potential) "winners" and "losers" that, in turn, constitute political potential for the articulation of their conflicting interests and demands by political parties, interest groups, and social movements. As shown in previous analyses, these new oppositions are not aligned with but rather cut across traditional structural and political cleavages (Kriesi et al. 2008, 2012).

Why should denationalization have the potential to create a new cleavage? The literature on globalization identified at least three types of conflict that contribute to the formation of winners and losers of denationalization: economic competition, cultural diversity, and political integration. In the first type, the argument is that globalization has intensified transnational economic competition; this has led to increasing social and economic risks for some members of advanced welfare states. Second, globalization and European integration also are responsible for a significant increase in cultural diversity within European societies. Since the 1960s, Western societies have seen massive immigration of groups that are, in many respects, distinct from the resident population. These migration processes may have various causes, but they all contribute to a strong increase in sociocultural diversity in European societies (Albrow 2001). By threatening the identity of resident populations, cultural diversity has the potential to create new political conflicts that transcend the conflicts produced in the course of industrialization and of creating the Western European nation-state.

A third source of conflict related to denationalization is political integration – that is, the transfer of political authority to institutions beyond the nation-state (Held et al. 1999; Grande and Pauly 2005). This is particularly true in the case of European integration, in which such a transfer jeopardizes national political sovereignty. These changes also create winners and losers in specific ways. On the one hand, winners and losers may result from differences in their identification with the national community. Thus, individuals who possess a strong identification with their national community and who are attached to its exclusionary norms will perceive a weakening of the national institutions as a loss. On the other hand, European integration may result in substantial fiscal transfers and economic losses. The transfer of competencies to the EU may produce direct losses by redistributing funds among member states. It also may cause economic grievances indirectly – for example, by prohibiting national subsidies or by enforcing domestic budget cuts. In the current euro crisis, all of these problematic aspects of political integration can be observed.

The new groups of winners and losers of denationalization created by these conflicts are not ideologically predefined, however. Rather, they constitute new political potentials, which can – and must – be articulated by political organizations. Given the heterogeneous composition of these groups, we cannot expect that the preferences formed as a function of this new antagonism will be closely aligned with the political divisions on which domestic politics traditionally has been based. As we can observe from the development of national party systems in Western Europe during the past two decades, this makes it difficult for established national political actors to organize these new potentials. The crucial questions, then, are as follows: How do these new political oppositions affect the structure of political conflict in Europe? How is this new cleavage related to European integration? Which political actors are most successful in exploiting these new potentials?

European integration and the new "demarcation–integration" cleavage

There is substantial empirical evidence that the emergence of new social groups of (potential) winners and losers of globalization has produced a new "demarcation–integration" (or "cosmopolitanism–nationalism") cleavage in Western European societies. This is not the proper place to present a full account of this transformation in all of its relevant aspects. In this chapter, we are mainly interested in the European dimension of this conflict and its political organization in the electoral arena and public debates. As we know from comparative analyses of various political arenas, it is in the national election arena that the new cleavage is organized and articulated most forcefully (Kriesi et al. 2012).

Figure 8.1 presents the results of a multidimensional scaling (MDS) analysis for national elections in six Western European countries (including Switzerland) in the 2000s.[6] The analysis covers two elections to national parliaments for each country; in the French case, the first ballot for the presidential election was included. The analysis shows both the positioning of the most salient issues (e.g., immigration and the welfare state) and the relevant political parties for each country. We drew lines between two contrasting issues in both dimensions and cluster boundaries to facilitate interpretation. Two aspects are most relevant for our analysis. First, our data clearly show a two-dimensional structure of the political space on an aggregate level, and these findings are reconfirmed for each country in each of the elections. The first of these two dimensions is the familiar socioeconomic conflict constituted by statist positions (i.e., welfare) on the left and pro-market positions (i.e., economic liberalism) on the right. The second dimension is constituted mainly by three issues: cultural liberalism and European integration, on the one hand, and immigration, on the other.

Second, the cultural dimension is clearly distinct from the religious cleavages and the conflicts between "libertarians" and "authoritarians," which shaped this dimension in the past. These results signify

---

[6] An MDS analysis weights the actors' position on a set of issues by the salience of the issues for the actors. For details of this procedure, see Kriesi et al. 2008, 71–3, and Kriesi et al. 2012, 58f.

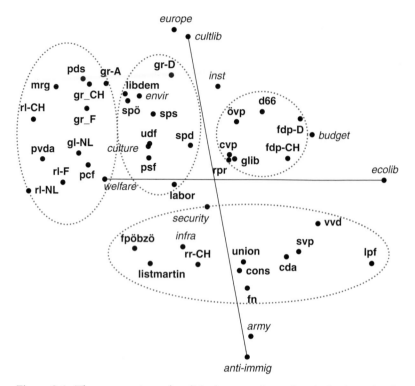

Figure 8.1. The structuring of political spaces in national elections in six Western European countries in the 2000s (A, CH, D, F, NL, UK).

Selected party abbreviations:
– *Radical left:* pds (PDS, *Partei des Demokratischen Sozialismus*; since 2007: *Die Linke*), pcf (PCF, *Parti Communiste Français*)
– *Greens:* gr-A (*Die Grünen Österreich*), gr-CH (*Grüne Partei der Schweiz*), gr-D (*Bündnis90/Die Grünen Deutschland*), gl (*GroenLinks*, the Netherlands)
– *Social Democrats:* spd (SPD, *Sozialdemokratische Partei Deutschlands*), pvda (PvdA, *Partij van de Arbeid*, the Netherlands), sps (SPS, *Sozialdemokratische Partei der Schweiz*), psf (PS, *Parti Socialiste*, France), labour (Labour Party, UK)
– *Christian Democrats/Conservatives:* union (CDU/CSU (*Christlich-Demokratische/Soziale Union, Germany*), cda (CDA, *Christen-Democratisch Appel*, the Netherlands), cvp (CVP, *Christlichdemokratische Volkspartei*; Switzerland), rpr (*Rassemblement pour la République*; France)
– *Liberals:* d66 (D'66, *Democraten'66*, the Netherlands), fdp (FDP, *Freie Demokratische Partei*; Germany), lib (FDP, *Freisinnig-Demokratische Partei*, Switzerland), libdem (Liberal Democratic Party, UK)
– *Populist Right:* fn (Front National, France), fpö (FPÖ, *Freiheitliche Partei Österreichs*), bzö (BZÖ, *Bündnis Zukunft Österreichs*), listmartin (*Liste Hans-Peter Martin*, Austria), lpf (LPF, *Lijst Pim Fortuyn*, the Netherlands), svp (SVP, *Schweizerische Volkspartei*).

the emergence of a new cleavage that has been constituted not by adding a completely new dimension to the political space but instead by redefining the cultural dimension in an existing two-dimensional political space.

Figure 8.1 also shows party clusters in this two-dimensional space. By the 2000s, we find four large groups of parties: two on the left and two on the right. These groups are rather heterogeneous in their composition and do not represent party families. On the left, we find two clearly discernible groups: a moderate, "cosmopolitan" group composed mostly of Social Democrats and Greens, as well as a more radical, "interventionist" fringe composed mostly of former Communists (e.g., *Parti Communiste Français* [PCF] and *Partei des Demokratischen Sozialismus* [PDS]). On the right, we find a collection of parties that share nationalist orientations but that are spread across the economic dimension. This group includes new radical right and Euroskeptic parties, such as the French Front National (FN), the Dutch *Lijst Pim Fortuyn* (LPF), and the Austrian *Liste Hans Peter Martin*; transformed mainstream parties that have adopted culturally protectionist and nationalist positions, such as the Swiss *Schweizerische Volkspartei* (SVP), the Austrian *Freiheitliche Partei Österreichs* (FPÖ), and the Austrian *Bündnis Zukunft Österreichs* (BZÖ); as well as Conservative and Christian Democratic parties. Moreover, there is a small neoliberal-cosmopolitan group composed of Liberal party group members and Christian Democratic parties in Austria and Switzerland.

This transformation of political conflict has several important implications for Europe. First, as the data in Table 8.1 show, European integration has become a salient and hotly contested issue in

---

(figure caption continued)
Selected issue abbreviations:
Army = support for armed forces; budget = support for rigid budgetary policy; cultlib (cultural liberalism) = support for the goals of new social movements; ecolib (economic liberalism) = opposition to market regulation and intervention; europe = support for European integration; immigration = support for tough immigration and integration policy; infra = infrastructure; security = support for more law and order; welfare = support for expansion of welfare.

For complete explanations of our categorization of party actors and issues, see Dolezal et al. 2012, 52–4.

Table 8.1. *Overall issue salience in national elections by decade (in percentages)*

Issue categories	Decade			Average 1990s and 2000s
	1970s	1990s	2000s	
Economic	**48.6**	**40.2**	**37.8**	**39.0**
Welfare state	17.2	19.1	19.5	19.3
Economic liberalism	20.8	12.4	9.5	10.9
Budgetary rigor	10.6	8.6	8.9	8.7
New cultural	**18.6**	**24.7**	**25.7**	**25.2**
Cultural liberalism	14.4	12.0	12.7	12.4
European integration	2.7	6.7	5.1	5.9
Immigration	1.5	6.0	7.9	6.9
Old cultural	**16.5**	**20.2**	**20.6**	**20.4**
Culture	7.4	7.2	6.3	6.7
Security	5.6	9.3	10.7	10.0
Army	3.5	3.7	3.7	3.7
Other	**16.3**	**14.9**	**15.9**	**15.4**
Ecology	4.5	5.5	6.5	6.0
Institutional reform	4.4	6.1	5.7	5.9
Infrastructure	7.5	3.4	4.5	3.6
Total	100%	100%	100%	100%
N	4,582	9,551	14,768	24,319

Note: Entries are the issue saliences in Austria, France, Germany, the United Kingdom, and the Netherlands, based on actor-issue sentences with national political parties as the subject. In each country, two elections in the 1970s, 1990s, and 2000s were examined. In this table, all countries and elections are weighted equally.

national-election campaigns since the 1990s, thereby making European integration an issue of "mass politics" in most member states (Hooghe and Marks 2009). As shown in the overview on the issue salience in national elections, European integration accounts for 5.9 percent of core sentences in the 1990s and 2000s. It is of similar importance as environmental issues (6.0 percent) and immigration (6.9 percent) but clearly less salient than economic issues. Compared to the 1970s, there is a marked increase of issue salience in all countries; however, compared to the 1990s, the salience of European integration declined in national elections in the 2000s from 6.7 to 5.1 percent.[7] Contrary to public debates more generally, controversies on the Constitutional Treaty did not cause a boost in the salience of European issues in national elections (Statham and Trenz 2013b). A review of values for individual countries (the data are not shown) reveals considerable cross-national variations. The salience of European issues is highest in the United Kingdom (8.8 percent) and lowest in Germany (4.2 percent). However, it must be emphasized that the salience of new cultural issues is still limited compared to (old) economic issues. The importance of economic issues has been declining since the 1970s, but the welfare state is still by far the most salient issue in all countries (19.3 percent of core sentences).

To fully understand the structuring power of new conflicts, we must examine the issues that constitute them and the positioning of actors in more detail. This holds true particularly for European integration. "Europe" is a multidimensional issue that includes both economic and cultural sub-issues (Hooghe and Marks 1999, 2009; Höglinger 2011). The positioning of political actors may vary across these dimensions and sub-issues. We analyzed public debates on European integration over a longer period (2004–2006) to uncover this internal structure of the European issue.[8] The period under examination should be highly instructive because it includes some of the most controverial debates in the history of European integration – namely, the Constitutional Treaty, the Eastern Enlargement, and the EU membership of Turkey. The results of our empirical analysis are summarized in the dotplots shown in Figure 8.2.[9]

In the first part of Figure 8.2, the aggregate results for European integration in the five countries are examined. In addition to the relevant parties, European and domestic public actors and interest

---

[7] Unfortunately, we do not yet have data on the most recent national elections in France and the Netherlands.

[8] The selection of articles for analyzing the debate on issues related to European integration was accomplished in a two-step procedure. In the first step, we identified relevant events in each country through yearbooks (e.g., *Keesing's World Record of Events*) and produced an extensive keyword list for each country. In the second step, we chronologically took a random sample of 1,200 articles per country. We then coded, at most, the first twenty core sentences of each article.

[9] The dotplots in Figure 8.2 represent averages of actors' positioning on issues based on our coding of core sentences. Values ranged from −1 to +1. A value of +1 indicates a fully supportive position on a specific issue.

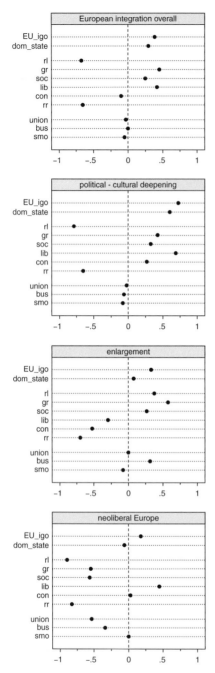

Figure 8.2. Actor positions on European integration (A, D, F, NL, UK).
Actor abbreviations: EU_igo (EU and international governmental actors); dom_state (domestic state actors); rl (radical left/left socialists); gr (Greens); soc (Social Democrats); lib (Liberals); con (Christian Democrats and Conservatives); rr (right-wing populists); union (unions); bus (business actors); smo (public-interest groups, including social movements)

groups are included. Most interesting here is the positioning of political parties, which shows the expected "inverted-U curve" (Hooghe et al. 2004): both the radical left and the radical right strongly oppose European integration, whereas the Greens, the Liberals, and the Social Democrats are supportive. On average, Conservative and Christian Democratic parties occupy moderately negative positions. As expected, actors from EU institutions and national governments are in favor of European integration; values for interest groups are less telling because their neutral positions, on average, mask strong variations on sub-issues.

In the following sections, we show the results for three of the four sub-issues that define the two dimensions of the European integration debate: (1) in the cultural dimension, the two key issues have been the extension of constitutional competencies and authoritative powers of EU institutions (i.e., the "deepening" of European integration); and (2) the "enlargement" of the EU (i.e., the inclusion of new member states). Both issues certainly have economic implications; however, public debates mostly have been dominated by a cultural logic in these cases. The debate on Turkey's EU membership is the clearest case in point. The two economic sub-issues are (1) the strengthening of "market-correcting" policies at the European level, which were debated under the heading of a "Social Market Europe"; and (2) the enforcement of further "market-making" policies (i.e., a "neoliberal Europe"). Most important, the positioning of political actors (political parties in particular) varies significantly across these sub-issues. (For a more detailed analysis, see Helbling et al. 2010 and Höglinger 2011.) For three of the four sub-issues, there are different actor constellations.[10] The positioning of actors toward a further "deepening" of European integration is similar to the general picture. Radical parties on the left and on the right strongly oppose a further transfer of competencies to the European level, whereas the other parties clearly support it. In contrast to the general picture, Conservative and Christian Democratic parties occupy supportive positions on this sub-issue as well – with one major exception, of course: the British Conservative Party (the data are not shown).

---

[10] Because the number of core sentences on "Social Market Europe" is significantly lower for most actors, we do not report these results.

These results are in strong contrast to the parties' positioning on the second cultural sub-issue (i.e., "enlargement"). Here, we find a clear left–right divide with the radical left, the Green parties, and the Social Democrats (except the Austrian SPÖ) in favor of further enlargement (including Turkey), whereas not only the radical right but also the Conservatives, Christian Democrats, and Liberals take negative positions. The parties' positioning on the most salient economic sub-issue (i.e., "neoliberal Europe") also shows a left–right divide. However, in this case, the left is seconded by the radical right, which also is strongly opposed to more market-making policies at the European level.

Having shown the structure of political conflicts on European integration, we now are interested in the territorial scope of these debates. Have these conflicts been integrated in a European public sphere, or did we observe more or less isolated national debates dominated by national political actors? We obtain an admittedly rough answer to this question by analyzing the relative importance of individual political arenas in public debates. Political arenas can be distinguished by their specific set of institutional norms and rules that guide the articulation and processing of political conflicts (for more details, see Helbling et al. 2012, 211ff.). On the basis of these norms and rules, we can distinguish several such arenas (e.g., the electoral arena and the protest arena).

Table 8.2 presents the findings on the three most relevant economic, cultural, and political globalization issues (i.e., immigration, economic liberalization, and European integration) from 2004 to 2006. Most important in our context is the contribution of the "international and supranational arena" to these debates. This arena includes actor statements mostly from the EU – but also from international organizations – to national debates. Thus, it can be considered an indicator of the degree of vertical transnationalization as defined by Koopmans and Statham (2010b, 38). This is certainly an imperfect measure of the overall degree of transnationalization because it does not cover horizontal forms; nevertheless, it is instructive. Our analysis allows an assessment of the relative importance of this arena in the European integration debate in comparison with other arenas and debates. Hence, there are two benchmarks that we can use to assess the degree of transnationalization – which is mostly Europeanization in this case. Two findings stand out. First, we find a remarkable degree of "vertical Europeanization" of public debates on European integration. Almost

Table 8.2. *Contribution of political arenas to public debates over globalization (in percentages)*

	All	Immigration	Economic liberalization	European integration
International/ supranational public authority arena	23.2	8.9	16.7	44.0
Domestic executive arena	19.5	25.2	24.8	8.5
Judicial arena	5.8	11.2	4.0	2.3
Electoral arena	18.8	22.8	12.3	21.4
Protest arena	7.2	14.8	6.0	0.7
Direct democratic arena	8.0	0.6	1.9	21.3
Administrative arena	6.4	6.5	12.0	0.9
Economy	7.3	0.3	21.6	0.1
Civil society	3.8	9.7	0.7	0.8
Total	*100*	*100*	*100*	*100*
N	18,237	4,087	5,376	8,774

Notes: Reported values are the relative shares of actor statements stemming from a particular political arena. Data are weighted by country and debate.

half of all statements on this issue (44.0 percent) were made by international or supranational actors, compared to 8.9 percent in the debate on immigration and 16.7 percent in the debate on economic liberalization. This is clear evidence that, in fact, a European public sphere exists, at least on European integration issues. Second, our data indicate the relevance of this arena compared to other political arenas. In the European integration debate, this arena clearly outnumbers the electoral arena and the direct democratic arena, although we had national parliamentary elections in each country (except France) and national referenda on European issues in two countries (i.e., France and the Netherlands) in this period. Our data also confirm the irrelevance of the protest arena and civil-society actors in the debate on European integration compared, for example, to the immigration debate.

To summarize, our analysis thus far has provided empirical evidence, first, for an intensification of political conflict on European integration in public debates and national elections; second, this politicization substantially contributed to a restructuring of political conflict in Western

Europe producing a new "demarcation–integration" cleavage; and, third, the politicization of European integration in public debates took place in a public sphere with a remarkable degree of vertical Europeanization.

Driving forces: political actors and conflicting cleavage coalitions

Who, then, comprise the driving forces of the new conflict? Which political actors are responsible for organizing the new demarcation–integration cleavage in Europe? Our comparative analysis of political debates on those issues that are constitutive for the new cleavage provides a detailed and nuanced picture of the actor constellations in these conflicts. To analyze these actor constellations, we introduced the concept of cleavage coalitions (Grande and Kriesi 2012, 20). Cleavage coalitions include those actors that share (more or less) identical positions on the issues constitutive of a cleavage. The advantage of this concept is that it includes a broad range of different actors from different arenas or "channels" of political mobilization. Therefore, cleavage coalitions are much broader than "party families" or "party coalitions," and they can be composed of different types of actors (e.g., parties, unions, public-interest groups, and domestic state actors) from different territorial levels. An analysis of contributions to public debates provides the opportunity to identify these cleavage coalitions.

In theory, we can distinguish four ideal-typical coalitions that combine the oppositions in the political space spanned by the cultural and economic axes in distinct ways: interventionist–cosmopolitan, neoliberal–cosmopolitan, neoliberal–nationalist, and interventionist–nationalist (Grande and Kriesi 2012, 22). The analysis of the electoral arena (see Figure 8.2) shows that the left parties were adherents of the interventionist–cosmopolitan coalition, although they were divided on the economic axes. The Liberal and Conservative/Christian Democratic parties, however, were divided on the cultural axes. Their members were found in a neoliberal–cosmopolitan coalition (i.e., most Liberal and some Conservative and Christian Democratic parties) as well as in the neoliberal–nationalist coalition (i.e., the right-wing populist parties and their functional equivalents among the Conservative and Christian Democratic parties). We would not necessarily expect

Figure 8.3. Cleavage coalitions in public debates on immigration, European integration, and economic liberalism: MDS analysis.

Issue abbreviations: ANTI_IMMIG = anti-immigration; INTEGRATION = integration of foreigners; XENO = xenophobia; ANTI_DOMLIB = anti-domestic liberalization; INT_LIB = international liberalization; DEEPENING = EU deepening; NO_ENLARGE = no EU enlargement; SM_EUROPE = social market Europe; NL_EUROPE = neoliberal Europe.

Actor abbreviations: EU_igo = EU and IGO actors; d_state = domestic state actors; com = Communists/left socialists; gr = Greens; soc = Social Democrats; lib = Liberals; con = Christian Democrats and Conservatives; rr = right-wing populists; smo = public-interest groups (including social movements).

exactly the same coalitions to be present in public debates on the three globalization issues because economic issues such as welfare-state policies, which have a strong influence in the national electoral arena, are not included here.

Figure 8.3 combines an MDS analysis for the three globalization issues with a cluster analysis of the MDS coordinates.[11] It allows us to identify simultaneously the structure of the political space, the issues responsible for its structuring, and the actor coalitions located in this space. Because we are mainly interested in conflicts on European integration in this chapter, we drew lines between the two economic and cultural sub-issues of European integration to facilitate interpretation. As shown in Figure 8.3, the conflict on European integration has a two-dimensional structure with "deepening" of integration and opposition against further "enlargement" constituting the cultural axis, and support for "social-market Europe" and "neoliberal Europe" forming the economic axis. The sub-issues of the other debates are more or less where expected: "integration" (i.e., positive attitudes toward integration of foreigners) and "anti-xenophobia" (i.e., opposition toward xenophobia) are close to deepening; and "anti-immigration" (i.e., refusal of further immigration) is on the opposite side of the political space. The three economic sub-issues (i.e., domestic liberalization, neoliberal Europe, and international liberalization) are positioned on the right-hand side of the political space opposite "social-market Europe." This reconfirms the embedding of the European integration conflict into the broader conflict on denationalization. In fact, the findings on the European integration debate alone produce a similar pattern (the data are not shown).

How are political actors positioned in this two-dimensional space? The five boldfaced, dashed ellipses correspond to the empirical cleavage coalitions identified by our cluster analysis. In detail, we find two coalitions with pro-European positions and three coalitions with anti-European positions on the cultural axis, as follows:

1. A *neoliberal–cosmopolitan coalition*, which articulates and organizes the "neoliberal consensus" in Western European societies. This group includes Liberal parties, state authorities, and business associations. As expected, Conservative and Christian Democratic parties are mostly absent in this coalition (except the

---

[11] K-means is a clustering algorithm that aims to find cluster centers that minimize the intra-class variance. In our analysis, we used an improved k-means-clustering algorithm called *k*-means++. K-means++ first calculates stable cluster centers and then performs the actual clustering.

Austrian *Österreichische Volkspartei* [ÖVP]). In strong contrast to our findings on national elections, however, we also find Green and Social Democratic parties (i.e., the German SPD and the British Labour Party) in this coalition. In national elections, these parties are part of interventionist coalitions on the left. Their change of coalitions in public debates on European integration and globalization issues can be explained by the strong influence of welfare-state issues in national election contests, on the one hand, and by the fact that these parties have been in government in the years under examination, on the other.

2. An *interventionist cosmopolitan coalition* with positive values on the cultural dimension and clearly negative (i.e., interventionist) positions on the economic dimension. This group includes some Green (i.e., the Netherlands and EU) and Social Democratic (i.e., Austria, France, and EU) parties; some social-movement organizations (SMOs) (i.e., Austria, France, and Germany); and the Dutch unions.

3. A *moderate nationalist coalition*, composed mainly of business associations, state actors, Christian Democratic and Conservative parties in the Netherlands, Germany, and France. In addition, we find French and German state actors, the French Liberals, and the British SMOs in this coalition. These actors combine moderately negative positions on the cultural dimension and a moderately interventionist position on the economic dimension.

4. An *interventionist–nationalist coalition* is united in supporting interventionist positions economically and protectionist policies culturally. Values on both dimensions are strongly negative. This coalition includes trade unions (except the Dutch), public-interest groups (including SMOs), the radical left in France and the Netherlands, and the Dutch radical right.

5. A *(neoliberal–)nationalist coalition* composed of the radical right in Austria and France and the Conservative Party and business associations in the United Kingdom. Contrary to our theoretical expectations, this group of actors does not show a clear neoliberal profile, however. The only actor with a clear positive value on this dimension is the British business association. It is obvious that the radical right has been moving toward interventionist positions in recent years and no longer shows positive values on the economic dimension.

Whereas the basic structure of these coalitions is in line with our theoretical expectations – except the discovery of a fifth, moderately nationalist coalition – their composition and strength are quite surprising for several reasons. Most remarkable is the strong population of the interventionist–nationalist corner of the political space. In our analysis of national elections, we found this space rather deserted until the end of the 1990s (Kriesi 2012, 99). Because analyses of the preferences and sociostructural characteristics of the losers of globalization revealed that a substantial share of them is located in this corner, we expected the radical left – unions as well as right-wing populists – moving in this direction (Grande and Kriesi 2012, 22). Our empirical analysis largely confirmed this expectation. In the globalization-related debates of the mid-2000s, this part of the political space was occupied with exactly the actors we expected: unions, the radical left, and a radical-right party. At the same time, the neoliberal–nationalist coalition has been shrinking. The only party with clear negative values on both dimensions is the British Conservative Party, which serves as a functional equivalent to the right-wing populist parties in Continental European countries without sharing their xenophobic attitude. Both the radical right and the Christian Democratic parties have been moving economically to the center of the political space. This seems to indicate that the "winning formula" of radical and populist parties has been changing from neoliberal to protectionist and interventionist economic positions.

The emergence of a moderately nationalist coalition indicates that the mainstream right was receptive to soft forms of nationalism on immigration issues and on European integration in the 2000s (Leconte 2010, 123). The membership of Christian Democratic and Conservative parties in France, Germany, and the Netherlands in this group is surprising at first sight. It is in striking contrast to claims that these parties "are moderately centre-right and pro-European" (Hix and Høyland 2011, 139). However, our analysis of party positions on European integration issues (see Figure 8.2) already has shown that the positions of these parties are moderately negative on European integration overall and that they are strongly negative on enlargement. A detailed analysis of the debate on Turkey's EU membership in Germany and Austria in the period 1995 to 2010 confirms these findings (see Kerscher 2011).

Our analysis of actor constellations also reveals that the radical-right parties – which are part of the (neoliberal–)nationalist coalition, the Austrian FPÖ/BZÖ, and the French FN – are still rather isolated in public debates. No relevant interest group or government actor force-fully supports their radical positions against immigration and Euro-pean integration.[12] The organized critics of globalization – the trade unions and SMOs – can be found mostly in two different cleavage coali-tions: unions in an interventionist–nationalist coalition and SMOs in an interventionist–cosmopolitan coalition. Our analysis also reveals that the critics of neoliberal globalization and European integration from unions and SMOs are clearly detached from the political par-ties with which they were most closely aligned historically (i.e., trade unions with Social Democratic parties and SMOs with Green parties). The most striking cases are unions in Germany and the United King-dom, on the one hand, and the Social Democratic parties, on the other, which we found at completely different places in the political space on these issues.

Regarding the ideological positioning of political parties on the new globalization issues, we see an unraveling of the mainstream party families. In Figure 8.3, party families are represented by light, dotted ellipses. Neither Social Democratic nor Christian Democratic and Con-servative parties consistently belong to the same cleavage coalition. Social Democrats are distributed along the economic axis, whereas Christian Democrats and Conservatives are spread out along the cul-tural axis. Consequently, we find Christian Democratic and Conser-vative parties in three of the five cleavage coalitions, although they dominate the moderate–nationalist coalition. The same holds for the smaller party families (except the radical left), which are quite con-sistent in their positions on the cultural axis but diverge on economic issues.

Overall, these findings indicate that the "demarcation" pole of the new cleavage has not yet been organized by a coherent political coali-tion that forcefully mobilizes the losers of globalization and the critics of European integration. Rather, there are competing cleavage coali-tions, each emphasizing specific nationalist and interventionist aspects

---

[12] In our MDS analysis, only the British business associations are located at the margins of this coalition, although at a clear distance from the radical-right parties.

of the new cleavage. Therefore, the articulation of the new cleavage becomes a matter of competing frames that are supported by different actors and cleavage coalitions.

Thus far, the radical right is most successful in this competition (Mudde 2007). Analyses of the framing of globalization debates show it to be the only political force that consistently articulates the preferences of globalization losers by using nationalistic frames. This is especially apparent in the debate on European integration, in which both economic and cultural sub-issues are at stake. If we omit the Swiss SVP, radical or populist-right parties use the same identity-based argument toward all issues (Helbling et al. 2010). By contrast, the economic logic of articulating and framing the new cleavage is only weakly present in the globalization debate.

The intense national debates on the "boundaries" of the EU – provoked by the decision on membership negotiations with Turkey – are most instructive in this respect (Höglinger 2011; for an overview on the debate in Germany, see Leggewie 2004). In this debate, the question of Turkey's EU membership was transformed into a question of the "cultural identity" of Europe. References to a "common geography," a "common history," and "common values" were made to permanently exclude Turkey from the EU (Risse 2010, 209–20). Turkey served as a symbolic code for the "Islamic East," which was sharply set apart from the "Christian West." In this debate, the populist right was particularly successful in mobilizing the use of identity-based arguments that emphasized the threat of mass immigration and Islamization. The political dangers of this debate are signified not least by the fact that Christian Democratic and Conservative parties, despite their more general pro-European commitment (except the British Conservative Party, of course), are firmly opposed to further EU Enlargement, particularly the accession of Turkey (see Figure 8.2). In short, the mobilization of European citizens on European issues has been achieved most successfully by the critics of the EU and by the defenders of national identity and sovereignty.

Radical-right parties were rewarded particularly in European elections for their anti-European positions. Although their success during the latest European elections was rather mixed across Europe (Hix and Marsh 2007; Minkenberg and Perrineau 2007), these elections provided a favorable political opportunity structure for some of them (e.g., the French FN and the British National Party). With proportional-representation systems in place in all of the EU member states we examined (i.e., Austria, France, Germany, the Netherlands, and the United Kingdom), institutional obstacles are significantly lower in countries such as France and the United Kingdom, where majoritarian electoral systems for a long time have prevented the entry of new challengers into the national parliament.

In addition, the politicization of the European integration process has produced a new type of anti-EU populism, most clearly in Austria and the United Kingdom. In Austria, the *Liste Hans Peter Martin* won 14.0 (2004) and 17.7 (2009) percent in the last two European elections, whereas the UK Independence Party ended up second (ahead of the Liberal Democrats and New Labour) with 16.5 percent of the votes in the last European election in the United Kingdom.[13] These two parties differ from the group of radical-right parties in Europe by taking more moderate positions on immigration issues; however, they share with the radical right a critique of the process of European integration, European institutions, and European policies.

How does the euro crisis fit into this picture?

The euro crisis certainly marks a critical threshold in the European integration process. It has significantly intensified political conflicts on national sovereignty and solidarity. On the one hand, the euro crisis has produced new redistributional conflicts between member states – framed as conflicts between "donor" and "debtor" states in public debates – and within states. On the other hand, the loss of national sovereignty has become a key topic in national debates on the euro crisis. The euro crisis not only has inspired far-reaching plans for further institutional integration, exemplified in debates on the establishment of a new supranational economic authority, which would require a substantial transfer of sovereignty from the member states of (at least) the Eurozone to the EU. Budgetary restrictions and austerity measures imposed, in particular, on so-called debtor states also restricted the budgetary rights of national parliaments. As a result, the euro crisis certainly has contributed to the politicization of the integration process. Europe has become a permanent and highly controversial topic in

---

[13] In the European elections in 1999 and 2004, UKIP won 7.0 percent (1999) and 16.8 percent (2004) of the votes.

212 Part II Consequences

Table 8.3. *Types of actors participating in the debate on the euro crisis compared to the debate on the constitutional treaty (2004–2006) (in percentages)*

Type of actor	Euro crisis	Constitutional treaty (2004–2006)
EU institutional + IMF	**27.7**	4.6
Foreign executive	**38.5**	6.1
National executive	10.9	18.3
Foreign party	7.8	**17.9**
National party	6.2	**35.6**
EU party	1.0	5.7
Others	8.0	11.8
Total	100.0%	100.0%
N	6,865	3,747

public debates. The crucial question, then, is how have these conflicts affected the structure of political conflict that has emerged in the past three decades? Has the euro crisis reinforced the economic dimension of political conflict, thereby reversing previous changes in the structure of political conflict? Has it expanded the scope of actors? Has it reconfigured existing actor constellations? It is not possible to answer all of these questions in full in this chapter. To round off the arguments presented in this chapter, we analyze three aspects on the basis of our data on the public debate on the euro crisis: (1) the types of actors paricipating in this debate, (2) the positions of political parties on the main issues, and (3) the changes in the actor constellations in this debate.[14]

Table 8.3 presents the overall distribution of actors involved in the euro crisis debate (December 2010–March 2012) in comparison with the debate on the Constitutional Treaty (2004–2006). Two results are striking. First, the euro crisis debate was dominated by executive actors to an extraordinary extent. It did not expand the scope of mass

---

[14] Unfortunately, our sample does not include one of the most heavily affected debtor countries (i.e., Greece). Therefore, it does not provide a full picture of the consequences of the euro crisis on the politicization of Europe. For the countries investigated, however, it is highly instructive because it allows comparisons with previous debates and national elections.

politics; rather, it strengthened national and supranational executives. These two types of actor comprise roughly 75 percent of the subjects of our core sentences; all other types of actor play a largely secondary role in this debate. This holds true particularly for political parties, which account for only about one seventh of the actors involved in the debate. This is in striking contrast to the debate on the Constitutional Treaty. In this debate, political parties played the major role, accounting for almost 60 percent of core sentences, whereas executive actors (i.e., supranational and foreign executives in particular) were of minor importance.

Second, the debate is characterized by a high degree of both vertical Europeanization (indicated by the prominence of supranational actors) and horizontal Europeanization (indicated by the prominence of national executives and foreign parties). Supranational actors (including international organizations such as the International Monetary Fund [IMF]) account for more than one quarter of core sentences (27.7 percent). With respect to national executives, it is not domestic executives (10.9 percent) that intervene most frequently in the debate but rather national executives from other countries (38.5 percent). For political parties as well, more than half of the party involvement (7.8 percent) refers to parties of other countries. Hence, the euro crisis debate seems to be absolutely exceptional with regard to its degree of Europeanization.

A more detailed review of the origin of actors (the data are not shown) reveals an important difference between Germany and the other countries. Whereas supranational actors are prominent in all countries, it is only in Germany that they are dwarfed by the national actors. This means that the German debate on the euro crisis was primarily a national debate, whereas in the other countries it was primarily a Europeanized debate dominated by supranational and German actors. It is important that the German national debate involved not only executive actors but also political parties in and out of government. The share of contributions from political parties to the German debate (17.2 percent) almost reached the government's share (19.5 percent). These figures clearly show the "German Europe" (Beck 2012) that has evolved in the course of the euro crisis in both of its meanings: Germany dominating political debates in other countries, on the one hand, and Germany leading a nationally oriented debate, on the other.

Which positions do these actors take on the major issues raised in the euro crisis debate? How controversial are the political measures decided and debated in the course of the euro crisis among the most relevant actors? To answer these questions, we classified the many issues discussed publicly into two major categories: crisis management and structural reforms. With respect to crisis management, we further distinguished between efforts expected to be made at the national level (e.g., a stricter enforcement of national budgetary discipline, calls for bankrupcy of insolvent states, or their exit from the Eurozone) and European efforts. European efforts included all those measures for the stabilization of the financial markets and the European economy that were taken by existing institutions within the preexisting constitutional framework. With regard to structural reforms, we distinguished between policy-related and constitutional issues – between what we call "fiscal deepening" and "institutional deepening." Whereas "fiscal deepening" refers to the introduction and the use of new policy instruments in the field of fiscal and monetary policy at the European level (e.g., "bailout packages", Eurobonds, and the Tobin tax), "institutional deepening" refers to institutional reforms at the European level that are adopted as a direct response to the euro crisis (e.g., fiscal compact, banking union, and proposals for the establishment of a new economic government for the EU). As a general rule, we considered those issues that require the change of treaties or the establishment of new treaties (or international agreements outside of the EU's constitutional framework) as "constitutional issues," whereas we classified a more extensive use of existing treaties in a specific policy area as "policy-related."

The results of our analysis are shown in Figures 8.4, 8.5, and 8.6.[15] Because it is not possible to discuss them in great detail here, we restrict our interpretation to three aspects. First, there seems to be broad consensus among political elites in the donor states on the necessity of national efforts in the debtor states and on the need for economic and financial stability measures at the European level. Although support clearly varies among actors, there are no actors (except the radical left)

---

[15] The dotplots in Figures 8.4, 8.5, and 8.6 represent averages of actors' positioning on issues based on our coding of core sentences. Values ranged from −1 to +1. A value of +1 indicates a fully supportive position on a specific issue.

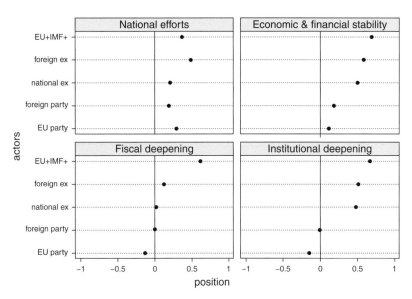

Figure 8.4. Positions of key actor types on sub-issues: mean values.

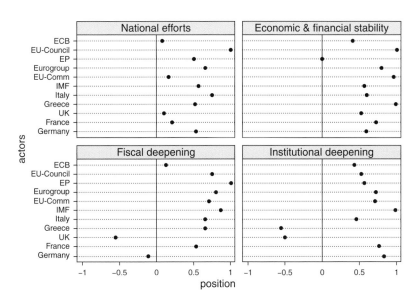

Figure 8.5. Positions of selected supranational actors and national governments on sub-issues: mean values.

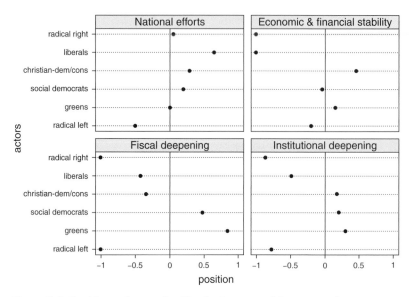

Figure 8.6. Positions of party families in the euro crisis: mean values.

that oppose such measures.[16] Figures 8.4 and 8.5 present an impressive view of the *executive elite consensus* in the euro crisis. Executive elites from supranational institutions and national governments not only take positive positions on measures for crisis management, they also support proposals for institutional and fiscal deepening. However, with regard to the latter, some qualifications are necessary. Most obvious is that by opposing both types of structural reforms, the UK government clearly occupies an outsider position. On institutional deepening, it is only second to the Greek government (although for different reasons); whereas on fiscal deepening, we also found the German government taking a moderately negative position.

Second, there are striking discrepancies between the positions of executive elites and those of political parties. Figure 8.6 shows the the positioning of the most relevant party families on the four issues of the euro crisis debate. Because of the rather small number of core sentences for the smaller parties (the radical left in particular), results should be interpreted with caution in these cases. In particular, with

---

[16] Because of the small number of core sentences, results for the radical left should be interpreted with caution, however.

regard to the structural reforms discussed previously, they are nevertheless quite interesting. If we omit the radical left, we find a left–right opposition that is most pronounced on fiscal deepening. On the one side, we find Social Democratic and Green parties supporting structural reforms, a further transfer of competencies to the EU, and new forms of transnational solidarity. On the other side, there is the radical right but also Liberals opposing them. The Christian Democrats and the Conservatives occupy mixed positions. They support measures for crisis management; however, with regard to institutional reforms, they take a negative position on fiscal deepening, which would imply far-reaching fiscal transfers between countries. In this context, we should consider that the Christian Democratic and Conservative parties were in office in the period of the euro crisis in every country we examined, which suggests a rather pro-integrationist position in general.

Third, a comparison with actor positions on the debates in the mid-2000s reveals that the euro crisis, in fact, has led to some repositioning of political parties on European integration issues. We find the Social Democrats, the Greens, and the radical right in the same position in both debates, and we find them consistently so on "deepening" and "enlargement" in the former debate and on "fiscal deepening" and "institutional deepening" in the latter. The most obvious change has taken place in the case of the Liberals. They were the most pro-European party family in the mid-2000s (with a moderately skeptical position on Eastern Enlargement), whereas they take clearly negative positions on structural reforms in the public debate on the euro crisis. The Christian Democratic and Conservative parties show the same ambiguous position in both debates. They were moderately supportive of "deepening" but firmly critical of further enlargement in the mid-2000s – as they are now on institutional and fiscal deepening, respectively. This seems to indicate that the "relative decline of pro-Europeanism among former federalist Christian Democrats" (Leconte 2010, 125f.), as observed in the mid-2000s, has not been a temporary phenomenon and due to unique issues such as Turkey's EU membership. Rather, it suggests that these parties in the meantime have developed more differentiated and conditional positions on European integration, which also allows them to take critical positions in public debates.

Finally, we turn to actor constellations and analyze how key actors are related to one another. For this analysis, we define the following

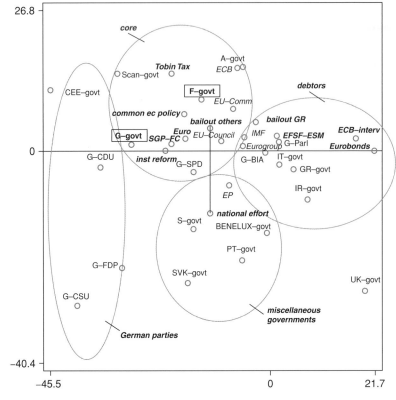

Figure 8.7. Configuration of the most important actors in the euro crisis.

Selected actor abbreviations:
G-CDU, G-CSU, G-FDP, G-SPD (= German parties CDU, CSU, FDP, SDP);
F-govt (= French government); *G-govt* (= German government); *CEE-govt* (=
governments of Central and Eastern European member states); *Scan-govt* (=
governments of Scandinavian EU members states); *GR-govt* (= Greek government); *IT-govt* (= Italian government); *SVK-govt* (= Slovakian government);
EU-Comm (= European Commission).

Selected issue abbreviations:
national effort (= national efforts); *bailout others* (= bailouts of Greece and
of other countries); *EFSF/ESM* (= creation and development of the financial
stabilization mechanism EFSF/ESM); *euro* (= general support for the euro);
SGP/FC (= negotiations of/agreements on the SGP, the Six-Pack, and the Fiscal Compact); *Tobin tax* (= proposition of the Tobin tax); *inst reform* (= a set
of additional institutional reforms); Eurobonds (= proposal of Eurobonds);
and *ECB-interv* (= issues referring to ECB interventions).

issues that cover roughly 75 percent of all the actor-issue sentences. The categories include national efforts, bailouts (of Greece and other countries), creation and development of the financial stabilization mechanism EFSF/ESM, general support for the euro, negotiations of/agreements on the Stability and Growth Pact (SGP) (i.e., the Six-Pack and the Fiscal Compact), proposal for the Tobin tax, and a set of additional institutional reforms, as well as the proposal for Eurobonds and issues referring to European Central Bank (ECB) interventions. We restricted the analysis to actors with at least fifty issue-specific statements on this set of issues. These include all of the major executive actors at the national and supranational levels, the European Parliament (EP), and a set of German actors (the major parties – CDU, CSU, FDP, SPD – as well as the parliament and business-interest associations (BIAs). We included additional German actors because there was a real national German debate, as discussed previously. To reveal the actor configuration, we applied the same MDS procedure as before.

The resulting actor configuration is presented in Figure 8.7. It is two-dimensional and basically represents the two-dimensional political space that we find in EU politics more generally (see Hooghe and Marks 1999, 2009). The opposite poles of the horizontal dimension are support of institutional reforms (SGP, fiscal compact, and other reforms; "inst reform") versus support of ECB interventions and Eurobonds. The vertical dimension distinguishes between efforts taken at the national level, on the one hand, and supranational activities such as bailouts and the Tobin tax, on the other. A cluster analysis of the resulting actors' configuration reveals the following four clusters[17]:

- The core group of national and supranational executive actors ("core") with the governments of the "German–French couple," the EU Commission, and the European Council (including the Council of Ministers). The Austrian and Scandinavian (N, DK, FIN) governments also belong to this group, as does the German SPD. This cluster is in favor of maintaining the euro, the bailout of other member states, and institutional reforms to defend the euro. However,

---

[17] In our analysis of the euro crisis debate, we used the same statistical techniques (i.e., MDS and cluster analysis) as before. Because of different issues and actors, we arrived at different actor constellations. For this reason, possibilities for comparisons with earlier debates are limited.

these actors are against new instruments for fiscal deepening such as
Eurobonds and more far-reaching ECB interventions.
- A "debtor cluster" constituted by the governments of the debtor
  countries (except Portugal) – that is, the governments of Greece,
  Ireland, and Italy; the Eurogroup; and the IMF.[18] This group is
  particularly in favor of additional fiscal measures and instruments
  such as bailouts, the EFSF/ESM, and Eurobonds. This group also
  supports institutional reforms (although with less emphasis).
- The German coalition parties (i.e., CDU, CSU, and FDP) constitute
  a separate cluster (with the governments of the Central and Eastern European [CEE] countries). This cluster provides, at best, tepid
  support for structural reforms, rejects bailouts and further ECB interventions, and was massively opposed to expanding the EFSF/ESM
  and introducing Eurobonds.
- A miscellaneous group of governments (i.e., Sweden, the Benelux
  countries, Slovakia, and Portugal), which also includes the EP. This
  group clearly emphasizes national efforts, although the majority of
  the group also supports the renewal of the SGP.

The British government is an outlier that does not belong to any
of these clusters. If anything, the position of the British government
is even more consistently negative than the position of the German
center-right parties.

The structure of the actors' configuration shows that the politicization of European integration in the euro crisis is the product of several
distinct conflict constellations. The debate over the euro crisis has
mainly reinforced the tensions among member states, which we find
spread across the entire political space. Furthermore, the debate over
the euro crisis has pitted a substantial number of national governments
and supranational actors against one another. This holds true not only
for the UK government but also for the cluster of miscellaneous governments (including the Benelux countries, Sweden, and Portugal) and
the governments of the CEE countries. It has given particular weight
to the "German–French couple." In the period covered (i.e., before the
change in the French presidency), the governments of the two countries maintained a close, positive relationship, which was buttressed
by the positive relationship between their two leading personalities:

---

[18] The German parliament and German business associations surprisingly also
belong to this cluster.

Angela Merkel and Nicolas Sarkozy. Finally, based on the German debate in particular, this analysis also pointed to significant domestic political tensions that have accompanied the tensions among the countries.

The German-actor constellation is very interesting in this regard, not the least because of the dominant role of the German government in the euro crisis. Our analysis reveals the repositioning of the Liberals on European integration issues and the precarious position of the Christian Democratic parties. Two of the coalition parties, the Bavarian Christian Social Union (CSU) and the liberal FDP, are remarkably distant from their own government's position. As a result, the German debate on the euro crisis has not been characterized by the difference between government and opposition. Rather, an informal "grand coalition" of the government (supported by the majority of the CDU) and the SPD was opposed by the CSU and the FDP. We also find this constellation in parliamentary voting on major decisions, in which Chancellor Merkel could not obtain the full support of her coalition partners.

Conclusions: toward a cosmopolitan politicization of Europe?

Our empirical results can be summarized in three points. First, they support our argument that the European integration process has significantly contributed to the emergence of a new demarcation integration (or cosmopolitan–nationalism) cleavage that, in turn, is expected to constitute the structural basis for an intensified and lasting politicization of European integration. Second, the results suggest that the politicization of Europe does not take place along the traditional left–right dimension as assumed, for example, by Simon Hix (2008). Rather, the politicization of Europe appears to be the result of a redefined cultural-conflict dimension. Until the euro crisis, it was the new radical-right parties (and, at elections to the EP, new anti-EU parties) that most actively contributed to this politicization. Third, our findings on the euro crisis do not invalidate these arguments; rather, they allow them to be accentuated. The euro crisis neither reversed existing conflict structures nor produced a completely new one. Instead, the new conflicts on national sovereignty and supranational solidarity were fought

within the existing conflict structures, thereby reproducing and ampli-
fying them. It is most interesting that it did not expand the scope of
actors; rather, it has been narrowing it.

Thus far, the politicization of European integration has not been
caused by the supporters of the European project in the first place, and
it has not taken the shape imagined by them. In election campaigns and
public debates, the critics of European integration and the defenders
of national identity and sovereignty have been significantly more successful in mobilizing European citizens. From a normative perspective
that promotes a "cosmopolitan Europe," the current politicization of
Europe must be interpreted as disappointing, if not frightening.

In such a perspective, an active civil society and strong social
movements are indispensable preconditions for European integration
becoming a cosmopolitan project (Delanty and Rumford 2005; Beck
and Grande 2007, chap. V). If this cosmopolitan politicization is too
weak, the European project is likely to be deformed. Moreover, such
a politicization requires that civil-society actors and organizations
actively constitute the cosmopolitan pole of the new cleavage. Our
empirical analysis of globalization debates (including the European
integration debate) reveals that this was not the case in the past. In
these debates, the cosmopolitan pole was occupied only by a small
group of actors composed mainly of Green parties and a few Social
Democratic parties (e.g., in Germany; see Figure 8.4). Most impor-
tantly, organized civil society (i.e., nongovernmental organizations,
SMOs, and trade unions) is not part of this cosmopolitan coalition
but instead is integrated in separate coalitions. These coalitions clearly
are opposed to the "neoliberal consensus" in the economic dimension.
However, in the cultural dimension – particularly on issues such as a
deepening of European integration and enlargement – the positions of
these coalitions diverge enormously, including radical Euroskeptical
claims. Our empirical findings on the euro crisis show that the crisis –
at least in the donor countries – has not strengthened organized civil
society. In the debate on the euro crisis, civil-society actors were almost
absent; to a remarkable extent, it was dominated by supranational and
national executives. The core group of executive actors was certainly
supportive of further integration, thereby representing a type of *executive cosmopolitanism*. As we can observe in the German case, this
executive cosmopolitanism rests on precarious political ground, however. The euro crisis further alienated at least parts of those parties

(i.e., the Christian Democrats and the Liberals), which were for a long time the strongest supporters of European integration.

Against this background, we assume that the emergence of a European public sphere is a necessary but not a sufficient precondition for a cosmopolitan politicization of the European integration process. As we can see in the euro crisis, the public debate can be dominated by executive actors to a remarkable extent. Moreover, our empirical findings suggest that both the intensity and the course of politicizing Europe will depend on the strength and the composition of the relevant cleavage coalitions at both poles of the new cosmopolitan–nationalist cleavage. In the past two decades, the radical right has demonstrated successfully that it is possible to politicize the European project, thereby making it an object of "mass politics." It is still an open question whether dissatisfaction with the current state of the EU also can be used to strengthen the European integration process.

PART III

Theoretical and normative implications

9 Identity, Europe, and the world beyond public spheres

JEFFREY T. CHECKEL

Europeanized public spheres affect politics.[1] This broad claim is accepted by all of the contributors to this book, even while they disagree on other issues: the precise extent of Europeanization in this area (a little or a lot); the way to measure public spheres (claims, frame, or discourse analysis); where precisely to look for such spheres (among elites and the quality media or a more bottom-up, civil-society view); and – finally – the politics being affected by them (party-political cleavages or identity politics). My purpose here is not to adjudicate among these disputes; the book's opening chapter does an excellent job of highlighting and justifying them while persuasively demonstrating the common ground shared by all (see Chapter 1). Thus, the collection is a state-of-the-art treatment of the subject matter – European public spheres – in the best sense of that phrase: telling the reader what we have learned but also where our knowledge is incomplete or disputed.

My chapter continues with this last point, making three arguments about these loose ends. First, the workings of public spheres are ultimately claims about the ability of language and communication to shape politics. Elsewhere, however, such linguistic approaches have been supplemented by analysts arguing that institutions, power, and practice are important as well; a similar move seems absent in work on public spheres (see Chapter 8). The result is incomplete arguments – for example, on the relationship of public spheres to changes in European identity.

Second, how well do arguments on European public spheres stand up cross-nationally? Within Europe this may be an issue, especially if we take Eastern Enlargement seriously.

Third, having established that Europeanized public spheres matter, future work needs to go a step further, exploring how much

---

[1] For comments on earlier drafts, I thank the project participants, Onur Bakiner, Martha Snodgrass, and, especially, Thomas Risse.

they matter. This will involve both a substantive and methods/design move. On the former, the implications of the euro/sovereign-debt crisis, which began in 2009, need to be addressed because they likely will weaken the causal force of Europeanized public spheres. On the latter, the challenge will be to establish baselines and relative weightings, to think counterfactually, and to craft more ambitious research designs.

Stated differently, this chapter is a modest attempt at mainstreaming findings on European public spheres through the perception of an outsider who has done considerable work on Europe but none per se on the subject at hand. How well do arguments about public spheres stand up when placed in a broader theoretical-empirical-methodological frame? Asking and offering answers to these questions can contribute to the all-important task of better specifying the scope conditions of the claims advanced in this book.

Public spheres and politics

This book views Europeanized public spheres as both dependent and independent variables. In Part I (see Chapters 2–5), they are the outcome or product, and we want to know what produces them – and how they might be measured. In Part II (see Chapters 6–8), contributors explore what public spheres cause or make possible. My concern is that the theory in both parts is underspecified in important ways; as a result, the politics from which public spheres emerge and to whose development they contribute lacks teeth.

First, one effect of public spheres in general and Europeanized public spheres in particular is to facilitate democratic politics. This is a strong claim advanced throughout the book; it is also not very controversial.[2] As Risse argues, a public sphere informs citizens about the political process, monitors and critically evaluates governance, and enables a public discourse in a democracy (Risse 2010, 108). No one asserts that public spheres cause or produce politics; rather, the more nuanced argument is that they act like an intervening variable.

---

[2] Although as Follesdal notes (see Chapter 10), it is a claim with a wrinkle because the contributors embrace two quite different conceptions of democracy – one emphasizing deliberative consensus and one more focused on political contestation.

The theoretical problem or gap is the implicit conceptualization of those democratic politics that Europeanized public spheres help to foster. For some contributors (see Chapters 4 and 7), it is an understanding of politics as communication, discourse, and deliberation. Yet, if a central goal of this book is to bring politics back in, then we need to consider other facets of it. Politics – in Europe or anywhere – is also about institutions, power, and daily lived practice. What is its role in shaping Europeanized public spheres? With regard to institutions, several chapters indeed view the media as an institution, one that both reflects and shapes public discourse (see Chapters 1, 2, and 7).

More could be discussed about this institutional factor, however. If one views Europeanized public spheres as the dependent variable, it is quite likely that the varying structure of domestic institutions across Europe would crucially affect their shape, form, and content. Here, I am not so much thinking of the media but rather the broader domestic institutional context in which it is embedded. Indeed, an older literature on domestic structures (Katzenstein 1976) predicted cross-national variation in process and outcomes as a function of the structure of political institutions – statist, liberal, and corporatist, for example. These arguments would help to make sense of the finding by Bennett, Lang, and Segerberg (see Chapter 5) that national-level issue networks in Germany – contrary to expectations – engage citizens more weakly than their EU-level counterparts. The answer to this puzzle lies in the "institutional incorporation of core civil-society" (see Chapter 5, p. 110, in this volume) – that is, within its corporatist domestic structure.

Institutions also may serve as amplifiers. Perhaps in particular countries, there are powerful organizations that promote a certain type of claims making (see Chapter 3) or discursive frames (see Chapter 4) that are then picked up by the media, eventually appearing in the public sphere. Consider two examples. In Turkey, the military has played a central role in politics for many years, albeit one that has weakened more recently. Could a Europeanized public sphere in Turkey thus be influenced by frames embedded in and promoted by it? In Scandinavia, gender equality seems hard wired into the social fabric of the countries. Would the content of Norway's or Sweden's Europeanized public sphere, therefore, not be shaped by gender's deep institutionalization in both discourse and public institutions?

The argument is simply that claims, frames, discourses, *and* institutions will be a stronger force than when the former act alone. This is a central finding among students of historical institutionalism (Sikkink 1991; Steinmo, Thelen, and Longstreth 1992), as well as proponents of more interpretive institutional analysis (Hopf 2012). In fact, my point is similar to the one made by Risse many years ago regarding the ideas literature, when he argued that ideas do not float freely (Risse-Kappen 1994); the same holds for public spheres.

It is also possible that national institutions cooperate across borders to foster islands of interaction that create their own frames and communities of understanding. These may support or undercut those generated by the media. We know that the EU has facilitated cross-border institutional connections and communities of this type (Fligstein 2008), and it may well be that they influence the formation and content of public spheres. In fact, this is precisely the conclusion of Bennett, Lang, and Segerberg, which looks beyond the quality media to analyze emerging Europeanized public spheres (see Chapter 5 in this volume). Stated differently, for future work to build constructively on this book's findings, we need to bring not only politics back in but institutions as well.

Regarding power, students of the EU and Europeanization often underestimate its importance. This book seems to be of two schools on the role of power. On the one hand, several contributors directly consider – in a theoretical sense – its role. The introduction, for example, offers a careful and nuanced discussion of the power asymmetries and structural power shaping public spheres (see Chapter 1). As Risse notes, the so-called selectivity of public spheres – that is, who can speak and who is allowed to listen – is partly a function of asymmetries in (personal) power. At a structural level, the power of media empires clearly also plays a role in shaping this selectivity (see Chapter 1).

It also matters whose media empire we speak about; some are simply much stronger in a material and financial sense. As Pfetsch and Heft argue in their theoretical overview of European public spheres, "communication patterns within Europe depend on the size and power of a country, thereby determining the transnational hierarchy of influence on news geography and flows of opinion" (see Chapter 2, p. 48, in this volume). These analyses help us to better understand public spheres as outcome and product – and the role of power in the process.

Unfortunately, contributors to the book too often fail to build on such insights in their own empirical explorations. For example, Kantner's analysis of the emergence of transnationalized discourse arenas in Europe is oddly silent on power (see Chapter 4). Yet, the very discourses and frames that she studies are often the product of clever, strategic individuals who exploit their personal skills and organizational power to make individual beliefs become collectively held frames, as demonstrated by the literature on norm entrepreneurs (Barnett and Finnemore 2004).

In their methodologically sophisticated exploration of media and European identity, Harrison and Bruter argue and document (experimentally) that good news about Europe is good news for European identity. Building on this finding, they then argue that there is a significant "scope for impact [on European identity] of any potential genuine information on Europe (e.g., through civic education)" (see Chapter 7, p. 185, in this volume). Yet, the reality of politics – in Europe as anywhere – is that such information will be distorted by individuals in positions of power, institutions with agendas of their own, and media empires, to name only a few. Without attention to such variables, the analysis seems more oriented to an (unreachable) normative ideal than to the day-to-day reality of a deeply politicized European project.

Let me be clear: by "power," I do not refer specifically to how a realist international relations scholar might understand the term; rather, my more mundane point is that power is always present in politics. This power can be material; it can be social (i.e., the disciplining power of dominant discourses); and it may operate through institutions (Barnett and Duvall 2005). The latter understanding of how power works should be especially relevant in a deeply institutionalized Europe.

Do EU institutions – in collaboration with or in opposition to national institutions – use their institutional power to privilege certain discourses and frames? Reaching back to a very old public-policy literature (Bachrach and Baratz 1962, 1963), we could ask whether these institutions have a critical power of non-decision and non-agenda setting – a power that might decisively shape the content of public spheres. They clearly have the financial wherewithal and willingness to affect the nongovernmental (NGO) sector, which, in turn, is influencing the content of public spheres (see Chapter 5).

Perhaps power in these multiple forms does not matter. However, it is best to rule it out through theoretical specification and empirical testing rather than through neglect or assumption. Otherwise, there is a risk of developing Euro centric arguments on public spheres that work only as applied to the European Union (EU) in Western Europe (see Chapter 8), as happened in earlier work on socialization (Checkel 2007).

If we now shift the focus and view Europeanized public spheres as independent variables, it is here that the book offers its most intriguing and, I argue, theoretically underspecified arguments. Consider the following statements:

It is in public debate that collective identities are constructed and reconstructed and publicly displayed, thereby creating political communities. (See Chapter 2, p. 30, in this volume)

[The public sphere is] a setting for communication and participation in collective action that can shape identities and interests, not only reflect them. (see Chapter 5, p. 114, in this volume)[3]

These arguments considerably surpass the idea that Europeanized public spheres facilitate a more democratic politics at the EU level. Now, they are exerting causal force on deep social structures: the identities of European actors.

This book is not alone in making such claims. Indeed, there is abundant evidence that identities and senses of identification in Europe are in flux – evidence that is all the more compelling because it comes from multiple disciplinary perspectives utilizing different methodological tools (Bruter 2005; Favell 2008; Fligstein 2008; Checkel and Katzenstein 2009b; Risse 2010). That Europeanized public spheres also would be playing a role makes intuitive sense. Such spheres are arenas of communication, and we know from a now well-developed constructivist literature that communication, language, and discourse can shape identities (Adler 2013).

Yet, theoretically, this is a rather narrow understanding of the processes that may influence identity. Indeed, I argue that one must engage other types of arguments to specify better the scope conditions for the book's public-sphere identity claims and to build a more integrated

---

[3] Calhoun 2003, 4.

understanding of the mechanisms shaping identity in contemporary Europe.

The starting point – to repeat the obvious – is Europeanized public spheres. They comprise one site in which collective identities emerge; this is a consensus view in the book, as the previous quotations suggest. Thus, to explain a change or evolution in European identity, a role must be accorded to public discourses, public spheres, communicative practices, communicative spaces, and communities of communication (see also Risse 2010, 5, 11, 63, 107, 168). I intentionally use the phrases "one site" and "a role" because no one claims that Europeanized public spheres carry all of the causal weight in shaping identities; rather, the challenge is better to specify and delimit their role.

In this regard, there are three issues to consider. First, without further specification, the argument resembles an old one from social psychology – that is, the contact hypothesis – in which communication and personal interactions produce a greater sense of group identification. However, most scholars now recognize that the hypothesis fails when we move from the laboratory-experimental setting of social psychology to the real world of politics, in the EU or elsewhere. In particular, whereas the *quantity* of contact does play a role, considerably more decisive is its *quality* (Beyers 2005). That is, deliberative settings, dominated by arguing and persuasion, are more likely to promote greater identification with the group. Thus, contributors to this book who embrace a Habermasian perspective may be on to something (see Chapter 4) because it emphasizes the importance of deliberative dynamics. Yet, even in this case, we would need to document not only the amount of deliberative communication; rather, the (empirical-methodological) challenge would be to look inside these Europeanized public spheres, searching for observable implications of possible identity change.

Second, it is equally plausible that identity change is produced not via communication among elites but rather by the daily lived experience and social practice of those same elites. From such a practice perspective, "it is not only who we are that drives what we do; it is also what we do that determines who we are" (Pouliot 2010, 5–6; see also Neumann 2002; Adler and Pouliot 2011). Perhaps those same individuals who have a European identity "lite" (Risse 2010) go to the beaches of southern Spain and – through daily practice – re-create their own national communities by establishing Norwegian (or German or British – choose your nationality) schools, by producing local editions of national newspapers or by constructing gated communities of co-nationals.

Such lived experience may undercut feelings of identification with Europe, even in the most likely case of young, upwardly mobile, well-educated Europeans. This is precisely the dynamic that Favell (2008, 2009) masterfully documents in his sociological-anthropological study of identity (non-)change among young European professionals in Brussels, Amsterdam, and London. Favell's findings are supported by studies of the Erasmus student-exchange program, with students reporting they never feel so Dutch (or German, or Polish . . .) as when they temporarily move abroad (Wilson 2011).[4]

My point is not to claim that social practice will always trump social communication as a mechanism of European identity formation. Rather, by engaging the broader literature on identity change, this book can sharpen its own arguments, better specifying the scope conditions for when social communication and Europeanized public spheres will matter. Most likely, this will be a case in which it is not either/or but rather both/and (Checkel 2013). That is, we will need to theorize social communication and social practice, as well as their interaction, if we want fully to understand changing identities and their relationship to Europeanized public spheres (see also Checkel and Katzenstein 2009b).

Third, an emphasis on identity change as occurring – at least partly – through social communication in public spheres all too easily can lead us to view such processes in nonviolent terms. Yet, in many other contexts (e.g., professional militaries, urban gangs, and rebel groups in civil war) and regions (e.g., the Middle East and Serbia under Milošević) identity change results from intimidation, hazing, violence, rape, and death (Wood 2008, 2010; Cohen 2013; see also Checkel 2011, 14–15). It may be the case that none of these dynamics is at work in contemporary Europe or, if present, they have little impact on the communities of communication forming in public spheres.

---

[4] More recently, Wilson's findings have been called into question by Stoeckel (2012). Both study Erasmus students and both use surveys and panel studies to examine changing patterns of identification, yet they come to nearly opposite conclusions! The broader lesson here may be the inability of survey instruments to measure identity reliably.

However – and to repeat my previous concern – this must be established empirically and not simply assumed away.

To summarize, this book makes powerful and innovative claims both on how transnationalized/Europeanized public spheres are being constructed and their impact on European politics and society. At the same time, new arguments – at least in their initial specification and testing – often over-reach theoretically and underperform in terms of research design. Future work easily can rectify the former by considering additional factors shaping and interacting with public spheres; I suggest several in this discussion.

On design, follow-on studies should be crafted explicitly to examine cases in which Europeanized public spheres fail to form; such non-events can help scholars to move a step further analytically, specifying the scope conditions of their arguments. In a partial move in this direction, several contributors compare European public spheres to national ones (see Chapters 3 and 5). This is an excellent strategy; in future work, it should be the norm and not the exception.

Public spheres and the borders of Europe

Are Europeanized public spheres coterminous with the borders of the old EU-15? Stated differently, how and in what ways do the 2004 and 2007 enlargements affect the arguments in this book about public spheres? One answer is that it is still too early to determine. Researchers are only now beginning to extend their media databases to the new member states (Diez Medrano 2009).

Still, it seems odd that most contributors to the book focus empirically on an entity – the EU-15 – that is no more.[5] Where will Europeanized public spheres stop? Will they eventually include the new Eastern European member states? What about European states – for example, Turkey, Ukraine, and Russia – with little chance of EU membership? Will the public spheres in these countries nonetheless be Europeanized through their partial association with the EU and its institutions?

[5] The exception is Kantner, whose data on Poland were only partly available for analysis (see Chapter 4). Two other chapters contain brief mentions of the new member states but only to summarize others' data (see Chapters 1 and 2).

Although some work on Europeanization has begun to theorize and collect data on the new member states (Schimmelfennig and Sedelmeier 2005), in many other cases we are left essentially with stories and data about Western Europe (Favell 2008; Fligstein 2008; Checkel and Katzenstein 2009b; Risse 2010). So, without hard data, what are the theoretical expectations for how inclusion of these missing Europeans might affect arguments about Europeanization or Europeanized public spheres? I see two possibilities: modernization and the return of history and domestic context.[6]

The modernization story predicts more of the same. That is, the partial Europeanization of public spheres seen in Western Europe and documented in this book will continue in the new member states. There may be some delay but, as the various mechanisms of Europeanization kick in – whether judicial (European Court of Justice rulings), legal (the *acquis*), material (structural adjustment funds), or normative (diffusion of models and standards) – we will see similar patterns emerge in Eastern Europe. The future is the past. The book's main theoretical chapter explicitly adopts this perspective, arguing that "in the course of time, differences in the Europeanization of old and new member states seem to vanish" (see Chapter 2, p. 45, in this volume).

I call this the "modernization story" because it basically sees the EU as a great development machine, wearing down and making more similar all member states. Everyone does not become the same – the Europeanization literature has never made such a claim – but partial Europeanization continues apace. This is a theory of Europeanization in which greater weight is placed on the European level.

The history and domestic-context story predicts a sharper break with current trends. Historically, the new member states have had a different relationship to Europe; they have unique historical memories that will not be Europeanized away (Case 2009). Religion (i.e., Catholicism and Orthodoxy) plays a different and more powerful role than in Western Europe, adding a confessional element to politics and processes of identification (Byrnes and Katzenstein 2006, *passim*; Checkel and Katzenstein 2009b, chaps. 1, 9). Stated differently,

---

[6] In the following discussion, my focus is on the new member states in Central and Eastern Europe. Although I may refer to the older members as the "EU-15" and the like, I am well aware that both historically (e.g., Germany and the United Kingdom) and at present (e.g., Northern Europe and Germany versus Southern Europe), important differences exist within Western Europe as well.

Eastern Enlargement has amplified the roles played by history and religion in the EU (see also Risse 2010, 209–13); the future is not the past. This is a theory of Europeanization in which, in the interaction between the European and national levels, the primary causal weight is with the latter. No other contributor to this book shares this view of Europeanization.[7]

Of course, either theory could be correct; the test will come as each is operationalized and assessed against new data. Furthermore, for this test to be fair, the data must come from at least two sources. One will be an extension of the sophisticated claims (see Chapter 3), discursive-framing (see Chapter 4), and panel studies (see Chapter 7) on display in this book. They capture the communicative and linguistic dimensions. However, equally important will be data collected from sociological-anthropological fieldwork because this will highlight the role of daily practice in also shaping European politics, public spheres, and identities (Favell 2008; Checkel and Katzenstein 2009b, chap. 1; Holmes 2009).

After these new data are collected and the dust settles, my own sense is that the second story will get it more right. Domestic politics matters as never before in relation to the EU. This is true in Western Europe, where Risse (2010; see also Chapter 6 in this volume) and others (Hooghe and Marks 2009; see also Chapter 8 in this volume) note the growing trend toward politicization of all things EU. It is true in Eastern Europe as well, with the added twist of different domestic contexts (see previous discussion). Over time, the EU clearly will interact with and possibly change historical memories and consciousness in the new member states. This is not an either/or situation. However, this will be a slow process, one that is even less linear than seen in Western Europe in the post-World War II period.[8]

If I am correct, this has implications for Europeanized public spheres as both dependent and independent variables. On the former, their construction will become more complicated because the media structures, politics, and domestic institutions of the new member states are different. It is true that the latter likely will see an increase in reporting on EU matters – indeed, it is already happening (see Chapter 2); however,

---

[7] However, two chapters highlight the importance of domestic politics in Western Europe (see Chapters 3 and 8).

[8] Thanks go to Thomas Risse for discussions on this point.

this will be refracted through a new – that is, not Western European – domestic context.

A central finding of this book is that the Europeanized public spheres we see today are partial and operate mainly if not entirely at the elite level; they coexist and, in many cases, are still dominated by their national counterparts (see Chapters 1, 3, and 5). They are a "fragile and fluid phenomenon" (see Chapter 2, p. 51, in this volume). If it took more than 55 years to attain this outcome among the old EU-15 in Western Europe, then the addition of twelve new member states – nearly all from a very different part of the Continent – at a minimum, will not lead to any acceleration of Europeanization in this area.

What about the causal effect of Europeanized public spheres – post-enlargement – on other aspects of European politics? On the one hand, politicization likely will continue apace. Contributors to this book, looking at Western Europe, are unanimous in this conclusion; the addition of member states from Central and Eastern Europe (CEE) should not change the general trend. However, these same contributors are divided when it comes to interpreting the results of this politicization.

Risse (see Chapter 6) is cautiously optimistic, whereas Grande and Kriesi (see Chapter 8) warn that opponents of integration are best positioned to exploit the new discursive possibilities offered by politicization and Europeanized public spheres. A key fact behind this difference is empirical domain, with Risse considering the EU and Europeanization and Grande and Kriesi including broader globalization dynamics. The latter – structural – force has produced new "cleavage coalitions," which have been exploited most successfully by Euroskeptic parties of the populist right (see Chapter 8, p. 191, in this volume). With the CEE countries fully exposed to these forces of globalization and denationalization (Zürn 2013) since at least the end of the Cold War, we might expect similar (and new) cleavage coalitions in these countries as well. Thus, Eastern Enlargement not only continues the process of politicization but also does so in a way that is likely further to strengthen opponents of the EU.[9]

---

[9] To be clear: This is my extrapolation of the Grande and Kriesi argument; their empirical data cover only Western Europe.

Moving beyond politicization, how might Eastern enlargement affect the ability of Europeanized public spheres to craft a sense of collective identification with Europe? On the one hand, as I argue above, Eastern Enlargement will increase politicization, or at least not slow it in any way. As Risse explains in Chapter 6, politicization and the growth of Europeanized public spheres means "debating European issues as *European* questions"; in turn, this is "likely to increase political identification levels with the EU" (see Chapter 6, p. 156, in this volume; emphasis in the original).

On the other hand, as suggested in the previous section, this is a rather top-down view of identity formation. It still may help to create a European identity lite – even in an enlarged EU – among a small cross-section of the elite. However, this top-down dynamic now will interact with additional types of bottom-up processes in the new member states, where historical memory and religion may craft different senses of identification. Even if history and religion do not matter, time will still play a role. The extent of Europeanization for those joining in 2004 (or 2007) inevitably will be – at least in the near term – less than for states that joined the EU many decades ago. Thus, in the short term (and perhaps longer), the overall effect will be a diminished role for Europeanized public spheres in the shaping of collective identification with Europe.

In summary, where we draw the borders of Europe has significant implications for both the operation and causal effects of Europeanized public spheres. For a Europe defined as the old EU-15, this book demonstrates beyond any doubt that something is happening. That is, public spheres – at least among elites – indeed are being Europeanized, creating new transnational communities of communication. For an EU of twenty-seven – that is, the EU existing today after the 2004 and 2007 enlargements – any conclusions are heavily constrained by data limitations. However, empirical extrapolation and theoretical logic suggest that, in this new EU, the construction of and effects wrought by Europeanized public spheres will be slower and weaker.

How much do public spheres really matter?

In this final section, I address two separate but related issues: (1) What are the cutting-edge challenges for future work on European public spheres? and (2) Will there be anything left to study after the euro/

sovereign-debt crisis eventually runs its course? First, if this book has shown that public spheres matter, then the challenge for future work is to develop metrics, designs, and methodological strategies to understand better how much they matter. If previous sections were criticisms of what the book has accomplished (or omitted), then my comments here are more forward-looking. If we think in terms of research programs, then the scholarship on European public spheres represents a maturing one. This typically means that the next steps are a mix of greater theoretical specification, sharper research designs, and more attention to methods – all in the service of obtaining answers to those "how much" questions.

In this regard, follow-on studies usefully could address four issues. First, we need explicit attention to and justification of baselines (see Chapters 1 and 10). To what are Europeanized public spheres being compared? National public spheres? Some ideal from political theory? The book begins to address this issue but more needs to be done.

In particular, Koopmans's approach – to compare national and European structures of political communication – should be replicated. As he notes, an important reason why debates about the Europeanization of public spheres have remained inconclusive is that "a standard of comparison is lacking" (see Chapter 3, p. 54, in this volume). Koopmans provides such a standard by theorizing and measuring, in similar ways, both the Europeanization of political communication and, within countries, its nationalization. This then allows him to compare directly "the structure of communication within national and European arenas, thereby putting our assessments of the (in)sufficiency of current degrees and forms of Europeanization on a more solid footing" (see Chapter 3, p. 55, in this volume). From a research-design perspective, this type of comparison would seem essential; unfortunately, only one other contribution – by Bennett, Lang, and Segerberg on civil-society networks (see Chapter 5) – adopts a similar approach.

That missing standard is why readers of this book will have difficulty interpreting the conclusions reached by its contributors and the degree to which they are comparable. How to compare, for example, Koopmans's nuanced, contextualized bottom line on the extent of Europeanized public spheres (see Chapter 3) with Kantner's finding of considerably more Europeanization in her study of transnational discourse arenas in the area of humanitarian interventions (see Chapter 4)? Part of the difficulty in making relative assessments is Kantner's lack of a national baseline in Europe. There is a baseline of sorts in her study, but it is measured by newspaper articles in the United States.

In fairness to Kantner, this criticism is somewhat misplaced. Her study is not only about the empirical measurement of Europeanized public spheres; it also has a strong normative element, in which it is more the very possibility of such public spheres and their implication for a more democratic European politics that matters (see Chapter 4). From this perspective, establishing the precise extent to which national public spheres still play a role (i.e., Koopmans's concern) is of less importance.

Second, to explore and fully understand the impact of Europeanized public spheres, we need a sense of relative weightings. For example, in their cleverly crafted panel study, Harrison and Bruter (see Chapter 7) show that news and images drawn from Europeanized media influence individual identity. This is an important finding but, at the same time, it begs the question of the degree to which media exposure – as opposed to other factors – is driving identity change.[10] We know from a rich and multidisciplinary literature that identities are shaped by a variety of forces, including media and communication (e.g., this book), structural economic flows (Favell 2009), schools and churches (Dawson and Prewitt 1969), national militaries (Winslow 1999), and – in many cases – violence and intimidation (Vigil 2003; Stretesky and Pogrebin 2007).

Given this multitude of forces shaping any individual's identity, the challenge for Harrison and Bruter (and certainly for many others) is to explore how much identity change results from media exposure as compared to these other factors. My strong suspicion is that media-driven change is being swamped by other mechanisms, many of which are anchored in powerful and deeply institutionalized national organizations (Checkel 2007, chap. 8).

Another related way to think about the analytic challenges described herein is to develop scope conditions for arguments about the causal effects of Europeanized public spheres. That is, what are the conditions under which an argument is likely to hold? Returning to the study by Harrison and Bruter, a crucial – albeit essentially implicit – scope

---

[10] Controlling for prior identities, which Harrison and Bruter carefully do (see Chapter 7), is not the same as considering the impact of other factors driving identity change.

condition for media-driven change in identity would appear to be the intensity of exposure. Almost in passing (and at the end of their chapter), the authors note that participants in their two-year panel study were "exposed to more news on Europe than the average European throughout an entire lifetime" (see Chapter 7, p. 185). Without such intense and high-volume exposure, I suggest, the argument relating media to identity change does not hold.

In Chapter 6, Risse thinks quite explicitly in terms of scope conditions, an intelligent move that allows him to nuance and delimit his claims. In particular, he advances two "scope conditions under which the Europeanization of public spheres is likely to increase the sense of community among Europeans" (see Chapter 6, p. 155, in this volume). For one, he argues that framing matters: "good news about the EU is good news for identity" (see Chapter 6, p. 155; see also Chapter 7). However – and following on the previous discussion – this might be more aptly phrased *lots* of good news about the EU is good news for identity, given the need for significant exposure.

Risse's other scope condition is somewhat unclear because it seems to override the first. In particular, he argues that whether or not the EU is portrayed in good or bad terms, the very act of "debating European issues as *European* questions . . . is also likely to increase political identification levels with the EU" (see Chapter 6, p. 156, in this volume; emphasis in original). This is intriguing, but the theoretical logic is unclear and no supporting empirical studies are cited, in contrast to his discussion of the first scope condition. Moreover, Risse concludes the analysis by noting that such debates may be part of a virtuous or vicious circle, with the latter leading to a "de-Europeanization of public spheres and their renationalization" (see Chapter 6, p. 156). Which, then, will it be and under what conditions?

Third, work on public spheres needs to ask the counterfactual question: Without the emergence of Europeanized public spheres, would the outcomes of interest – politics, collective identification with Europe – be any different? Counterfactuals are thought experiments; asking and answering them does not prove anything. In this sense, they are a forward-looking exercise: How could we design future research to deal with the issues they raise? As a case in point, we can take Europeanized public spheres and identity in Europe and ask the counterfactual. Without any such public spheres, would the outcome – the tentative emergence of a European identity lite – be any different?

Contributors to this book likely would answer "Yes, the outcome would be different; Europeanized public spheres have had a discernible causal impact on people's identification with Europe." I would answer "No, the outcome would be the same because there are other factors at work: strategic efforts by the EU to craft such an identity, social practice and lived experience, the creation of small horizontal communities of common identification à la Fligstein (2008) – producing the same outcome, a European identity lite."

Where does this leave us? Having thought counterfactually, the contributors and I likely would agree that the outcome was overdetermined, with multiple mechanisms at work, all contributing to the same result: the creation of a secondary sense of identification with Europe. The challenge in follow-on research would be to think at an early point of research designs that could better address such causal complexity, or to use methodological tools such as process tracing (Bennett and George 2005, chap. 10; Bennett and Checkel 2014, chap. 1), qualitative comparative analysis (Ragin and Rihoux 2009), or agent-based modeling (Nome and Weidmann 2013) that could better disentangle the competing mechanisms.

My arguments here, it should be noted, resonate with those of Pfetsch and Heft. Whereas they are looking more at the input side – what contributes to the growth of Europeanized public spheres – their advice is the same: that is, a greater focus on research design in future work (see Chapter 2).

Fourth – and another point about design – we need designs that are less EU-centric, and especially less EU-15-centric. This simply reiterates a call for studies that include all EU member states, including the twelve new ones added since 2004. Yes, these more ambitious designs must await the collection of data in the new members – data, as argued previously, that should come from surveys and panel studies as well as techniques more informed by sociology and anthropology. This interdisciplinary mix of techniques offers more powerful answers to central questions, whether about politics more generally (Schatz 2009) or the creation and effects of Europeanized public spheres.

More ambitiously, designs would extend beyond the EU and Europeanization, which would sharpen our arguments on Europeanized public spheres as both independent and dependent variables. On the latter – and as Grande and Kriesi argue and document (see Chapter 8) – the politicization that many contributors to this book see as an enabling condition of Europeanized public spheres is also empowering new domestic political actors and cleavages who are no advocates of the integration process. Spurred by the workings of longer-term globalization dynamics, their (negative) role would be missed if we focused only on the effects of Europeanization.

Regarding Europeanized public spheres as the independent variable, scholars need to learn the same lesson as those studying European identity: the EU is not "the only game in town" (Favell 2008; Checkel and Katzenstein 2009b). Europeanized public spheres play some role in shaping senses of identification in Europe; this is an important finding of this book. Yet, "some role" will remain vague and under-specified until research is specifically designed to capture the multiple causal factors shaping identity on the Continent.

Perhaps, however, the foregoing – a set of suggestions for how future work on Europeanized public spheres can sharpen its designs and findings – is not necessary. That is, we will not need more studies about them because none will exist after the euro/sovereign-debt crisis runs its course. At some point, the "Angela Merkel is Hitler" and "all Greeks are corrupt thieves" discourse will rupture and undermine Europe's emergent transnationalized arenas of communication. This is certainly not a view to which contributors of this book subscribe. Indeed, as Risse argues conceptually (see Chapter 1) and as Koopmans documents empirically (see Chapter 3), the increasing politicization of all things EU caused by the euro crisis, at a minimum, is not undermining and perhaps may be further strengthening Europeanized public spheres.

With two caveats, I concur with these findings. First, and at risk of sounding like a broken record, an EU of twenty-seven is likely different in many ways from an EU of fifteen. Until we have systematic data that include the new member states when exploring the euro crisis/politicization/public-sphere nexus, all conclusions must remain tentative. For example, Koopmans's extension of his data to cover the euro crisis unfortunately is limited only to Germany (see Chapter 3).

Second, this same process of intense politicization – along with continuing, broader, global dynamics – is empowering new political forces and actors in Europe (see Chapter 8). When we ask what Europeanized public spheres cause or make possible, these new dynamics mean that such spheres face increasingly tough competition. The causal relationship of Europeanized public spheres to identity – to consider just one example – will be further weakened by the euro crisis, as new actors offer their own, often countervailing, views on European identity (Checkel and Katzenstein 2009b).

In summary, "bringing politics back in" to the study of public spheres, which is both this book's central goal and its main achievement, suggests that the euro crisis may be simultaneously strengthening transnational arenas of communication while empowering new forces that will limit those same arenas' influence.

Conclusions

This book demonstrates that Europeanized public spheres affect politics, which is no small feat – especially in an era when the euro/sovereign-debt crises have highlighted the continuing centrality of power, political leadership, and material interests in the European project. As the opening chapters argue, vibrant public spheres are an essential prerequisite of democratic politics, including those in the EU (see Chapters 1 and 2). Most of the remaining chapters – using diverse analytic starting points and different methodologies and examining a range of issue areas and actors – then go on to show that transnational communication in Europe is occurring. From the standpoint of normative-democratic theory, the book has done its job, documenting that a crucial ingredient of a more democratic EU exists and is (slowly) growing.

If we move from the realm of normative to problem-solving theory, then here the book also delivers, with a core argument that is both powerful and succinct. Simply stated, it is language – transnationalized communication, in this case – that helps to shape the world around us. This is a refreshing formulation for students of integration, one that frees our thinking about Europe and its future from older theoretical debates – neofunctionalism versus intergovernmentalism as the most obvious. Certainly, Risse and collaborators offer no general theory of their own to explain the broad workings of public spheres and their relationship to the integration process. However, the days of grand theorizing – whether about Europe or more generally – seem to be over (Sil and Katzenstein 2010a, 2010b; Checkel 2013).

Yet, at the same time, the book is less successful in theorizing at a level below grand, general theories – that is, in articulating a partial, middle-range (George 1993) framework for explaining Europeanized public spheres. To understand fully how, whether, and under which conditions public spheres shape politics – questions at the heart of middle-range and problem-solving theory – the core argument will need further specification.

At a minimum, this will require greater attention to institutions, power, and daily practice. Institutions matter in at least two ways: (1) the media as an often powerful institution (e.g., media conglomerates); and (2) how different structures of political institutions across countries can lead to differential input into public spheres. Power also plays two roles: (3) the traditional role of differentials in material power; and (4) institutional power, where institutions work to privilege certain discourses and frames that subsequently are rearticulated in public spheres. Finally, daily practice is (5) an additional arena in which activities and behaviors may counter dynamics playing out in Europeanized public spheres. Of these five factors, the book addresses (1) and (3) but chiefly in the introductory and theory chapters (see Chapters 1 and 2); only (1) is addressed in the empirical essays and then in only one instance (see Chapter 7).

Beyond theory, further work on design and method will sharpen analytic claims about Europeanized public spheres by delimiting their scope. If this discussion sounds like a call for a normal science of research on public spheres, then readers will have interpreted correctly my fundamental bottom line. In stating this, I realize that work on public spheres has a strong normative and – for some – critical-theory element to it; this is necessary and welcome. Yet, greater attention to problem-solving theory and method as well as empirical testing can only strengthen that critical project. Such a synergy stands at the cutting edge in the broader international relations literature (Price and Reus-Smit 1998; Price 2008a, 2008b) and, it is to be hoped, in future work on European public spheres as well.

10 | Democracy, identity, and European public spheres

ANDREAS FOLLESDAL

An underlying concern that motivates much normative and empirical research on the Europeanization of public spheres is its crucial importance for democratic decision making.[1] The empirical findings of this book conclude that, indeed, there is evidence of such Europeanization in the form of political contestation about matters European. Several authors point to the present debates surrounding the euro crisis as a particularly illustrative case in point (see Chapter 2). Indeed, the euro debates underscore the need to better understand the intricate conceptual and causal linkages between four different elements of these debates: the nature of these political and quasi-constitutional conflicts; discussions of their causes and solutions in public arenas by elites and citizens; contested democratic standards and ideals; and appeals to the need for a shared European identity, at least for solutions to this and other crises. How should we assess these trends of Europeanization of public spheres? What are their implications for European integration or Euroskepticism, for the prospects of a "European identity," and for the contours of a more legitimate and democratic European Union (EU)? Specifically, what is the significance for democracy and for the future EU of increased politicization in the sense of contestation in various public spheres among political parties about the European polity and regimes – including the territory and competencies of the EU – as addressed by Risse (see Chapter 6), Pfetsch and Heft (see Chapter 2), and others in this book (see also De Wilde 2011)?

[1] This chapter was written under the auspices of ERC Advanced Grant 269841 MultiRights on the Legitimacy of Multi-Level Human Rights Judiciary – www.MultiRights.net; and partly supported by the Research Council of Norway through its Centres of Excellence Funding Scheme, project number 223274 – PluriCourts The Legitimacy of the International Judiciary – www.PluriCourts.net. I am also grateful to the editor and for many constructive comments received during the authors' workshops in Berlin.

This final chapter considers some of these linkages from the vantage point of democratic theory. Is such contestation about "constitutional" issues as those raised by the euro crisis evidence of regrettable Euroskepticism, which in turn indicates the absence of a European identity (see Chapter 7)? Should a European identity be fostered so as to motivate increased solidarity among EU citizens and their member states – for example, in response to the euro crisis? If so, is such a shared identity best identified as or promoted by a grand project that commands consensus, as European Commission President Barroso recommended (Barroso 2005)? Or is identity better fostered by more contestation?

I present a normative case for more contestation, both about policies and the EU polity in the form of Euroskepticism, as part of the requisite solutions – albeit without assuming that such politicization will further integration (*pace* Grande and Kriesi, Chapter 8). I also suggest that there is a third option in addition to either unfortunate corrosion and fragmentation of the EU (Majone 1998, 2001; Bartolini 2006) or "normalization" of policy contestation (see Chapter 6) – namely, permanent salient contestation about constitutional matters, of which the euro crisis may be only one.

I elaborate this option by a focus on deliberative theories of democracy that agree that citizens' sense of justice and political judgments are – or at least should be – developed and maintained in institutionally specified arenas where "citizens or their representatives actually seek to give one another mutually acceptable reasons to justify the laws they adopt" (Gutmann and Thompson 2004; cf. Cohen 1997). Such arenas may include mass media as well as the newer social media, exploited, for example, by dynamic issue networks (see Chapter 5). The deliberation in these arenas, of course, should concern and affect factual beliefs and instrumental issues about the best choice of means or strategies for given ends. It is important that the discussions also should shape individuals' ultimate values, including their conceptions of a legitimate political order, citizenship, and the common good. I assume that these are components of what is sometimes referred to as a "European identity" (Cohen 1997; Elster 1998; Pettit 2001).

The first section of this chapter disentangles two sets of reasons that such deliberative theories may offer for valuing a public sphere. One reason is to regard consensus seeking as a central objective and mechanism for key participants; another reason is that constrained contestation is a central objective and mechanism, in which political parties, media, and somewhat independent experts play central roles. These two sets of reasons, of course, are not mutually exclusive, yet they may incline scholars of European public spheres to look for somewhat different indicators and standards.

The second section considers some of these implications with regard to several issues: developments toward a European identity and a more legitimate division of competencies between EU bodies and member states. These topics include questions of more intergovernmentalism or more supranational governance; whether Turkey and other candidates should be member states of the EU; which states should be part of Euro-Europe and how to address the present and future euro crisis; and the choice of actions to make the EU more democratic and more legitimate. I draw on lessons from comparative federalism on the assumption that the EU will maintain several salient federal, multilevel features.

The third section draws certain conclusions. One outcome concerns Euroskepticism in the sense discussed in this book (see Chapter 1), which, I argue, will remain on the political agenda. That is, whatever the division of competencies and allocation of influence over EU decisions, there will be actors opposed to the present "constitutional bargain" urging either more authority to the central bodies or more toward the member units, and possibly about the geographical domain of the EU. Such high-stake politics concerning frames such as the political system and the polity is characteristic of federal political orders, especially during the period when formerly independent states come together to form a federation, but also as a permanent feature. Consensus on these issues is even less realistic due to the asymmetric nature of the EU, such as the different membership of the EU and of Euro-Europe. Both of these features challenge the prospects of a shared "European identity" of the type specified in this book – or so I argue.

A methodological note on measuring politicization in the public sphere

Many scholars assume that Europeanization of public spheres in the sense specified by Risse (see Chapter 1) is of value. However, there is disagreement about whether the present level of such Europeanization is sufficient or optimal, for several reasons. One reason may be that some empirical findings seem to be at odds with one another (see

Chapters 3 and 4). Two other sources of disagreement also are worth mentioning. First, such disagreements may be due to underlying choices of different plausible baselines. Others may concern assessments of whether contestation about the polity and the regime is desirable, and whether the standard of comparison is with the most vibrant national political public spheres of ideal theory or compared to actual public debates in actual European democracies – and, if so, unitary or federal (see Chapters 3 and 4).

Second, diverging views about what to make of the Europeanization of public spheres may be due to differing conceptions of the public sphere; the editor's choice in this regard is but one among several. Here, the public sphere is understood as "an open forum of communication for everybody who wants to say something or listen to what other speakers have to say" (see Chapter 1, p. 6, citing Neidhardt 1994, 7; in this volume). These arenas should but often fail to secure critical discussion insulated from social and economic pressures, in which participants treat one another as equals, cooperating to reach agreement on laws and other matters of common concern. These processes of public discourse – which surely include much debate and contestation – in turn influence all or most formal law-making in legislative bodies (Habermas 1996c, 110, 135; Gutmann and Thompson 2004).

Other scholars may define "public sphere" in ways closer to Rawls's narrower "public political forum": the discourse of judges and government officials and the oratory and statements of candidates to public office. I assume the latter to include the important arenas of intra- and inter-party discussion and contestation (Michelman 1996, 314–15; Rawls 1999, 134). The topics of such deliberations are limited (at least in the first instance) to the law-making system and other central issues of "constitutional essentials and basic justice" (Rawls 1993, xxi; Dryzek 2000; Michelman 2000, 1066–67). Whereas normal legislation falls outside of this narrower scope, I assume that other such constitutional topics would include aspects of the polity or regime as a whole: for instance, which states should be members of the EU, which competencies they should have, and the wisdom of establishing the euro.

There seems to be broad agreement that politicization of EU issues indicates the normal workings of a political order (Kriesi et al. 2008; De Wilde 2011). However, agreement ends concerning politicization regarding the polity and particular regimes such as the euro. Insofar as such issues count as framing questions of policies, a central question emerges: What are we to make of such ongoing contestation? Is this polarizing constitutional politicization an expression of worrisome Euroskepticism, sightings of a healthy process toward a more democratic EU – or a warning of ultimately destabilizing fragmentation?

The role of a public sphere in consensus-oriented and contest-oriented democratic theory

Many democratic theorists agree that political salience of issues is endogenous to the political process (see Chapter 6 in this volume; Follesdal and Hix 2006). Thus, European and domestic media attention to issues and multilevel political contestation mutually may feed one another so that transnationalization of public spheres in Europe comprises both enabling conditions for EU politicization and the result of such political contestation (Kriesi et al. 2008; see also Chapter 7 in this volume).

This agreement notwithstanding, a public sphere may have several competing roles or functions within a democracy: as an arena for arriving at agreement or for contestation among competitors. One set of reasons to value a public sphere draws on aspects of deliberative theories of democracy that urge actors to be consensus-oriented in a certain sense. The objective of participants in a public sphere is to resolve disagreements through deliberation within institutions that should facilitate deliberation, as unconstrained as possible by extraneous factors such as brute force and eloquence. The aim of the actors should be consensus, brought about by deliberation in such public arenas that should facilitate reasoned changes in beliefs and values. These changes include both epistemic updates about likely outcomes, beliefs, and preferences of other actors – and, therefore, likely actions and coalitions – as well as the transformation of ultimate values, self-perception, objectives that ensure that the interests of the self go beyond self-interest to include solidarity, justice, and so forth. One result is to foster a version of collective identity among the interlocutors in the sense of shared values and beliefs. Along this line of argument, the standard for assessing the emergence and quality of the public sphere is the extent of reasoned consensus among individuals, political parties, and other civil-society actors. Empirically, such an approach might lead us to determine whether institutions are closer or further from the ideal deliberative procedure (e.g., an "ideal speech situation") in which outstanding philosophy seminars would come close to such an ideal. The ideal procedure should "mirror" such conditions (Cohen 1997, 79). Some authors hold, for instance, that there is an assumption for political discourse that legal questions have single correct answers (Habermas 1996c, 1491–95) or a limited set of answers suitable for a fair compromise (Bohman 1998; McCarthy 1998; Bohman and Regh 2011). Remaining disagreements are due to either lack of time or lack of goodwill among some of the participants. Among the implications of this view may be that increased levels of disagreement would seem to indicate that such a public sphere is further from being realized, especially if the disagreements concern the proper frame of reference or criteria of relevance (Habermas 1998a; Van de Steeg and Risse 2010).

A very different reason to value public spheres hones in on the contestation among political parties, corrected by independent media and experts. Proponents of such an account also may regard themselves as offering a deliberative theory of democracy – one that defends

> …a complementary rather than antagonistic relation of deliberation to many democratic mechanisms that are not themselves deliberative. These nondeliberative mechanisms, such as aggregation through voting as well as fair bargaining and negotiation among cooperative antagonists, involve coercive power in their mechanisms of decision. Yet they can and must be justified deliberatively. (Mansbridge et al. 2010, 64)

Thus, several democratic theorists hold that a central benefit of democratic, majoritarian rule is that it more reliably than alternatives serves to identify or create normatively acceptable decisions. A central mechanism for this epistemic benefit is "genuine competition by decision makers for the votes of those who are actually affected by their decisions" (Dahl 1971; Shapiro 2003, 7). Competitive elections on this view are crucial to make policies and elected officials responsive to the preferences of citizens (Powell 2000) – and to shape these preferences. Electoral contests provide incentives for elites to develop rival policy ideas and propose rival candidates for political office. This identification of new alternatives is crucial: "the definition of the alternatives is the supreme instrument of power" (Schattschneider 1960, 68). Competition among parties with different platforms that express alternative, somewhat consistent conceptions of public interest and public policies helps voters to realize which choices may be made and provides alternatives (Manin 1987, 338–68). On this line of argument, political parties are not motivated primarily by a search for consensus but rather for contested positions that can command votes. An important concern, then, is how well the institutions allow for contestation among parties and opportunities for an opposition to form and criticize the powers that be. An important role for the public sphere is to allow such disagreements to arise and to provide opportunities for new cleavages and conflicts among political parties that seek the votes of the electorate. European integration has created new groups of "winners" and "losers," which old and new parties may court (see Chapter 8). That is, the public spheres should foster politicization (see Chapter 6 in this volume; see also De Wilde 2011, 566–67). At the same time, the public spheres must allow the competing parties, media, and independent voices to arrest unfounded claims. Here, various old and new media play crucial roles. They can serve as independent critical watchdogs on governments and parties, engaging citizens not only as observers but also as players. Moreover, the media contribute in complex games as autonomous elements of the political parties' strategies – and vice versa.

On this account, competing proposals for frames of reference or criteria of relevance may well be on the agenda. Indeed, such contestation helps citizens to understand the difference between the present government and the (democratic) political order (Shapiro 1996, 2003) – and what may be secured by changing aspects of this order, the regime – or the polity. A viable opposition is central to determine and partially order such feasible institutional alternatives according to normative principles. If citizens cannot identify alternative leaders or policy agendas, it is difficult for them to determine whether leaders could have done better or to identify who is responsible for policies. This account also values how such contestation fosters preference formation, by both epistemic updates – that is, correction of mistaken beliefs and the acquisition of new information – and transformation of ultimate values, self-perceptions, and views about the proper objectives of the political order. Such socialization is due in part to the expression and modification of policy platforms and party ideologies that citizens witness as observers to such competitions. These effects of political discourse for identity formation are widely acknowledged, not only among communicatively oriented deliberative democrats – although they sometimes seem to ignore that much of this is a shared democratic heritage (Weale 1999, 37). Where different theorists disagree is instead in their assessment of the risks, possibilities, and best institutions for regulating such preference formation and modification in a normatively preferred direction (Schumpeter 1976; Riker 1982; Follesdal 2000; Schmitter 2000; Shapiro 2003).

Attentive readers will observe that these two alternative modes, through which a public sphere serves democratic ends, are largely compatible. That is, there is room for both within plausible theories of democracy, and there is room for plausible democratic theories that include both deliberative and aggregative elements. Such a theory would value both deliberative and "post-deliberative" contestatory democratic elements. The right to political participation of this form may be assigned an intrinsic value as well as an instrumental role in ensuring just outcomes more reliably than other modes of governance. However, compared to the arguments that value consensus-oriented benefits of the public spheres, the contestation-oriented arguments suggest strikingly different standards for assessing the existence of a European public sphere worth keeping and enhancing. The institutions should have as their objective to facilitate such contestation – although not necessarily as unconstrained as possible. In such a properly working public sphere, disagreements arise and political cleavages and conflicts are fostered by political parties chasing electoral votes. They seek to mobilize preferences about policy issues and to create salient disagreements, not least about what is at stake in terms of frames of reference. Media actors also will seek out and focus on political conflicts, as well as scrutinize whether some issues are deliberately kept off the political agenda by cartels of parties who only stand to lose by more attention to certain issues. In the European setting, the euro crisis illustrates how such scrutiny and challenge increasingly occur in a multilevel space: domestic and European actors target actors at other levels (see Chapter 3).

To illustrate how findings may be interpreted differently along these two sets of arguments, consider if empirical research were to find a lack of visible or vocal disagreement about the polity or other constitutional essentials. Is this a sign that the desired consensus process has run its course in the European public spheres? Or is it, to the contrary, an indication that such arenas are not (yet) fully developed and utilized in a truly democratic manner?

Implications of such politicization for a European identity

One of the overall findings of this book is the gradual Europeanization of public spheres, interdependent with the emerging politicization of European affairs (see Chapter 1) – although some may note
that the requisite impact of such politicization on representative
democratic institutions at the EU level appears to be missing (see
Chapter 4). However, the findings of this book concerning the outcome of such politicization for a European identity are ambivalent.
Will such politicization and increased salience of EU politics foster a
European identity?

One scenario is that politicization in Europeanized public spheres
indeed will foster a European collective identity (see Chapter 6). Several scholars hold that a crucial intervening variable for this scenario
is the extent of party mobilization that will foster political cleavages.
However, one of these potential cleavages is Euroskepticism understood as opposition to "constitutional" issues concerning the polity.

This gives rise to a second scenario. Several contributors in this book
point out that the growth of political parties supporting Euroskepticism will run counter to the development of a European identity
(see Chapters 7 and 8). Politicization and emerging European public
spheres thus will hinder the desired European identity.

Here, I offer considerations in support of a third scenario in which
we may expect polarizing constitutional politicization about the polity
and the regimes of the EU for a long time to come, with implications
for the sort of meager shared identity that may be hoped for in the
multilevel political order that is the EU.

Both the consensus- and the contest-oriented arguments for a public
sphere described previously acknowledge the need to create and maintain a collective identity for several reasons, of which at least three
merit mention here. First, ordinary citizens are sometimes asked to
refrain from benefits in order to support other members of the citizenry. Second, some will lose out in a majoritarian decision because
they find themselves in the minority. Yet, they are still expected to
comply, for instance, from a motivation that they believe the system is fair, that they may get their turn when others will be losers
but still comply, and that the burden on them of complying is not
too harsh (Barry 1991). Third, law makers, treaty negotiators, and
the various domestic and EU officials must be trusted not only to

promote the interests of their own constituency unbridled but also to consider the interests of other Europeans when crafting treaties, legislation, and policies. Therefore, they and the citizens who vote them into office must be guided in part by such other-regarding values and commitments. The result is that both accounts of the value of public spheres must attend to mechanisms to maintain some meta-agreement that constrains the political disagreements, even those disagreements that concern the constitutional essentials (i.e., about the polity, such as Turkish membership, aspects of the euro regime, and the extent of supranational governance). This may amount to an agreed meta-ideology – a consensus of sorts – about the values of democratic decision making and human rights. However, regarding the contestation-oriented account, the shared European identity may emerge as quite meager. Indeed, insofar as there are few shared frames of reference in the form of agreement about the polity, some may question whether there is, indeed, politicization of the appropriate type (see Chapter 4). Will a meager identity then suffice? A central question then becomes, of course, suffice for what? What should be the baseline of comparison?

It seems that at least one central social function of such an identity is to ensure stable compliance (e.g., with majority decisions) by the minority that loses. The public reactions to the euro crisis and the various partial solutions proposed illustrate that such compliance cannot be taken for granted. For our purposes, it seems especially helpful to draw lessons from comparative federalism on the assumption that the EU will maintain several salient federal, multilevel features.

From the point of view of federal political theory, the EU clearly has several federal elements (Follesdal 2007). One of the central challenges of such political orders is how they merit and facilitate trust and trustworthiness among citizens committed to uphold a normatively legitimate political order. Comparative studies of federalism warn of a higher level of ongoing contestation concerning the constitution and its values and interpretation than in unitary political orders (Lemco 1991; Filippov, Ordeshook, and Shvetsova 2004). Thus, stabilizing mechanisms are more important to prevent the disintegration of the political order and citizen disenchantment. These stabilizing mechanisms also may have to accommodate and correct great imbalances and conflicts of various types. Among the most contentious conflicts are typically the objectives of the federal level – witness, in the EU, disagreements among member states about how "deep" the EU should be with regard to such matters as social rights and foreign policy – and monetary and fiscal policies. Ironically, the grounds of shared values and goals may be especially weak in federations, given their frequent genesis as solutions to intractable problems otherwise resolved by a unitary political order. In particular, many scholars underscore the need to develop an overarching loyalty to the federation as a whole, if the political order is not to disintegrate (Linz 1999; Filippov, Ordeshook, and Shvetsova 2004).

The challenge of building such an overarching loyalty is difficult in many federations but is especially demanding in the EU, which is regarded as a political order with federal elements. That union consists of well-established member states that, in principle, could exist independently and that therefore have been prepared to bargain even harder about many particular choices (Filippov, Ordeshook, and Shvetsova 2004, 315). A European party system that could foster such cross-cutting loyalties is underdeveloped (Filippov, Ordeshook, and Shvetsova 2004, 321; see also Hix 2008). Furthermore, because the decision-making arrangements of the EU are exceedingly complex with a high number of veto points, stasis is a permanent risk.

For our purposes, three central points are worth underscoring. First, federations in this broad sense do not require "post-national" citizens. The challenge of federations instead is to be self-sustaining in order to create and maintain political loyalty among the citizenry toward *both* the own member unit *and* the federal-level institutions, officials, and citizens. In the EU, the task therefore is to ensure that EU citizens and political authorities maintain dual political loyalties, toward both compatriots and authorities of their own member state and an overarching loyalty toward the EU citizenry and authorities as a whole. This has implications for the choice of a baseline to assess the requisite European identity. It is not a zero-sum game vis-à-vis national identity, and it is not obvious that either should be dominant overall. Indeed, a plurality of citizens in most member states holds dual identities anyway (Risse 2010). Perhaps we should not expect all conflicts between them to fade – some tensions well may remain between segments of EU citizens, some of whom regard their disagreement as one among

"Europeans *as Europeans*" and other times addressing conflicts as "Germans against Greeks" (see Chapter 6).

Second, in *asymmetric* federations, disagreements will always remain about the objectives of the central authority. In these federal arrangements, member units have pooled different competencies; therefore, citizens and authorities of different member units will hold correctly that the objectives of the central unit are different across the member units. This has been discussed in the study of European integration as a polycentric or variable geometry feature of the EU. One implication is that the conception of European – or EU – identity well may be legitimately different depending on whether the person is a member of Schengen Europe, of Euro-Europe, and so so forth – or not. Such differences create different legitimate expectations of solidarity and intervention across member states: witness the debates about the root causes of the present euro crisis and whether solutions should focus on internal adjustment in some member states or on ways to restructure the modus operandi of the European Central Bank (ECB).

Third, comparative studies of federalism suggest that federal arrangements are more subject to constitutional contestation than unitary political orders (e.g., Lemco 1991; Bakvis, Baier, and Brown 2009). These topics include which competencies should be enjoyed by central authorities and how member states should influence such decisions – and sometimes questions of which member units to include in the polity. Insofar as the EU maintains federal features, these constitutional frames are likely to remain more contested than in unitary political orders. How to ensure that the ECB remains sufficiently independent in relevant ways, yet under sufficient indirect democratic control, is only one example. It is not only in the EU that leaders tend to transform and reframe some policy issues into constitutional issues (see Chapter 6) – this is typical in federations. This is both good news and bad news. It is good news because this phenomenon is not unique to the EU because it is also typical of political orders with federal elements. The bad news for those concerned with stability is that federal orders also suffer a higher risk of instability, of two types: they tend toward fragmentation – indeed, secession – or complete centralization. In short, we should expect the same type of constitutional contestation for the EU, for at least three reasons. Such contestation is first, of course, more frequent when federations "come together" than when they are seeking to "hold together." Second, contestation and the absence of a shared identity are more likely for the EU because it is asymmetric: citizens of different member states will correctly have different views about what the EU should be doing because the domestic–EU division of competencies differs among the states (e.g., concerning the euro) and the obligations that follow from such pooled competencies. Third, a further source of potentially destabilizing constitutional contestation is Article 50 of the Treaty of the European Union that explicitly recognizes member states' right to withdraw from the EU, which is unusual in political orders with federal features. Therefore, we should expect politicization and "normal politics" in the EU often to escalate into constitutional issues if not to constitutional crises (see Chapter 6).

This comparative exercise thus underscores the need for a European identity as well as European politicization – and suggests that contestation about constitutional frames is only to be expected. At the same time, it is an open question what the shared European identity should consist of and how to assess spreading Euroskepticism in the Europeanized public spheres about precisely such issues.

Conclusions: the type of European public spheres worth keeping

What conclusions can we draw from the findings of this book, combined with the distinction between two reasons to value the public spheres and the lessons from federalism? At least two issues seem important with regard to the euro crisis, not the least of which is for future research.

The first conclusion concerns baselines of satisfactory levels of Europeanized public spheres and a European identity. The lessons from federal studies underscore that it may be difficult to specify this baseline. First, we seem to have no agreement on the minimum threshold of public-sphere activity for a domestic democracy to work in a legitimate way (see Chapters 1 and 4). Second, there is a risk that we cannot sufficiently calibrate the Europeanization of the public spheres when we ask, as in the introductory chapter (see Chapter 1, p. 18, in this volume), "How salient do Europe and the EU have to become in the various public spheres in order to qualify as Europeanization?" (see Chapter 1, p. 18, in this volume). When we regard the EU as a political and legal order with federal elements, it seems impossible and, arguably, not helpful to try to identify such a threshold. Not only is there no clear zero-sum game or relative importance between domestic and EU-level public-sphere deliberations. In addition, the answer would seem to be in part a matter of which competencies and policies the EU bodies pursue. Insofar as such contestation is endogenous to the politicization process, few external standards seem available. Thus, it seems unreasonable to hold that there should be the same amount of contestation at both levels: this is a matter of how much policy and legislation is determined at which level. We also must consider which issue areas are within the scope of responsibility for the member states and which for the EU, as Koopmans illustrates with the case of the German federal experience regarding educational policies (see Chapter 3). The euro regime is a particularly vexing challenge because some but not all member states are directly subject to it, whereas non-euro member states also are drawn into the discussions and may become part of agreed solutions, more or less willingly.

The second conclusion concerns likely future scenarios. The direction of political contestation among political parties clearly should remain on the agenda. For instance, the findings of Grande and Kriesi (see Chapter 8) give rise to several scenarios. They note the emergence of several Euroskeptical coalitions that are otherwise quite dissimilar, composed of trade unions, radical-right parties, and Conservative and Christian Democratic parties (see Chapter 8). I suggest that such Euroskepticism, which seeks to return some competencies to the member states or which wants to stop further membership, should not surprise us. Contestation about these constitutional issues is part of ordinary politics in political orders with federal elements, especially during the "coming-together" phase of emerging federations. The euro crisis may be only the first of several deep conflicts: in the future, we may expect more skepticism about the euro but also about the extent or lack of a strong common-defense policy, fiscal policies, or social rights in the workplace.

These comparative lessons should not foster optimism about the future stability of the EU. In particular, further scenarios remain open. The scenario I describe herein would envision political parties at the EU level integrating the various single-issue networks and pressure groups identified by Bennett, Lang, and Segerberg (see Chapter 5). However, other quite different scenarios also are possible. Consider whether political parties at the European level become further de-linked from domestic parties and turn into more single-issue lobbyists – for example, concerning the dismantling of EU competencies in one or more sectors. This may be a shrewd response to the disagreements among the various coalitions that Grande and Kriesi observe – although they deem it unlikely (see Chapter 8). If this happens, such political parties at the EU level no longer serve the valuable functions identified by the contestatory democratic argument for a public sphere.

To conclude, it seems clear that the main findings of this book support the claims of democratic theory, brought to bear on political orders with federal elements. In a complex, interlocking, multilevel political order such as the EU (Scharpf 1985), citizens clearly need Europeanization of national public spheres in the form of parallel national debates about European matters. Representatives of national bodies partake in centralized decision making, and national parliaments and other arenas of debate may check EU bodies in significant ways to maintain the proper division of responsibilities between member states and the EU level (e.g., in the form of the "yellow card" procedure) (Cooper 2006).

EU-level arenas are important for debating issues that are contested at the European level as well as where there is a risk that some individuals or states suffer unreasonably from one particular decision or from the systemic effects of several decisions, each of which appears innocuous. A problem for the EU is that there have been few if any vehicles for encouraging such Europe-wide debates – for example, about structural reforms of the European economy or about other politically contested issues that can develop from and mobilize political opposition. In a well-functioning democracy, rival groups of elites (including political parties) have incentives to present and defend competing policy positions based on a contested conception of the European interest, within shared frames about the political and legal order and its objectives. This book provides evidence that such European public spheres indeed exist, but I suggest that some of the requisite shared, overarching norms and values are hitherto unclear. Therefore, although some parts of a European identity seem to be in place, it seems that a *full* European identity, possibly *unique* to EU citizens, has yet to emerge (Follesdal 2009a, 2009b). In the absence of such full-fledged democratic contestation, within a shared meta-agreement, the EU is less capable of assessing and addressing central issues of institutional design and policy making (Follesdal and Hix 2006, 549). How to handle this and future euro crises is one case in point. However, I suggest that politicization of constitutional issues is likely to remain in the EU – and even flourish – with the Europeanization of public spheres.

Bibliography

Adam, Silke. 2007a. "Domestic Adaptions of Europe: A Comparative Study of the Debates on EU Enlargement and a Common Constitution in the German and French Quality Press." *International Journal of Public Opinion Research* 19 (4): 409–33.

Adam, Silke. 2007b. *Symbolische Netzwerke in Europa: Der Einfluss der nationalen Ebene auf europäische Öffentlichkeit. Deutschland und Frankreich im Vergleich.* Köln: Halem.

Adam, Silke. 2008a. "Do Mass Media Portray Europe as a Community? German and French Debates on EU Enlargement and a Common Constitution." *Javnost – The Public* 15 (1): 91–112.

Adam, Silke. 2008b. "Medieninhalte aus der Netzwerkperspektive: Neue Erkenntnisse durch die Kombination von Inhalts-und Netzwerkanalyse." *Publizistik* 53 (2): 180–99.

Adam, Silke, and Michaela Maier. 2011. "National Parties as Politicizers of EU Integration? Party Campaign Communication in the Run-Up to the 2009 European Parliament Election." *European Union Politics* 12 (3): 431–53.

Adam, Silke, and Barbara Pfetsch. 2009. "Europa als Konflikt in nationalen Medien – Zur Politisierung der Positionen in der Integrationsdebatte." In Barbara Pfetsch and Frank Marcinkowski (eds.), *Politik in der Mediendemokratie: PVS-Sonderheft 42.* Wiesbaden: VS Verlag, pp. 559–84.

Adler, Emanuel. 2013. "Constructivism in International Relations: Sources, Contributions and Debates." In Walter Carlsnaes, Thomas Risse, and Beth Simmons (eds.), *Handbook of International Relations.* 2nd edn. London: Sage Publications, pp. 112–44.

Adler, Emanuel, and Vincent Pouliot (eds.). 2011. *International Practices.* New York: Cambridge University Press.

Albrow, Martin. 2001. "Society as Social Diversity: The Challenge for Governance in the Global Age." In Organisation for Economic Co-operation and Development (OECD) (ed.), *Governance in the 21st Century.* Paris: OECD, pp. 179–219.

Anduiza, Eva, Camilo Cristancho, and Jose Sabucedo. 2014. "Mobilization through Online Social Networks: The Political Protest of the Indignados in Spain." *Information, Communication & Society* 17 (6): 750–64.

Ansolabehere, Steven, and Shanto Iyengar. 1995. *Going Negative.* New York: Free Press.

Bachrach, Peter, and Morton Baratz. 1962. "Two Faces of Power." *American Political Science Review* 56 (4): 947–52.

Bachrach, Peter, and Morton Baratz. 1963. "Decisions and Nondecisions: An Analytic Framework." *American Political Science Review* 57 (3): 632–42.

Bain, Jessica, and Martin Holland (eds.). 2007. *European Union Identity: Perceptions from Europe and Asia.* Baden-Baden: Nomos.

Bakvis, Herman, Gerald Baier, and Doug Brown. 2009. *Contested Federalism: Certainty and Ambiguity in the Canadian Federation.* Oxford: Oxford University Press.

Balme, Richard, and Didier Chabanet. 2008. *European Governance and Democracy: Power and Protest in the EU.* Lanham, MD: Rowman and Littlefield.

Barnett, Michael, and Raymond Duvall. 2005. "Power in International Politics." *International Organization* 59 (1): 39–75.

Barnett, Michael, and Martha Finnemore. 2004. *Rules for the World: International Organizations in Global Politics.* Ithaca, NY: Cornell University Press.

Barroso, José Manuel. 2005. "Building an Open Europe in Times of Change." In *European Ideas Network*, speech at European Ideas Network, Lisbon, September 22.

Barry, Brian. 1991. "Is Democracy Special?" In Brian Barry (ed.), *Democracy and Power.* Oxford: Oxford University Press, pp. 24–60.

Bartolini, Stefano. 2005. *Restructuring Europe.* Oxford: Oxford University Press.

Bartolini, Stefano. 2006. "Should the Union Be Politicized? Prospects and Risks." *Notre Europe Policy Paper* 19: 28–50.

Bechtel, Michael, Jens Hainmueller, and Yotam M. Margalit. 2012a. *Sharing the Pain: What Explains Public Opinion Towards International Financial Bailouts?* MIT Political Science Department Working Paper. Cambridge, MA: The MIT Press.

Bechtel, Michael, Jens Hainmueller, and Yotam M. Margalit. 2012b. *Studying Public Opinion on Multidimensional Politics: The Case of the Eurozone Bailouts.* MIT Political Science Department Working Papers. Cambridge, MA: The MIT Press.

Beck, Nathaniel, and Jonathan N. Katz. 1995. "What to Do (and Not to Do) with Time-Series Cross-Section Data." *American Political Science Review* 89 (3): 634–47.

Beck, Ulrich. 2006. *The Cosmopolitan Vision.* Cambridge: Polity Press.

Beck, Ulrich. 2012. *Das deutsche Europa.* Berlin: Suhrkamp.

Beck, Ulrich, and Edgar Grande. 2007. *Cosmopolitan Europe*. Cambridge: Polity Press.

Bennett, Andrew, and Jeffrey T. Checkel (eds.). 2014. *Process Tracing: From Metaphor to Analytic Tool*. Cambridge: Cambridge University Press.

Bennett, Andrew, and Alexander George. 2005. *Case Studies and Theory Development in the Social Sciences*. Cambridge, MA: The MIT Press.

Bennett, W. Lance. 2003. "Communicating Global Activism: Strengths and Vulnerabilities of Networked Politics." *Information, Communication & Society* 6 (2): 143–68.

Bennett, W. Lance. 2012. *News: The Politics of Illusion*. 9th edn. New York: Pearson/Longman.

Bennett, W. Lance, Kirsten Foot, and Michael Xenos. 2011. "Narratives and Network Organization: A Comparison of Fair Trade Systems in Two Nations." *Journal of Communication* 61: 219–45.

Bennett, W. Lance, Sabine Lang, Alexandra Segerberg, and Henrike Knappe. 2011. "Public Engagement vs. Institutional Influence Strategies: Comparing Trade and Environmental Advocacy Networks at the National and EU Levels in Germany and the UK." Paper presented at the 6th European Consortium for Political Research. Reykjavik: University of Iceland, August 25–27.

Bennett, W. Lance, and Alexandra Segerberg. 2011. "Digital Media and the Personalization of Collective Action: Social Technology and the Organization of Protests against the Global Economic Crisis." *Information, Communication & Society* 14: 770–99.

Bennett, W. Lance, and Alexandra Segerberg. 2013. *The Logic of Connective Action: Digital Media and the Personalization of Contentious Politics*. Cambridge and New York: Cambridge University Press.

Beyers, Jan. 2005. "Multiple Embeddedness and Socialization in Europe: The Case of Council Officials." *International Organization* 59 (4): 899–936.

Beyers, Jan, and Bart Kerremans. 2004. "Bureaucrats, Politicians, and Societal Interests: How is European Policy Making Politicized?" *Comparative Political Studies* 37 (10): 1119–50.

Bohman, James. 1998. "The Coming of Age of Deliberative Democracy." *Journal of Political Philosophy* 6 (4): 400–25.

Bohman, James, and William Regh. 2011. "Jürgen Habermas." In Edward N. Zalta (ed.), *The Stanford Encyclopedia of Philosophy* (Winter 2011 Edition). Available at http://plato.stanford.edu/archives/win2011/entries/habermas.

Boomgaarden, Hajo G., Jens Vliegenthart, Claes H. De Vreese, and Andreas R. T. Schuck. 2010. "News on the Move: Exogenous Events and News

Coverage of the European Union." *Journal of European Public Policy* 17 (4): 506–26.

Börzel, Tanja A. 2005. "Europeanization: How the European Union Interacts with its Member States." In Simon Bulmer and Christian Lequesne (eds.), *The Member States of the European Union.* Oxford: Oxford University Press, pp. 45–69.

Börzel, Tanja A. (ed.) 2009. *Coping with Accession to the European Union: New Modes of Environmental Governance, Palgrave Studies in European Union Politics.* Houndmills, Basingstoke, UK: Palgrave Macmillan.

Börzel, Tanja A., and Thomas Risse. 2007. "Europeanization: The Domestic Impact of EU Politics." In Knud Erik Jorgensen, Mark A. Pollack, and Ben Rosamond (eds.), *Handbook of European Union Politics.* London: Sage Publications, pp. 483–504.

boyd, danah, and Jeffrey Heer. 2006. "Profiles as Conversation: Networked Identity Performance on Friendster." In *Proceedings of Hawai'i International Conference on System Sciences (HICSS-39).* Kauai, HI: IEEE Computer Society, January 4–7, 2006.

Brannigan, Augustine. 2004. *The Rise and Fall of Social Psychology: The Use and Misuse of the Experimental Method.* New York: de Gruyter.

Brüggemann, Michael. 2008. *Europäische Öffentlichkeit durch Öffentlichkeitsarbeit? Die Informationspolitik der Europäischen Kommission.* Wiesbaden: VS Verlag.

Brüggemann, Michael. 2009. *"Der Mythos vom Dialog mit den Bürgern: Der Beitrag der Europäischen Kommission zur Schaffung einer europäischen Öffentlichkeit."* TranState Working Papers No. 84. Bremen: Sonderforschungsbereich 597 "Staatlichkeit im Wandel".

Brüggemann, Michael, Andreas Hepp, Katharina Kleinen-von Königslöw, and Hartmut Wessler. 2009. "Transnationale Öffentlichkeit in Europa: Forschungsstand und Perspektiven." *Publizistik* 54: 391–414.

Bruter, Michael. 2005. *Citizens of Europe? The Emergence of a Mass European Identity.* Houndmills, Basingstoke, UK, and New York: Palgrave Macmillan.

Bruter, Michael. 2009. "Time Bomb: The Dynamic Effect of News and Symbols on the Political Identity of European Citizens." *Comparative Political Studies* 42 (December): 1498–36.

Bruter, Michael. 2011. "Europolity? Seven Paradoxes about European Identity." Salzburg Paper on European Integration, No. 03–11.

Bruter, Michael, and Sarah Harrison. 2009. *The Future of our Democracies?* Houndmills, Basingstoke, UK: Palgrave Macmillan.

Bruter, Michael, and Sarah Harrison. 2012. "How European Do You Feel?" Report presented at the UK Houses of Parliament on a Mass Study on European Identity.

Byrnes, Timothy, and Peter J. Katzenstein (eds.). 2006. *Religion in an Expanding Europe*. New York: Cambridge University Press.

Calhoun, Craig. 2003. "The Democratic Integration of Europe: Interests, Identity and the Public Sphere." In Mabel Berezein and Martin Schain (eds.), *Europe without Borders: Remapping Territory, Citizenship and Identity in a Transnational Age*. Baltimore, MD, and London: The Johns Hopkins University Press, pp. 243–74.

Campbell, Donald T., and Julian Stanley. 1963. *Threats to Validity: Experimental and Quasi-Experimental Designs for Research*. Chicago: Rand McNally.

Capoccia, Giovanni. 2002. "Anti-System Parties: A Conceptual Reassessment." *Journal of Theoretical Politics* 14 (1): 9–35.

Case, Holly. 2009. "Being European: East and West." In Jeffrey T. Checkel and Peter J. Katzenstein (eds.), *European Identity*. Cambridge: Cambridge University Press, pp. 111–31.

Cederman, Lars-Erik 2001. "Nationalism and Bounded Integration: What it Would Take to Construct a European Demos." *European Journal of International Relations* 7 (2): 139–74.

Checkel, Jeffrey T. 1999. "Norms, Institutions and National Identity in Contemporary Europe." *International Studies Quarterly* 43 (1): 83–114.

Checkel, Jeffrey T. (ed.). 2007. *International Institutions and Socialization in Europe*. Cambridge: Cambridge University Press.

Checkel, Jeffrey T. 2011. "The Social Dynamics of Civil War: Insights from Constructivist Theory." Simons Papers in Security and Development, No. 10. Vancouver: School for International Studies, Simon Fraser University.

Checkel, Jeffrey T. 2013. "Theoretical Pluralism in IR: Possibilities and Limits." In Walter Carlsnaes, Thomas Risse, and Beth Simmons (eds.), *Handbook of International Relations*, 2nd edn. London: Sage Publications, pp. 220–42.

Checkel, Jeffrey T., and Peter J. Katzenstein. 2009a. "The Politicization of European Identities." In Jeffrey T. Checkel and Peter J. Katzenstein (eds.), *European Identity*. Cambridge: Cambridge University Press, pp. 1–25.

Checkel, Jeffrey T., and Peter J. Katzenstein (eds.). 2009b. *European Identity*. Cambridge: Cambridge University Press.

Cohen, Dara Kay. 2013. "Female Combatants and the Perpetration of Violence: Wartime Rape in the Sierra Leone Civil War." *World Politics* 65 (3): 383–415.

Cohen, Joshua. 1997. "Deliberation and Democratic Legitimacy." In James Bohman and William Rehg (eds.), *Deliberative Democracy:*

Essays on Reason and Politics. Cambridge, MA: The MIT Press, pp. 67–91.

Cooper, Ian. 2006. "The Watchdogs of Subsidiarity: National Parliaments and the Logic of Arguing in the EU." *Journal of Common Market Studies* 44 (2): 281–304.

Cowles, Maria Green, James A. Caporaso, and Thomas Risse (eds.). 2001. *Transforming Europe: Europeanization and Domestic Change.* Ithaca, NY: Cornell University Press.

Crespy, Amandine. 2010. "'When 'Bolkestein' is Trapped by the French Anti-Liberal Discourse: A Discursive-Institutionalist Account of Preference Formation in the Realm of EU Multi-Level Politics." *Journal of European Public Policy* 17 (8): 1253–70.

CREST. 1998. *British Elections Panel Studies.* Available at http://www.crest.ox.ac.uk/intro.htm.

Dahl, Robert A. 1971. *Polyarchy: Participation and Opposition.* New Haven, CT: Yale University Press.

Dawson, Richard, and Kenneth Prewitt. 1969. *Political Socialization.* Boston: Little, Brown.

De Vreese, Claes H. 2004. *Framing Europe: Television News and European Integration.* Amsterdam: Aksant.

De Vreese, Claes H. 2007a. "A Spiral of Euroscepticism: The Media's Fault?" *Acta Politica* 42: 271–86.

De Vreese, Claes H. 2007b. "The EU as a Public Sphere." *Living Reviews in European Governance.* Available at http://europeangovernance.livingreviews.org/Articles/lreg-2007-3.

De Vreese, Claes, Susan Banducci, Holli Semetko, and Hajo Boomgaarden. 2006. "The News Coverage of the 2004 European Election Campaign in 25 Countries." *European Union Politics* 7 (4): 477–504.

De Vreese, Claes H., and Hajo Boomgaarden. 2009. "A European Public Sphere: Media and Public Opinion." In Inka Salovaara-Moring (ed.), *Manufactoring Europe: Spaces of Democracy, Diversity and Communication.* Göteborg: Nordicom, pp. 117–28.

De Vreese, Claes H., Hajo Boomgaarden, and Holli Semetko. 2011. "(In)Direct Framing Effects: The Effects of News Media Framing on Public Support for Turkish Membership in the European Union." *Communication Research* 38 (2): 179–205.

De Vreese, Claes H., Jochen Peter, and Holli Semetko. 2001. "Framing Politics at the Launch of the Euro: A Crossnational Comparative Study of Frames in the News." *Political Communication* 18: 107–22.

De Wilde, Pieter. 2011. "No Polity for Old Politics? A Framework for Analyzing the Politicization of European Integration." *Journal of European Integration* 33 (5): 559–75.

De Wilde, Pieter. 2012. "Politicization of the EU Budget: Conflict and the Constraining Dissensus." *West European Politics* 35 (5): 1075–94.

De Wilde, Pieter, Hans Jörg Trenz, and Asimina Michailidou. 2010. *Contesting EU Legitimacy: The Prominence, Content, and Justification of Euroscepticism During 2009 EP Election Campaigns*. ARENA Working Paper 14. Oslo: Centre for European Studies, University of Oslo.

De Wilde, Pieter, and Michael Zürn. 2012. "Can the Politicization of European Integration be Reversed?" *Journal of Common Market Studies* 50 (S1): 137–53.

Delanty, Gerard, and Chris Rumford. 2005. *Rethinking Europe: Social Theory and the Implications of Europeanization*. London: Routledge.

Della Porta, Donatella, and Manuela Caiani. 2006. "The Europeanization of Public Discourse in Italy: A Top-Down Process?" *European Union Politics* 7 (1): 77–112.

Della Porta, Donatella, and Manuela Caiani. 2009. *Social Movements and Europeanization*. Oxford: Oxford University Press.

Della Porta, Donatella, and Lorenzo Mosca. 2007. "In Movimiento: 'Contamination' in Action and the Italian Global Justice Movement." *Global Networks: A Journal of Transnational Affairs* 7 (1): 1–28.

Déloye, Yves, and Michael Bruter (eds.). 2007. *Encyclopaedia of European Elections*. Houndmills, Basingstoke, UK: Palgrave Macmillan.

Deutsch, Karl W. 1953. *Nationalism and Social Communication: An Inquiry into the Foundations of Nationality*. Cambridge, MA: The MIT Press.

Diez Medrano, Juan. 2009. "The Public Sphere and the European Union's Political Identity." In Jeffrey T. Checkel and Peter J. Katzenstein (eds.), *European Identity*. Cambridge: Cambridge University Press, pp. 81–110.

Directorate-General for Communication. 2012. *Two Years to Go to the 2014 European Elections. European Parliament Eurobarometer (EB/EP 77.4). Analytic Synthesis*. Brussels: European Parliament.

Doerr, Nicole. 2008. "Listen Carefully: Democracy Brokers at the European Social Forums." Dissertation. Florence, Italy: Department of Social and Political Science, European University Institute.

Doerr, Nicole. 2009. "How European Protest Transforms Institutions of the Public Sphere: Discourse and Decision-Making in the European Social Forum Process." KFG Working Paper Series, September 2009. Berlin: Kolleg-Forschergruppe (KFG). "The Transformative Power of Europe," Free University Berlin.

Dolezal, Martin, Swen Hutter, and Bruno Wüest. 2012. "Exploring the New Cleavage across Arena and Public Debates: Design and Methods." In Hanspeter Kriesi, Edgar Grande, Martin Dolezal, et al. (eds.), *Political*

Conflict in Western Europe. Cambridge: Cambridge University Press, pp. 36–63.

Dryzek, John S. 2000. *Deliberative Democracy and Beyond: Liberals, Critics, Contestations*. Oxford: Oxford University Press.

Easton, David. 1965. *A Systems Analysis of Political Life*. New York: John Wiley & Sons.

Eder, Klaus. 2000. "Zur Transformation nationalstaatlicher Öffentlichkeit in Europa. Von der Sprachgemeinschaft zur issuespezifischen Kommunikationsgemeinschaft." *Berliner Journal für Soziologie* 10: 167–84.

Eder, Klaus, and Cathleen Kantner. 2000. "Transnationale Resonanzstrukturen in Europa: Eine Kritik der Rede vom Öffentlichkeitsdefizit." In Maurizio Bach (ed.), *Die Europäisierung nationaler Gesellschaften: Sonderheft der Kölner Zeitschrift für Soziologie und Sozialpsychologie*. Opladen: Westdeutscher Verlag, pp. 307–31.

Eder, Klaus, and Cathleen Kantner. 2002. "Interdiskursivität in der europäischen Öffentlichkeit." *Berliner Debatte Initial* 13 (5/6): 79–88.

Eder, Klaus, and Hans-Jörg Trenz. 2007. "Prerequisites of Transnational Democracy and Mechanisms for Sustaining it: The Case of the European Union." In Beate Kohler-Koch and Berthold Rittberger (eds.), *Debating the Democratic Legitimacy of the European Union*. Lanham, MD: Rowman & Littlefield, pp. 165–81.

Eilders, Christiane, and Katrin Voltmer. 2003. "Zwischen Deutschland und Europa: Eine empirische Untersuchung zur Europäisierung der meinungsführenden deutschen Tageszeitungen." *Medien und Kommunikationswissenschaft* 51 (2): 250–70.

Elster, Jon (ed.). 1998. *Deliberative Democracy*. Cambridge: Cambridge University Press.

Entman, Robert. 1993. "Framing: Toward Clarification of a Fractured Paradigm." *Journal of Communication* 4 (4): 51–8.

Erbe, Jessica. 2005. "'What Do the Papers Say?' How Press Reviews Link National Media Arenas in Europe." *Javnost – The Public* 12 (2): 75–92.

Erbe, Jessica. 2006. "Integration der politischen Öffentlichkeit in Europa durch Vernetzung: Der Fall der grenzüberschreitenden Presseschauen in Deutschland." In Wolfgang R. Langenbucher and Michael Latzer (eds.), *Europäische Öffentlichkeit und medialer Wandel: Eine transdisziplinäre Perspektive*. Wiesbaden: VS Verlag, pp. 156–78.

Erbe, Jessica. 2012. *Der europäische Blick: Presseschauen und die Verbindung nationaler Öffentlichkeiten*. Baden-Baden: Nomos.

Eriksen, Erik O. 2005. "An Emerging European Public Sphere." *European Journal of Social Theory* 8 (3): 341–63.

Eriksen, Erik O. 2007. "Conceptualising European Public Spheres: General, Segmented and Strong Publics." In John E. Fossum and Philip

R. Schlesinger (eds.), *The European Union and the Public Sphere: A Communicative Space in the Making.* Abingdon, UK, and New York: Routledge, pp. 23–43.

European Commission. 2011. "Spring 2011: Europeans, the European Union and the Crisis." *Standard Eurobarometer 75.* Brussels: European Commission.

European Commission. 2012. "Public Opinion in the European Union, Spring 2012." *Standard Eurobarometer 77.* Brussels: European Commission.

European Commission. 2013. "Public Opinion in the European Union: First Results." *Standard Eurobarometer 79.* Brussels: European Commission.

European Parliament. 2011. *Europeans and the Crisis: European Parliament Eurobarometer Summary.* Brussels: Directorate General for Communications, Public Opinion Monitoring Unit.

Everson, Michelle, and Ellen Vos (eds.). 2009. *Uncertain Risks Regulated.* London: Routledge.

Favell, Adrian. 2008. *Eurostars and Eurocities: Free Movement and Mobility in an Integrating Europe.* Oxford: Blackwell.

Favell, Adrian. 2009. "Immigration, Migration, and Free Movement in the Making of Europe." In Jeffrey T. Checkel and Peter J. Katzenstein (eds.), *European Identity.* Cambridge: Cambridge University Press, pp. 167–92.

Favell, Adrian, and Virginie Guiraudon (eds.). 2011. *Sociology of the European Union.* Houndmills, Basingstoke, UK, and New York: Palgrave Macmillan.

Featherstone, Keith, and Claudio Radaelli (eds.). 2003. *The Politics of Europeanization.* Oxford: Oxford University Press.

Ferree, Myra M., William A. Gamson, Jürgen Gerhards, and Dieter Rucht (eds.). 2002. *Shaping Abortion Discourse: Democracy and the Public Sphere in Germany and the United States.* Cambridge: Cambridge University Press.

Filippov, Mikhail, Peter C. Ordeshook, and Olga Shvetsova. 2004. *Designing Federalism: A Theory of Self-Sustainable Federal Institutions.* Cambridge: Cambridge University Press.

Fligstein, Neil. 2008. *Euroclash: The EU, European Identity, and the Future of Europe.* New York: Oxford University Press.

Fligstein, Neil, Alina Polyakova, and Wayne Sandholtz. 2012. "European Integration, Nationalism and European Identity." *Journal of Common Market Studies* 50 (51): 106–22.

Follesdal, Andreas. 2000. "Subsidiarity and Democratic Deliberation." In Erik Oddvar Eriksen and John Erik Fossum (eds.), *Democracy in the European Union: Integration through Deliberation?* London: Routledge, pp. 85–110.

Follesdal, Andreas. 2007. "Toward Self-Sustaining Stability? How the Constitutional Treaty Would Enhance Forms of Institutional and National Balance." *Regional and Federal Studies* 17 (3): 353–74.

Follesdal, Andreas. 2009a. "If There is No Common and Unique European Identity, Should We Create One?" In Nils Holtug, Kasper Lippert-Rasmussen, and Sune Laegaard (eds.), *Multiculturalism and Nationalism in a World of Immigration.* Houndmills, Basingstoke, UK: Palgrave Macmillan, pp. 194–227.

Follesdal, Andreas. 2009b. "Universal Human Rights as a Shared Political Identity: Impossible? Necessary? Sufficient?" *Metaphilosophy* 40 (1): 65–76.

Follesdal, Andreas, and Simon Hix. 2006. "Why There is a 'Democratic Deficit' in the EU: A Response to Majone and Moravcsik." *Journal of Common Market Studies* 44 (3): 533–62.

Foot, Kirsten A., and Steven M. Schneider. (eds.). 2006. *Web Campaigning.* Cambridge, MA: The MIT Press.

Fossum, John Erik, and Philip Schlesinger (eds.). 2007. *The European Union and the Public Sphere: A Communicative Space in the Making?* London and New York: Routledge.

Franklin, Mark, and Cees Van der Eijk. 2006. "The Sleeping Giant: Potential for Political Mobilization of Disaffection in Europe." In Wouter Van der Brug and Cees Van der Eijk (eds.), *European Elections and Domestic Politics: Lessons from the Past and Scenarios for the Future.* Notre Dame, IN: University of Notre Dame Press, pp. 189–208.

Fraser, Nancy. 1992. "Rethinking the Public Sphere: A Contribution to the Critique of Actually Existing Democracy." In Craig Calhoun (ed.), *Habermas and the Public Sphere.* Cambridge, MA: The MIT Press, pp. 109–42.

Gamson, William A. 1992. *Talking Politics.* Cambridge: Cambridge University Press.

Gamson, William A., and Andre Modigliani. 1989. "Media Discourse and Public Opinion on Nuclear Power: A Constructionist Approach." *American Journal of Sociology* 95 (1): 1–37.

George, Alexander. 1993. *Bridging the Gap: Theory and Practice in Foreign Policy.* Washington, DC: U.S. Institute of Peace Press.

Gerhards, Jürgen. 1993. "Westeuropäische Integration und die Schwierigkeit der Entstehung einer europäischen Öffentlichkeit." *Zeitschrift für Soziologie* 22 (2): 96–110.

Gerhards, Jürgen. 2000. "Europäisierung von Ökonomie und Politik und die Trägheit der Entstehung einer europäischen Öffentlichkeit." In

Maurizio Bach (ed.), *Die Europäisierung nationaler Gesellschaften: Sonderheft der Kölner Zeitschrift für Soziologie und Sozialpsychologie*. Opladen: Westdeutscher Verlag, pp. 277–305.

Gerhards, Jürgen. 2002. "Das Öffentlichkeitsdefizit der EU im Horizont normativer Öffentlichkeitstheorien." In Hartmut Kaelble, Martin Kirsch, and Alexander Schmidt-Gernig (eds.), *Transnationale Öffentlichkeiten und Identitäten im 20. Jahrhundert*. Frankfurt am Main: Campus, pp. 135–58.

Gerhards, Jürgen, and Silke Hans. 2012. *Virtuelle Transnationalisierung: Partizipation der EU-Bürger an einer transnationalen europäischen Öffentlichkeit*. Arbeitspapier 27, Berliner Studien zur Soziologie Europas, Freie Universität Berlin.

Gerhards, Jürgen, and Holger Lengfeld. 2013. *Wir, ein europäisches Volk? Sozialintegration Europas und die Idee der Gleichheit aller europäischen Bürger*. Wiesbaden: Springer VS Verlag für Sozialwissenschaften.

Gerhards, Jürgen, and Friedhelm Neidhardt. 1991. "Strukturen und Funktionen moderner Öffentlichkeit: Fragestellungen und Ansätze." In Stefan Müller-Doohm and Klaus Neumann-Braun (eds.), *Öffentlichkeit, Kultur, Massenkommunikation: Beiträge zur Medien- und Kommunikationssoziologie*. Oldenburg: BIS, pp. 31–89.

Gerhards, Jürgen, Anke Offerhaus, and Jochen Roose. 2009. "Wer ist verantwortlich? Die Europäische Union, ihre Nationalstaaten und die massenmediale Attribution von Verantwortung für Erfolge und Misserfolge." In Frank Marcinkowski and Barbara Pfetsch (eds.), *Politik in der Mediendemokratie: Sonderheft 42 der Politischen Vierteljahresschrift*. Wiesbaden: VS Verlag, pp. 529–58.

Gerhards, Jürgen, and Jörg Rössel. 1999. "Zur Transnationalisierung der Gesellschaft der Bundesrepublik. Entwicklungen, Ursachen und mögliche Folgen für die europäische Integration." *Zeitschrift für Soziologie* 28 (5): 325–44.

Gerhards, Jürgen, and Mike S. Schäfer. 2010. "Is the Internet a Better Public Sphere? Comparing Old and New Media in the USA and Germany." *New Media & Society* 12 (1): 143–60.

Gitlin, Todd. 1980. *The Whole World Is Watching: Mass Media in the Making and Unmaking of the New Left*. Berkeley: University of California Press.

Grande, Edgar, and Hanspeter Kriesi. 2012. "The Transformative Power of Globalization and the Structure of Political Conflict in Western Europe." In Hanspeter Kriesi, Edgar Grande, Martin Dolezal, et al. (eds.), *Political Conflict in Western Europe*. Cambridge: Cambridge University Press, pp. 3–35.

Grande, Edgar, and Louis W. Pauly (eds.). 2005. *Complex Sovereignty: Reconstituting Political Authority in the 21st Century*. Toronto, Canada: Toronto University Press.

Grimm, Dieter. 1995. "Does Europe Need a Constitution?" *European Law Journal* 1 (3): 282–302.

Grossman, Emiliano, and Cornelia Woll. 2011. "The French Debate over the Bolkestein Directive." *Comparative European Politics* 9 (3): 344–66.

Gutmann, Amy, and Dennis Thompson. 2004. *Why Deliberative Democracy?* Princeton, NJ: Princeton University Press.

Habermas, Jürgen. 1980 (1962). *Strukturwandel der Öffentlichkeit: Untersuchungen zu einer Kategorie der bürgerlichen Gesellschaft*. Darmstadt and Neuwied: Luchterhand.

Habermas, Jürgen. 1981. *Theorie des kommunikativen Handelns*. 2 vols. Frankfurt am Main: Suhrkamp.

Habermas, Jürgen. 1992. *Faktizität und Geltung: Beiträge zur Diskurstheorie des Rechts und des demokratischen Rechtsstaats*. Frankfurt am Main: Suhrkamp.

Habermas, Jürgen. 1996a. "Braucht Europa eine Verfassung? Eine Bemerkung zu Dieter Grimm." In Jürgen Habermas, *Die Einbeziehung des Anderen: Studien zur politischen Theorie*. Frankfurt am Main: Suhrkamp, pp. 185–91.

Habermas, Jürgen. 1996b. "Three Normative Models of Democracy." In Sheila Benhabib (ed.), *Democracy and Difference: Contesting the Boundaries of the Political*. Princeton, NJ: Princeton University Press, pp. 21–30.

Habermas, Jürgen. 1996c. *Between Facts and Norms*. Cambridge, MA: The MIT Press.

Habermas, Jürgen. 1996d. *Die Einbeziehung des Anderen*. Frankfurt am Main: Suhrkamp.

Habermas, Jürgen. 1998a. "Does Europe Need a Constitution? Remarks on Dieter Grimm." In Jürgen Habermas, *The Inclusion of the Other: Studies in Political Theory*. Cambridge, MA: The MIT Press, pp. 155–61.

Habermas, Jürgen. 1998b. *The Inclusion of the Other: Studies in Political Theory*. Cambridge, MA: The MIT Press.

Habermas, Jürgen. 2006a. *The Divided West*. Cambridge: Polity Press.

Habermas, Jürgen. 2006b. "Political Communication in Media Society: Does Democracy Still Enjoy an Epistemic Dimension? The Impact of Normative Theory on Empirical Research." *Communication Theory* 16 (4): 411–26.

Habermas, Jürgen. 2006c. *Time of Transitions*. Cambridge: Polity Press.

Habermas, Jürgen. 2011. *Die Verfassung Europas*. Berlin: Suhrkamp.

Habermas, Jürgen. 2013. "Demokratie oder Kapitalismus? Vom Elend der nationalstaatlichen Fragmentierung in einer kapitalistisch integrierten Weltgesellschaft." *Blätter für deutsche und internationale Politik* 5: 59–70.

Habermas, Jürgen, and Jacques Derrida. 2003. "February 15, or What Binds Europeans Together: A Plea for a Common Foreign Policy, Beginning in the Core of Europe." *Constellations* 10 (3): 291–7.

Harrison, Jackie. 2010. "European Social Purpose and Public Service Communication." In Christina Bee and Emanuela Bozzini (eds.), *Mapping the European Public Sphere: Institutions, Media and Civil Society.* Farnham, UK, and Burlington, VT: Ashgate, pp. 99–113.

Haug, Christoph. 2010. "Public Spheres within Movements: Challenging the (Re)search for a European Public Sphere." In Simon Teune (ed.), *The Transnational Condition: Protest Dynamics in an Entangled Europe.* New York and Oxford: Berghahn Books, pp. 67–88.

Hecock, Douglas R. 2006. "Electoral Competition, Globalization, and Subnational Education Spending in Mexico: 1999–2004." *American Journal of Political Science* 50 (4): 950–61.

Helbling, Marc, Dominic Hoeglinger, and Bruno Wüest. 2010. "How Political Parties Frame European Integration." *European Journal of Political Research* 49 (4): 495–521.

Helbling, Marc, Dominic Hoeglinger, and Bruno Wüest. 2012. "The Impact of Arenas in Debates over Globalization." In Hanspeter Kriesi, Edgar Grande, Martin Dolezal, et al. (eds.), *Political Conflict in Western Europe.* Cambridge: Cambridge University Press, pp. 207–28.

Held, David, Anthony McGrew, David Goldblatt, and Jonathan Perraton. 1999. *Global Transformations: Politics, Economics and Culture.* Stanford, CA: Stanford University Press.

Herman, Edward S., and Noam Chomsky. 1988. *Manufacturing Consent: The Political Economy of the Mass Media.* New York: Pantheon Books.

Hix, Simon. 2005. *Political System of the European Union.* Houndmills, Basingstoke, UK: Palgrave Macmillan.

Hix, Simon. 2006. "Why the EU Needs (Left-Right) Politics? Policy Reform and Accountability Are Impossible Without It." Policy Paper No. 19. Paris: Notre Europe.

Hix, Simon. 2008. *What's Wrong with the European Union and How to Fix It.* Cambridge: Polity Press.

Hix, Simon, and Bjørn Høyland. 2011. *The Political System of the European Union.* 3rd edn. Houndmills, Basingstoke, UK: Palgrave Macmillan.

Hix, Simon, and Michael Marsh. 2007. "Punishment or Protest? Understanding European Parliamentary Elections." *Journal of Politics* 69 (2): 495–510.

Höglinger, Dominic. 2011. *Struggling with the Intricate Giant: How European integration is Being Politicized in Western Europe.* Unpublished PhD thesis, University of Zürich.

Holmes, Douglas. 2009. "Experimental Identities (after Maastricht)." In Jeffrey T. Checkel and Peter J. Katzenstein (eds.), *European Identity.* Cambridge: Cambridge University Press, pp. 52–80.

Holznagel, Bernd. 1999. *Der spezifische Funktionsauftrag des Zweiten Deutschen Fernsehens (ZDF): Bedeutung, Anforderungen und Unverzichtbarkeit unter Berücksichtigung der Digitalisierung, der europäischen Einigung und der Globalisierung der Informationsgesellschaft, ZDF Schriftenreihe 55.* Mainz: Zweites Deutsches Fernsehen.

Hooghe, Liesbet, and Gary Marks. 1999. "Making of a Polity: The Struggle over European integration." In Herbert Kitschelt, Peter Lange, Gary Marks, and John Stephens (eds.), *Continuity and Change in Contemporary Capitalism.* Cambridge: Cambridge University Press, pp. 70–97.

Hooghe, Liesbet, and Gary Marks. 2005. "Calculation, Community, and Cues: Public Opinion on European Integration." *European Union Politics* 6 (4): 419–43.

Hooghe, Liesbet, and Gary Marks. 2006. "Europe's Blues: Theoretical Soul-Searching after the Rejection of a European Constitution." *PS: Politics and Political Science* 39 (April): 247–50.

Hooghe, Liesbet, and Gary Marks (eds.). 2007a. "Understanding Euroscepticism." *Special Issue of Acta Politica*, Vol. 42. Houndmills, Basingstoke, UK: Palgrave Macmillan.

Hooghe, Liesbet, and Gary Marks. 2007b. "Sources of Euroscepticism." *Acta Politica* 42 (2–3): 119–27.

Hooghe, Liesbet, and Gary Marks. 2009. "A Postfunctionalist Theory of European Integration: From Permissive Consensus to Constraining Dissensus." *British Journal of Political Science* 39 (1): 1–23.

Hooghe, Liesbet, Gary Marks, and Carole J. Wilson. 2004. "Does Left/Right Structure Party Positions on European Integration?" In Gary Marks and Marco R. Steenbergen (eds.), *European Integration and Political Conflict.* Cambridge: Cambridge University Press, pp. 120–40.

Hopf, Ted. 2012. *Reconstructing the Cold War.* New York: Oxford University Press.

Hovland, Carl. 1959. "Reconciling Conflicting Results Derived from Experimental and Survey Studies of Attitude Change." *American Psychologist* 14: 8–17.

Hovland, Carl, Arthur Lumsdaine, and Fred Sheffield. 1949. *Experiments on Mass Communication.* Princeton, NJ: Princeton University Press.

Hutter, Swen, and Edgar Grande. 2012. "Politicizing Europe in the National Electoral Arena: A Comparative Analysis of Five European Countries,

1970 to 2010." Paper presented at PoIEU Project Meeting, November 24, Florence, Italy.

Iyengar, Shanto. 2002. *Experimental Designs for Political Communication Research: From Shopping Malls to the Internet.* Paper presented at the Workshop in Mass Media Economics, London. Accessed January 29, 2009. Available at http://pcl.stanford.edu/common/docs/research/iyengar/2002/expdes2002.pdf.

Iyengar, Shanto, Mark Peters, and Donald Kinder. 1982. "Experimental Demonstrations of the 'Not-So-Minimal' Consequences of Television News Programs." *American Political Science Review* 76 (4): 848–58.

Jansen, Dorothea. 2002. *Einführung in die Netzwerkanalyse.* Opladen: Leske+Budrich.

Jentges, Erich, Hans-Jörg Trenz, and Regina Vetters. 2007. "Von der politischen zur sozialen Konstitutionalisierung Europas: Verfassungsgebung als Katalysator europäischer Vergesellschaftung?" *Politische Vierteljahresschrift* 48 (4): 705–29.

Kantner, Cathleen. 2003. "Öffentliche politische Kommunikation in der Europäischen Union: Eine hermeneutisch-pragmatistische Perspektive." In Ansgar Klein, Ruud Koopmans, Ludger Klein, et al. (eds.), *Bürgerschaft, Öffentlichkeit und Demokratie in Europa.* Opladen: Leske+Budrich, pp. 215–29.

Kantner, Cathleen. 2004. *Kein modernes Babel: Kommunikative Voraussetzungen europäischer Öffentlichkeit.* Wiesbaden: VS Sozialwissenschaften.

Kantner, Cathleen. 2006. "Die thematische Verschränkung nationaler Öffentlichkeiten in Europa und die Qualität transnationaler politischer Kommunikation." In Kurt Imhof, Roger Blum, Heinz Bonfadelli, and Otfried Jarren (eds.), *Demokratie in der Mediengesellschaft.* Wiesbaden: VS Sozialwissenschaften, pp. 145–60.

Kantner, Cathleen. 2011. "Debating Humanitarian Military Interventions in the European Public Sphere." *RECON Online Working Paper.* Oslo: ARENA, University of Oslo.

Kantner, Cathleen, Amelie Kutter, Andreas Hildebrandt, and Mark Püttcher. 2011. "How to Get Rid of the Noise in the Corpus: Cleaning Large Samples of Digital Newspaper Texts." In *International Relations Online Working Paper.* Stuttgart: Stuttgart University.

Kantner, Cathleen, Amelie Kutter, and Swantje Renfordt. 2008. *The Perception of the EU as an Emerging Security Actor in Media Debates on Humanitarian and Military Interventions (1990–2006).* RECON Online Working Paper, 2008/19. Oslo: ARENA, University of Oslo.

Karpf, David. 2012. *The MoveOn Effect: The Unexpected Transformation of American Political Advocacy.* New York: Oxford University Press.

Katzenstein, Peter J. 1976. "International Relations and Domestic Structures: Foreign Economic Policies of Advanced Industrial States." *International Organization* 30 (1): 1–45.

Kerscher, Alena Debora. 2011. Der Beitritt der Türkei zur Europäischen Union. Ein Vergleich der öffentlichen Debatten in Deutschland und Österreich von 1995 bis 2010. University of Munich: Unpublished Masters thesis.

Kevin, Deirdre. 2003. *Europe in the Media: A Comparison of Reporting, Representation and Rhetoric in National Media Systems in Europe.* London: Lawrence Erlbaum.

Kielmansegg, Peter G. 1996. "Integration und Demokratie." In Markus Jachtenfuchs and Beate Kohler-Koch (eds.), *Europäische Integration.* Opladen: Leske+Budrich, pp. 47–72.

Kleinen-von Königslöw, Katharina. 2010a. "Die Mehrfachsegmentierung der europäischen Öffentlichkeit." TranState Working Papers No. 138. Bremen: Sonderforschungsbereich 597 "Staatlichkeit im Wandel."

Kleinen-von Königslöw, Katharina. 2010b. "Europe for the People? The Europeanization of Public Spheres in the Tabloid Press." In David Tréfás and Jens Lucht (eds.), *Europe on Trial: Shortcomings of the EU with Regard to Democracy, Public Sphere, and Identity.* Innsbruck: Studienverlag, pp. 44–59.

Kleinen-von Königslöw, Katharina, and Johanna Möller. 2009. "Nationalisierte Europäisierung: Die Entwicklung der polnischen Medienöffentlichkeit nach 1989." *Jahrbuch Nordost Archiv* 18: 101–39.

Kleinnijenhuis, Jan, Jan A. De Ridder, and Ewald M. Rietberg. 1997. "Reasoning in Economic Discourse: An Application of the Network Approach to the Dutch Press." In Carl W. Roberts (ed.), *Text Analysis for the Social Sciences: Methods for Drawing Statistical Inferences from Texts and Transcripts.* Mahwah, NJ: Lawrence Erlbaum Associates, pp. 191–207.

Kleinnijenhuis, Jan, and Paul Pennings. 2001. "Measurement of Party Positions on the Basis of Party Programmes, Media Coverage and Voter Perceptions." In Michael Laver (ed.), *Estimating the Policy Positions of Political Actors.* London: Routledge, pp. 162–82.

Kohler-Koch, Beate. 2011. "Zivilgesellschaftliche Partizipation: Zugewinn an Demokratie oder Pluralisierung der europaeischen Lobby?" In Beate Kohler-Koch and Christine Quittkat (eds.), *Die Entzauberung partizipativer Demokratie: Zur Rolle der Zivilgesellschaft bei der Demokratisierung von EU-Governance.* Frankfurt and New York: Campus, pp. 241–71.

Koopmans, Ruud. 2007. "Who Inhabits the European Public Sphere? Winners and Losers, Supporters and Opponents in Europeanised Political Debates." *European Journal of Political Research* 46 (2): 183–210.

Koopmans, Ruud. 2010. "Winners and Losers, Supporters and Opponents in Europeanized Public Debates." In Ruud Koopmanns and Paul Statham (eds.), *The Making of a European Public Sphere: Media Discourse and Political Contention.* New York: Cambridge University Press, pp. 97–121.

Koopmans, Ruud, and Jessica Erbe. 2004. "Towards a European Public Sphere? Vertical and Horizontal Dimensions of Europeanized Political Communication." *Innovation: The European Journal of Social Science Research* 17 (2): 97–118.

Koopmans, Ruud, Jessica Erbe, and Martin F. Meyer. 2010. "The Europeanization of Public Spheres: Comparisons across Issues, Time, and Countries." In Ruud Koopmans and Paul Statham (eds.), *The Making of a European Public Sphere: Media Discourse and Political Contention.* New York: Cambridge University Press, pp. 63–96.

Koopmans, Ruud, and Barbara Pfetsch. 2006. "Obstacles or Motors of Europeanization? German Media and the Transnationalization of Public Debate." *Communications* 31 (2): 115–38.

Koopmans, Ruud, and Paul Statham (eds.). 2010a. *The Making of a European Public Sphere: Media Discourse and Political Contention.* Cambridge: Cambridge University Press.

Koopmans, Ruud, and Paul Statham. 2010b. "Theoretical Framework, Research Design, and Methods." In Ruud Koopmans and Paul Statham (eds.), *The Making of a European Public Sphere: Media Discourse and Political Contention.* Cambridge: Cambridge University Press, pp. 34–59.

Koopmans, Ruud, and Ann Zimmermann. 2010. "Transnational Political Communication on the Internet: Search Engine Results and Hyperlink Networks." In Ruud Koopmans and Paul Statham (eds.), *The Making of a European Public Sphere: Media Discourse and Political Contention.* Cambridge: Cambridge University Press, pp. 171–94.

Kriesi, Hanspeter. 1998. "The Transformation of Cleavage Politics: The 1997 Stein Rokkan Lecture." *European Journal of Political Research* 33 (2): 165–85.

Kriesi, Hanspeter. 2012. "Restructuring the National Political Space: The Supply Side of National Electoral Politics." In Hanspeter Kriesi, Edgar Grande, Martin Dolezal, et al. (eds.), *Political Conflict in Western Europe.* Cambridge: Cambridge University Press, pp. 96–126.

Kriesi, Hanspeter, and Edgar Grande. 2012. "The Euro-Crisis: A Boost to Politicization of European Integration?" Paper presented at EUDO

2012 Dissemination Conference on The Euro Crisis and the State of European Democracy, Florence, Italy, November 22 and 23.

Kriesi, Hanspeter, Edgar Grande, Martin Dolezal, Marc Helbling, Dominic Höglinger, Swen Hutter, and Bruno Wuest. 2012. *Political Conflict in Western Europe.* Cambridge: Cambridge University Press.

Kriesi, Hanspeter, Edgar Grande, Romain Lachat, Martin Dolezal, Simon Bornschier, and Timotheos Frey. 2008. *West European Politics in the Age of Globalization.* Cambridge: Cambridge University Press.

Kriesi, Hanspeter, Anke Tresch, and Margit Jochum. 2010. "Going Public in the European Union: Action Repertoires of Collective Political Actors." In Ruud Koopmanns and Paul Statham (eds.), *The Making of a European Public Sphere: Media Discourse and Political Contention.* Cambridge: Cambridge University Press, pp. 223–44.

Kroeger, Sandra. 2008. "Nothing but Consultation: The Place of Organised Civil Society in EU Policy Making across Policies." *European Governance Papers (EUROGOV) C-08–03.* Available at www.connex-network/org/eurogov/pdf/egp-connex-C-08-03.pdf.

Kuhn, Theresa, and Florian Stoeckel. 2014. "When European Integration Becomes Costly: The Euro Crisis as a Test of Public Support for European Economic Governance." *Journal of European Public Policy.*

Kutter, Amelie, and Cathleen Kantner. 2012. "Corpus-Based Content Analysis: A Method for Investigating News Coverage on War and Intervention." In *International Relations Online Working Paper.* Stuttgart: Stuttgart University.

Laffan, Brigid, and Jane O'Mahony. 2004. *Multilevel Governance: Mis-Fit, Politicisation and Europeanisation: The Implementation of the Habitats Directive.* OEUE Phase 2, Occasional Paper. Dublin: Dublin European Institute, University College Dublin.

Lang, Sabine. 2012. *NGOs, Civil Society, and the Public Sphere.* New York and London: Cambridge University Press.

Latour, Bruno. 2005. *Reassembling the Social: An Introduction to Actor-Network Theory.* Oxford: Oxford University Press.

Lauf, Edmund, and Jochen Peter. 2004. "EU-Repräsentanten in Fernsehnachrichten: Eine Analyse ihrer Präsenz in 13 EU-Mitgliedsstaaten vor der Europawahl 1999." In Lutz M. Hagen (ed.), *Europäische Union und mediale Öffentlichkeit: Theoretische Perspektiven und empirische Befunde zur Rolle der Medien im europäischen Einigungsprozess.* Köln: Halem, pp. 162–77.

Leconte, Cécile. 2010. *Understanding Euroscepticism.* Houndmills, Basingstoke, UK: Palgrave Macmillan.

Leggewie, Claus. 2004. *Die Türkei und Europa.* Frankfurt am Main: Suhrkamp.

Lemco, Jonathan. 1991. *Political Stability in Federal Governments.* New York: Praeger.

Lengfeld, Holger, Sara Schmidt, and Julia Häuberer. 2012. *Solidarität in der europäischen Fiskalkrise: Sind die EU-Bürger zu finanzieller Unterstützung von hoch verschuldeten EU-Ländern bereit? Erste Ergebnisse aus einer Umfrage in Deutschland und Portugal.* Hamburg Reports on Contemporary Societies – HRCS, 5. Hamburg: Universität Hamburg.

Liebert, Ulrike (ed.). 2007. "Europe in Contention: Debating the Constitutional Treaty." *Special Issue of Perspectives on European Politics and Society.* Vol. 8 (September). London: Routledge.

Linz, Juan J. 1999. "Democracy, Multinationalism and Federalism." In Wolfgang Merkel (ed.), *Demokratie in Ost und West.* Frankfurt am Main: Suhrkamp, pp. 382–401.

Locher, Birgit. 2007. *Trafficking in Women in the European Union: Norms, Advocacy Networks and Policy Change.* Wiesbaden. VS Verlag.

Luhmann, Niklas. 1971. "Öffentliche Meinung." In Niklas Luhmann *Politische Planung: Aufsätze zur Soziologie von Politik und Verwaltung.* Opladen: Westdeutscher Verlag, pp. 9–34.

Luhmann, Niklas. 2000. *Die Politik der Gesellschaft.* Frankfurt am Main: Suhrkamp.

Madeker, Ellen. 2008. *Türkei und europäische Identität: Eine wissenssoziologische Analyse der Debatte um den EU-Beitritt.* Wiesbaden: VS Verlag für Sozialwissenschaften.

Majone, Giandomenico 1998. "State, Market and Regulatory Competition: Lessons for the Integrating World Economy." In Andrew Moravcsik (ed.), *Centralization or Fragmentation? Europe Facing the Challenges of Deepening, Diversity, and Democracy.* New York: Council on Foreign Relations, pp. 94–123.

Majone, Giandomenico. 2001. "Regulatory Legitimacy in the United States and the European Union." In Kalypso Nicolaidis and Robert Howse (eds.), *The Federal Vision: Legitimacy and Levels of Governance in the US and the EU.* Oxford: Oxford University Press, pp. 252–74.

Manin, Bernard. 1987. "On Legitimacy and Political Deliberation." *Political Theory* 15: 338–68.

Mansbridge, Jane J., James Bohman, Simone Chambers, David Estlund, Andreas Follesdal, Archon Fung, et al. 2010. "The Place of Self-Interest and the Role of Power in Deliberative Democracy." *Journal of Political Philosophy* 18 (1): 64–100.

Marks, Gary, and Marco R. Steenbergen 2004. *European Integration and Political Conflict, Themes in European Governance.* Cambridge: Cambridge University Press.

Markus, Gregory B. 1982. "Political Attitudes during an Election Year: A Report on the 1980 NES Panel Study." *American Political Science Review* 76 (3): 538–60.

Marres, Noortje. 2006. "Net-Work Is Format Work: Issue Networks and the Sites of Civil Society Politics." In Jodi Dean, John Asherson, and Geert Lovink (eds.), *Reformatting Politics: Information Technology and Global Civil Society*. New York: Routledge, pp. 3–18.

Marres, Noortje, and Richard Rogers. 2005. "Recipe for Tracing the Fate of Issues and their Publics on the Web." In Bruno Latour and Peter Weibel (eds.), *Making Things Public: Atmospheres of Democracy*. Cambridge, MA: The MIT Press, pp. 922–35.

McCarthy, Thomas. 1998. "Legitimacy and Diversity: Dialectical Reflections on Analytical Distinctions." In Michel Rosenfeld and Andrew Arato (eds.), *Habermas on Law and Democracy*. Berkeley: University of California Press, pp. 115–53.

McCombs, Maxwell E., and Donald L. Shaw. 1972. "The Agenda-Setting Function of the Mass Media." *Public Opinion Quarterly* 36: 176–87.

McNair, Brian. 2000. *Journalism and Democracy: An Evaluation of the Political Public Sphere*. London and New York: Routledge.

Meijers, Maurits. 2013. *The Euro-Crisis as a Catalyst of the Europeanization of Public Spheres? A Cross-Temporal Study of the Netherlands and Germany*. LSE "Europe in Question" Discussion Paper Series, 62, London: London School of Economics and Political Science.

Meyer, Christoph O. 1999. "Political Legitimacy and the Invisibility of Politics: Exploring the European Union's Communication Deficit." *Journal of Common Market Studies* 37 (4): 617–39.

Meyer, Christoph O. 2002. *Europäische Öffentlichkeit als Kontrollsphäre: Die Europäische Kommission, die Medien und politische Verantwortlichkeit*. Berlin: Vistas.

Meyer, Christoph O. 2007. "The Constitutional Treaty Debates as Revelatory Mechanisms: Insights for Public Sphere Research and Re-Launch Attempts." RECON Online Working Paper. Oslo: ARENA, University of Oslo.

Meyer, Christoph O. 2009. "Does European Union Politics become Mediatized? The Case of the European Commission." *Journal of European Public Policy* 16 (7): 1047–64.

Meyer, Jan-Henrik. 2009. "Transnational Communication in the European Public Sphere." In Wolfram Kaiser, Brigitte Leucht, and Morten Rasmussen (eds.), *The History of the European Union: Origins of a Trans- and Supranational Polity 1950–1972*. London and New York: Routledge, pp. 110–28.

Meyer, Jan-Henrik. 2010. *The European Public Sphere: Media and Transnational Communication in European Integration, Studies on the History of European Integration*. Stuttgart: Franz Steiner Verlag.

Michelman, Frank I. 1996. "Between Facts and Norms: Jürgen Habermas." *Journal of Philosophy* 93: 307–15.

Michelman, Frank I. 2000. "W(h)ither the Constitution?" *Cardozo Law Review* 21: 1063–83.

Milavsky, J. Ronald, Ronald C. Keppler, Horst H. Stipp, and William Rubens. 1982. "Television and Aggression: Results of a Panel Study." *The Public Opinion Quarterly* 48 (3): 701–5.

Minkenberg, Michael, and Pascal Perrineau. 2007. "The Radical Right in the European Elections 2004." *International Political Science Review* 28 (1): 29–55.

Monroe, Kristen. 1978. "Economic Influences on Presidential Popularity." *Public Opinion Quarterly* 42 (3): 360–69.

Mudde, Cas. 2007. *Populist Radical Right Parties in Europe*. Cambridge: Cambridge University Press.

Neidhardt, Friedhelm. 1994. "Öffentlichkeit, öffentliche Meinung, soziale Bewegungen." In Friedhelm Neidhardt (ed.), *Öffentlichkeit, öffentliche Meinung, soziale Bewegungen*. Opladen: Westdeutscher Verlag, pp. 7–41.

Neidhardt, Friedhelm. 2006. "Europäische Öffentlichkeit als Prozess. Anmerkungen zum Forschungsstand." In Wolfgang R. Langenbucher and Michael Latzer (eds.), *Europäische Öffentlichkeit und medialer Wandel: Eine transdisziplinäre Perspektive*. Wiesbaden: VS Sozialwissenschaften, pp. 46–61.

Neidhardt, Friedhelm, Ruud Koopmans, and Barbara Pfetsch. 2000. "Konstitutionsbedingungen politischer Öffentlichkeit: Der Fall Europa." In *WZB-Jahrbuch*. Berlin: Wissenschaftszentrum Berlin für Sozialforschung, pp. 263–93.

Nelson, Thomas E., Rosalee A. Clawson, and Zoe M. Oxley. 1997. "Media Framing of a Civil Liberties Conflict and its Effect on Tolerance." *American Political Science Review* 91 (3): 567–83.

Neumann, Iver. 2002. "Returning Practice to the Linguistic Turn: The Case of Diplomacy." *Millennium – Journal of International Studies* 31 (3): 627–51.

Nome, Martin Austvoll, and Nils B. Weidmann. 2013. "Conflict Diffusion via Social Identities: Entrepreneurship and Adaptation." In Jeffrey T. Checkel (ed.), *Transnational Dynamics of Civil War*. Cambridge: Cambridge University Press, pp. 173–204.

Oberhuber, Florian, Christoph Bärenreuter, Michal Krzyzanowski, Heinz Schönbauer, and Ruth Wodak. 2005. "Debating the European

Constitution: On Representations of Europe/the EU in the Press." *Journal of Language and Politics* 4 (2): 227–71.

Olsen, Johan P. 2002. "The Many Faces of Europeanization." *Journal of Common Market Studies* 40 (5): 921–52.

Peter, Jochen, and Claes H. De Vreese. 2003. "Agenda-Rich, Agenda-Poor: A Cross-National Comparative Investigation of Nominal and Thematic Public Agenda Diversity." *International Journal of Public Opinion Research* 15 (1): 44–64.

Peter, Jochen, and Claes H. De Vresse. 2004. "In Search of Europe: A Cross-National Comparative Study of the European Union in National Television News." *The Harvard International Journal of Press/Politics* 9 (3): 3–24.

Peters, Bernhard. 1993. *Die Integration moderner Gesellschaften*. Frankfurt am Main: Suhrkamp.

Pettit, Philipp. 2001. "Deliberative Democracy and the Discursive Dilemma." *Philosophical Issues* 11: 268–299.

Pfetsch, Barbara. 2008. "Agents of Transnational Debate across Europe: The Press in Emerging European Public Sphere." *Javnost – The Public* 15 (4): 21–40.

Pfetsch, Barbara, and Silke Adam. 2008. "Die Akteursperspektive in der politischen Kommunikationsforschung: Fragestellungen, Forschungsparadigmen und Problemlagen." In Barbara Pfetsch and Silke Adam (eds.), *Massenmedien als politische Akteure: Konzepte und Analysen*. Wiesbaden: VS Verlag, pp. 9–26.

Pfetsch, Barbara, Silke Adam, and Barbara Eschner. 2008. "The Contribution of the Press to Europeanization of Public Debates: A Comparative Study of Issue Salience and Conflict Lines of European Integration." *Journalism: Theory, Practice & Criticism* 9 (4): 465–92.

Pfetsch, Barbara, Silke Adam, and Barbara Eschner. 2010. "The Media's Voice over Europe: Issue Salience, Openness, and Conflict Lines in Editorials." In Ruud Koopmanns and Paul Statham (eds.), *The Making of a European Public Sphere: Media Discourse and Political Contention*. New York: Cambridge University Press, pp. 151–70.

Pouliot, Vincent. 2010. *International Security in Practice: The Politics of NATO-Russia Diplomacy*. New York: Cambridge University Press.

Powell, G. Bingham. 2000. *Elections as Instruments of Democracy: Majoritarian and Proportional Visions*. New Haven, CT: Yale University Press.

Price, Richard. 2008a. "Moral Limit and Possibility in World Politics." *International Organization* 62 (2): 191–220.

Price, Richard (ed.). 2008b. *Moral Limit and Possibility in World Politics*. Cambridge: Cambridge University Press.

Price, Richard, and Christian Reus-Smit. 1998. "Dangerous Liaisons? Critical International Theory and Constructivism." *European Journal of International Relations* 4 (3): 259–94.

Przeworski, Adam, and Henry Teune. 1970. *The Logic of Comparative Social Inquiry*. New York: John Wiley & Sons.

Puntscher Riekmann, Sonja, and Doris Wydra. 2013. "Representation in the State of Emergency: Parliaments Against Governments?" *Journal of European Integration* 35 (5): 565–82.

Ragin, Charles, and Benoit Rihoux (eds.). 2009. *Configurational Comparative Methods: Qualitative Comparative Analysis (QCA) and Related Techniques*. London: Sage Publications.

Rauh, Christian. 2013. "A Widening Audience, Ever More Interested and Active? The Public Politicization of European Integration in the EU6, 1990–2011." Unpublished manuscript. Berlin: WZB – Social Science Research Center Berlin.

Rawls, John. 1993. *Political Liberalism*. New York: Columbia University Press.

Rawls, John. 1999. "The Idea of Public Reason Revisited." In John Rawls, *The Law of Peoples*. Cambridge, MA: Harvard University Press, pp. 129–80.

Renfordt, Swantje. 2011. *Framing the Use of Force: An International Rule of Law in Media Reporting. A Comparative Analysis of Western Debates about Military Interventions, 1990–2005*. Baden-Baden: Nomos.

Riker, William H. 1982. *Liberalism against Populism*. San Francisco, CA: W.H. Freeman.

Risse, Thomas. 2000. "'Let's Argue!' Communicative Action in International Relations." *International Organization* 54 (1): 1–39.

Risse, Thomas. 2002. "Zur Debatte um die (Nicht-) Existenz einer europäischen Öffentlichkeit: Was wir wissen, und wie es zu interpretieren ist." *Berliner Debatte Initial* 13 (5/6): 15–23.

Risse, Thomas. 2010. *A Community of Europeans? Transnational Identities and Public Spheres*. Ithaca, NY, and London: Cornell University Press.

Risse, Thomas. 2013. *Solidarität unter Fremden? Europäische Identität im Härtetest*. KFG Working Paper Series, 50. Berlin: Freie Universität Berlin.

Risse, Thomas, Maria G. Cowles, and James A. Caporaso. 2001. "Europeanization and Domestic Change: Introduction." In Maria G. Cowles, James A. Caporaso, and Thomas Risse (eds.), *Transforming Europe: Europeanization and Domestic Change*. Ithaca, NY, and London: Cornell University Press, pp. 1–20.

Risse-Kappen, Thomas. 1994. "Ideas Do Not Float Freely: Transnational Coalitions, Domestic Structures, and the End of the Cold War." *International Organization* 48 (2): 185–214.

Rogers, Richard. 2004. *Information Politics on the Web.* Cambridge, MA: The MIT Press.

Rokkan, Stein. 1999. *State Formation, Nation-Building and Mass Politics in Europe.* Oxford: Oxford University Press.

Roskos-Ewoldsen, David, Beverly Roskos-Ewoldsen, and Francesca Dillman-Carpentier. 2002. "Media Priming: A Synthesis." In Jennings Bryant and Dolf Zillmann (eds.), *Media Effects: Advances in Theory and Research.* Mahwah, NJ: Erlbaum, pp. 97–120.

Sanders, David, and Pippa Norris. 2005. "The Impact of Political Advertising in the UK 2001 Election." *Political Research Quarterly* 58: 525–36.

Scharkow, Michael, and Jens Vogelgesang. 2009. "Effects of Domestic Media Use on European Integration." *Communications* 34: 73–91.

Scharpf, Fritz W. 1985. "Die Politikverflechtungs-Falle: Europäische Integration und deutscher Föderalismus im Vergleich." *Politische Vierteljahresschrift* 26 (4): 324–50.

Scharpf, Fritz W. 1988. "The Joint-Decision Trap: Lessons from German Federalism and European Integration." *Public Administration* 66: 239–78.

Scharpf, Fritz W. 2009. "Legitimacy in the Multilevel European Polity." *European Political Science Review* 1 (2): 173–204.

Scharpf, Fritz W. 2010. "The Joint-Decision Trap Revisited." In Fritz W. Scharpf (ed.), *Community and Autonomy: Institutions, Policies, and Legitimacy in Multilevel Europe.* Frankfurt am Main: Campus.

Scharpf, Fritz W. 2013. *Political Legitimacy in a Non-Optimal Currency Area.* KFG Working Paper Series. Berlin: Free University Berlin.

Schattschneider, Elmer Eric. 1960. *The Semi-Sovereign People: A Realist's View of Democracy in America.* New York: Holt, Rinehart and Winston.

Schatz, Edward (ed.). 2009. *Political Ethnography: What Immersion Contributes to the Study of Power.* Chicago: University of Chicago Press.

Schimmelfennig, Frank. 2003. *The EU, NATO, and the Integration of Europe: Rules and Rhetoric.* Cambridge: Cambridge University Press.

Schimmelfennig, Frank, and Ulrich Sedelmeier (eds.). 2005. *The Europeanization of Central and Eastern Europe.* Ithaca, NY: Cornell University Press.

Schmidt, Vivien A. 2006. *Democracy in Europe: The EU and National Polities.* Oxford: Oxford University Press.

Schmidt, Vivien A., and Claudio Radaelli. 2004. "Policy Change and Discourse in Europe: Conceptual and Methodological Issues," *West European Politics* 27 (2): 183–210.

Schmitter, Philippe C. 2000. *How to Democratize the European Union – and Why Bother?* London: Rowman & Littlefield.

Schuck, Andreas R.T., and Claes H. De Vreese. 2006. "Between Risk and Opportunity: News Framing and its Effects on Public Support for EU Enlargement." *European Journal of Communication* 21 (3): 5–32.

Schuck, Andreas R.T., Georgios Xezonakis, Matthijs Elenbaas, Susan A. Banducci, and Claes H. De Vreese. 2011. "Party Contestation and Europe on the News Agenda: The 2009 European Parliamentary Elections." *Electoral Studies* 30 (1): 41–52.

Schumpeter, Joseph A. 1976. *Capitalism, Socialism and Democracy.* London: Allen and Unwin.

Scott, John (ed.). 1991. *Social Network Analysis: A Handbook.* London: Sage Publications.

Sears, David O. 1986. "College Sophomores in the Laboratory: Influences of a Narrow Database on the Social Psychology View of Human Nature." *Journal of Personality and Social Psychology* 51: 515–30.

Semetko, Holli A., Claes H. De Vreese, and Jochen Peter. 2000. "Europeanised Politics – Europeanised Media? European Integration and Political Communication.", *West European Politics* 23 (4): 121–41.

Shapiro, Ian. 1996. *Democracy's Place.* Ithaca, NY: Cornell University Press.

Shapiro, Ian. 2003. *The State of Democratic Theory.* Princeton, NJ: Princeton University Press.

Sikkink, Kathryn. 1991. *Ideas and Institutions: Developmentalism in Brazil and Argentina.* Ithaca, NY: Cornell University Press.

Sil, Rudra, and Peter Katzenstein. 2010a. "Analytic Eclecticism in the Study of World Politics: Reconfiguring Problems and Mechanisms across Research Traditions." *Perspectives on Politics* 8 (2): 411–31.

Sil, Rudra, and Peter Katzenstein. 2010b. *Beyond Paradigms: Analytical Eclecticism in the Study of World Politics.* New York: Palgrave Macmillan.

Statham, Paul. 2010a. "What Kind of Europeanized Public Politics." In Ruud Koopmans and Paul Statham (eds.), *The Making of a European Public Sphere: Media Discourse and Political Contention.* Cambridge: Cambridge University Press, pp. 277–306.

Statham, Paul. 2010b. "Making Europe News: Journalism and Media Performance." In Ruud Koopmans and Paul Statham (eds.), *The Making of a European Public Sphere: Media Discourse and Political Contention.* Cambridge: Cambridge University Press, pp. 125–50.

Statham, Paul, Ruud Koopmans, Anke Tresch, and Julie Firmstone. 2010. "Political Party Contestation: Emerging Euroscepticism or Normalisation of Eurocriticism?" In Ruud Koopmans and Paul Statham (eds.), *The Making of a European Public Sphere: The Europeanisation of Media Discourse and Political Contention.* Cambridge: Cambridge University Press, pp. 327–65.

Statham, Paul, and Hans-Jörg Trenz. 2013a. "How European Union Politicization Can Emerge through Contestation: The Constitution Case." *Journal of Common Market Studies* 51 (5): 965–80.

Statham, Paul, and Hans-Jörg Trenz. 2013b. *The Politicization of Europe: Contesting the Constitution in the Mass Media.* London: Routledge.

Steffek, Jens, and Patrizia Nanz. 2008. "Emergent Patterns of Civil Society Participation in Global and European Governance." In Jens Steffek, Claudia Kissling, and Patrizia Nanz (eds.), *Civil Society Participation in European and Global Governance: A Cure for the Democratic Deficit?* Houndmills, Basingstoke, UK: Palgrave Macmillan, pp. 1–29.

Steiner, Jürg, André Bächtiger, Markus Spörndli, and Marco Steenbergen. 2004. *Deliberative Politics in Action: Analyzing Parliamentary Discourses.* Cambridge: Cambridge University Press.

Steinmo, Sven, Kathleen Thelen, and Frank Longstreth (eds.). 1992. *Structuring Politics: Historical Institutionalism in Comparative Analysis.* Cambridge: Cambridge University Press.

Stoeckel, Florian 2009. "The European Public Sphere, the Media, and Support for European Integration." *Berliner Studien zur Soziologie Europas* 20. Berlin: Free University Berlin.

Stoeckel, Florian. 2012. "Becoming Europeans? The Effect of Transnational Interactions on Identification with Europe." Unpublished paper. Chapel Hill, NC: University of North Carolina, Department of Political Science.

Stretesky, Paul, and Mark Pogrebin. 2007. "Gang-Related Gun Violence: Socialization, Identity, and Self." *Journal of Contemporary Ethnography* 36 (1): 85–114.

Taggart, Paul, and Aleks Szczerbiak (eds.). 2005/2008. *Opposing Europe? The Comparative Party Politics of Euroscepticism*, Vols. 1 and 2. Oxford: Oxford University Press.

Tarrow, Sidney. 2001. "Contentious Politics in a Composite Polity." In Doug Imig and Sidney Tarrow (eds.), *Contentious Europeans: Protest and Politics in an Emerging Polity.* Oxford: Rowman & Littlefield, pp. 233–52.

Thorhallsson, Baldur. 2000. *The Role of Small States in the European Union.* Aldershot, UK: Ashgate.

Tobler, Stefan. 2010. *Transnationalisierung nationaler Öffentlichkeit. Konfliktinduzierte Kommunikationsverdichtungen und kollektive Identitätsbildung in Europa.* Wiesbaden: VS Verlag.

Trenz, Hans-Jörg. 2002. *Zur Konstitution politischer Öffentlichkeit in der Europäischen Union. Zivilgesellschaftliche Subpolitik oder schaupolitische Inszenierung?* Baden-Baden: Nomos.

Trenz, Hans-Jörg. 2004. "Media Coverage on European Governance: Exploring the European Public Sphere in National Quality Newspapers." *European Journal of Communication* 19 (3): 291–319.

Trenz, Hans-Jörg. 2005. *Europa in den Medien: Die europäische Integration im Spiegel nationaler Öffentlichkeit.* Frankfurt am Main: Campus.

Trenz, Hans Jörg. 2007. "'Quo Vadis Europe?' Quality Newspapers Struggling for European Unity." In John Erik Fossum and Philip Schlesinger (eds.), *The European Union and the Public Sphere: A Communicative Space in the Making?* London and New York: Routledge, pp. 89–109.

Trenz, Hans Jörg. 2008. "In Search of the European Public Sphere: Between Normative Overstretch and Empirical Disenchantment." RECON Online Working Papers. Oslo: ARENA, University of Oslo.

Trenz, Hans-Jörg. 2010. "The Europeanisation of Political Communication: Conceptional Clarifications and Empirical Measurement." In Christina Bee and Emanuela Bozzini (eds.), *Mapping the European Public Sphere: Institutions, Media and Civil Society.* Farnham, UK, and Burlington, VT: Ashgate, pp. 15–29.

Van de Steeg, Marianne. 2000. "An Analysis of the Dutch and Spanish Newspaper Debates on EU Enlargement with Central and Eastern European Countries: Suggestions for a Transnational Public Sphere." In Barbara Baerns and Juliana Raupp (eds.), *Information und Kommunikation in Europa.* Berlin: Vistas, pp. 61–87.

Van de Steeg, Marianne. 2003. "Bedingungen für die Entstehung von Öffentlichkeit in der EU." In Ansgar Klein, Ruud Koopmanns, Hans-Jörg Trenz, et al. (eds.), *Bürgerschaft, Öffentlichkeit und Demokratie in Europa.* Opladen: Leske+Budrich, pp. 169–90.

Van de Steeg, Marianne. 2005. "The Public Sphere in the European Union: A Media Analysis of Public Discourse on EU Enlargement and on the Haider Case." PhD dissertation, Florence, Italy: European University Institute, Department of Social and Political Sciences.

Van de Steeg, Marianne. 2006. "Does a Public Sphere Exist in the European Union? An Analysis of the Content of the Debate on the Haider Case." *European Journal of Political Research* 45 (4): 609–34.

Van de Steeg, Marianne. 2010. "Theoretical Reflections on the Public Sphere in the European Union: A Network of Communication or a Political Community?" In Christina Bee and Emanuela Bozzini (eds.), *Mapping the European Public Sphere: Institutions, Media and Civil Society.* Farnham, UK, and Burlington, VT: Ashgate, pp. 31–45.

Van de Steeg, Marianne, Valentin Rauer, Sylvain Rivet, and Thomas Risse. 2003. "The EU as a Political Community: A Media Analysis of the 'Haider Debate' in the European Union." In *Annual Meeting of the European Union Studies Association (EUSA)*, Nashville, TN.

Van de Steeg, Marianne, and Thomas Risse. 2010. "The Emergence of a European Community of Communication: Insights from Empirical Research on the Europeanization of Public Spheres." KFG Working Paper Series 15, Free University Berlin.

Van der Eijk, Cees, and Mark Franklin. 1996. *Choosing Europe.* Ann Arbor: Michigan University Press.

Venables, John. 2005. *Making Headlines: News Values and Risk Signals in Journalism.* Huntingdon, UK: ELM Publications.

Vetters, Regina. 2007. "Vor Ort in Europa: Ein Vergleich der EU-Berichterstattung deutscher Qualitäts- und Regionalzeitungen." *Medien & Kommunikationswissenschaft* 3: 355–71.

Vigil, James Diego. 2003. "Urban Violence and Street Gangs." *Annual Review of Anthropology* 32: 225–42.

Vliegenthart, Jens, Andreas R. Schuck, Hajo G. Boomgaarden, and Claes H. De Vreese. 2008. "News Coverage and Support for European Integration 1990–2006." *International Journal of Public Opinion Research* 20 (4): 415–39.

Warleigh, Alex. 2003. "Informal Governance: Improving EU Democracy?" In Thomas Christensen and Simona Piattoni (eds.), *Informal Governance in the European Union.* London: Edward Elgar, pp. 22–35.

Weale, Albert. 1999. *Democracy.* New York: St. Martin's Press.

Weßels, Bernhard. 2007. "Discontent and European Identity: Three Types of Euroscepticism." *Acta Politica* 42: 287–306.

Wessels, Wolfgang, Andreas Maurer, and Jürgen Mittag (eds.). 2003. *Fifteen into One? The European Union and its Member States.* Manchester, UK, and New York: Manchester University Press.

Wessler, Hartmut, Bernhard Peters, Michael Brüggemann, Katharina Kleinen von Königslow, and Stefanie Sifft. 2008. *Transnationalization of Public Spheres, Transformations of the State.* Houndmills, Basingstoke, UK: Palgrave Macmillan.

Wilson, Iain. 2011. "What Should We Expect of 'Erasmus Generations'?" *Journal of Common Market Studies* 49 (5): 1113–40.

Wimmel, Andreas. 2006. *Transnationale Diskurse in Europa: Der Streit um den Türkei-Beitritt in Deutschland, Frankreich und Großbritannien.* Frankfurt am Main and New York: Campus.

Winslow, Donna. 1999. "Rites of Passage and Group Bonding in the Canadian Airborne." *Armed Forces & Society* 25 (3): 429–57.

Wittmer, Dennis. 1992. "Ethical Sensitivities and Managerial Decision-Making: An Experiment." *Journal of Public Administration Research and Theory* 2 (4): 443–62.

Woelke, Jens, Christian Steininger, and Torsten Maurer. 2010. "Zur Realität europäischer Öffentlichkeit: Die Darstellung der EU in Informationssendungen des deutschen und österreichischen Fernsehens." In Horst Pöttker and Christian Schwarzenegger (eds.), *Europäische Öffentlichkeit und journalistische Verantwortung: Journalismus International*. Köln: Halem, pp. 40–75.

Wood, Elisabeth Jean. 2008. "The Social Processes of Civil War: The Wartime Transformation of Social Networks." *Annual Review of Political Science* 11: 539–61.

Wood, Elisabeth Jean. 2010. "Sexual Violence during War: Variation and Accountability." In Alette Smeulers and Elies van Sliedregt (eds.), *Criminal Justice: An Interdisciplinary Approach*. Antwerp, the Netherlands: Intersentia Publishers.

Zaller, John. 1992. *The Nature and Origins of Mass Opinion*. Cambridge: Cambridge University Press.

Zippel, Kathrin. 2006. *The Politics of Sexual Harassment: A Comparative Study of the United States, the European Union, and Germany*. New York: Cambridge University Press.

Zürn, Michael. 1998. *Regieren jenseits des Nationalstaats: Globalisierung und Denationalisierung als Chance*. Frankfurt am Main: Suhrkamp.

Zürn, Michael. 2014. "The Politicization of World Politics and its Effects: Eight Propositions." *European Political Science Review* 6 (1): 47–71.

Zürn, Michael. 2013. "Globalization and Global Governance." In Walter Carlsnaes, Thomas Risse, and Beth Simmons (eds.), *Handbook of International Relations*, 2nd edn. London: Sage Publications, pp. 401–25.

Zürn, Michael, and Matthias Ecker-Ehrhardt (eds.). 2013. *Die Politisierung der Weltpolitik: Umkämpfte Internationale Institutionen*. Berlin: Suhrkamp.

Index